Citizenship and Gender in Britain, 1688–1928

Citizenship and Gender in Britain, 1688–1928 explores the history of citizenship in Britain during a period when admission to the political community was commonly thought about in terms of gender.

Between the Glorious Revolution of 1688 and the Equal Franchise Act of 1928 the key question in British politics was what sorts of men – and subsequently women – should be admitted to citizenship, particularly in terms of parliamentary suffrage. This book makes new links between the histories of gender and politics, and surveys exciting recent work in these areas. By examining central topics such as political masculinity, electoral culture, party politics and women's suffrage through this lens, it expands not only the remit of gender history but encourages the reader to rethink how we approach the history of politics. It explores the close connections between gender, nation and class in Britain, and advocates a new cultural history of politics for the period between the seventeenth and twentieth centuries.

Citizenship and Gender in Britain, 1688–1928 is essential reading for students of early modern and modern British history, gender history and political history.

Matthew McCormack is Professor of History at the University of Northampton. He has published widely on masculinity, politics and war. His previous books include *The Independent Man: Citizenship and Gender Politics in Georgian England* (2005) and *Embodying the Militia in Georgian England* (2015).

Citizenship and Gender in Britain, 1688–1928

Matthew McCormack

LONDON AND NEW YORK

First published 2019
by Routledge
2 Park Square, Milton Park, Abingdon, Oxon OX14 4RN

and by Routledge
52 Vanderbilt Avenue, New York, NY 10017

Routledge is an imprint of the Taylor & Francis Group, an informa business

© 2019 Matthew McCormack

The right of Matthew McCormack to be identified as author of this work has been asserted by him in accordance with sections 77 and 78 of the Copyright, Designs and Patents Act 1988.

All rights reserved. No part of this book may be reprinted or reproduced or utilised in any form or by any electronic, mechanical, or other means, now known or hereafter invented, including photocopying and recording, or in any information storage or retrieval system, without permission in writing from the publishers.

Trademark notice: Product or corporate names may be trademarks or registered trademarks, and are used only for identification and explanation without intent to infringe.

British Library Cataloguing-in-Publication Data
A catalogue record for this book is available from the British Library

Library of Congress Cataloging-in-Publication Data
Names: McCormack, Matthew, author.
Title: Citizenship and gender in Britain, 1688–1928 / Matthew McCormack.
Description: Abingdon, Oxon ; New York, NY : Routledge, 2019. | Includes bibliographical references and index. |
Identifiers: LCCN 2019003536 (print) | LCCN 2019019836 (ebook) | ISBN 9781315144139 (eBook) | ISBN 9781138501058 (hardback : alk. paper) | ISBN 9781138501065 (pbk. : alk. paper)
Subjects: LCSH: Citizenship—Great Britain—History. | Sex—Political aspects—Great Britain—History. | Political participation—Great Britain—History. | Women—Political activity—Great Britain—History. | Great Britain—Politics and government.
Classification: LCC JN906 (ebook) | LCC JN906 .M377 2019 (print) | DDC 323.60941/0903—dc23
LC record available at https://lccn.loc.gov/2019003536

ISBN: 978-1-138-50105-8 (hbk)
ISBN: 978-1-138-50106-5 (pbk)
ISBN: 978-1-315-14413-9 (ebk)

Typeset in Galliard
by codeMantra

Toby's book

Contents

List of figures	viii
List of tables	ix
Acknowledgements	x
Introduction: what is citizenship?	1
1 The state and the public sphere	12
2 Political masculinities, 1688–1837	35
3 The British electoral tradition	51
4 Patriotism and revolution, 1776–1819	67
5 Women and political campaigning	87
6 Reform, domesticity and citizenship, 1820–48	104
7 Feminism and citizenship	119
8 Popular politics in the age of mass party, 1837–1901	133
9 Citizenship, society and the state	152
10 Votes for women, 1865–1928	167
Conclusion	184
Index	191

List of figures

1.1	Isaac Cruikshank, 'Debating Society. (Substitute for Hair Powder)' (1795)	27
1.2	Anon., 'March 1829' (1829)	31
2.1	Early Georgian political ideologies	41
3.1	'Candidates Canvassing for Seats in Parliament' (1818)	57
3.2	William Hogarth, 'Chairing the Member' (1754–55)	60
3.3	'The Devonshire Amusement' (1784)	64
4.1	Charles Williams, 'The Consequence of Invasion or the Hero's Reward' (1 August 1803)	79
4.2	George Cruikshank, 'Liberty Suspended! with the Bulwark of the Constitution!' (March 1817)	83
5.1	Isaac Cruikshank, 'The Abolition of the Slave Trade' (1792)	94
5.2	George Cruikshank, 'The Belle Alliance or the Female Reformers of Blackburn!!!' (1819)	97
5.3	'The Blanket Hornpipe, by Signor Non Ricordo' (1820)	99
6.1	John Leech, 'A Physical Force Chartist Arming for the Fight', *Punch*, 26 August 1848	116
7.1	James Gillray, 'Fashion Before Ease, or A good Constitution sacrificed for a Fantastick Form' (1793)	123
8.1	John Tenniel, 'Mill's Logic; Or, Franchise for Females', *Punch*, 30 March 1867	139
8.2	John Tenniel, 'Rival Stars', *Punch*, 14 March 1868	142
8.3	William Currey, 'William Gladstone woodcutting' (1877)	143
9.1	'The Census Enumerator in a Gray's Inn Lane Tenement', *Illustrated Times* 7 (1861), 242	154
10.1	'The Cat and Mouse Act Passed by the Liberal Government' (WSPU poster, 1914)	174
10.2	'The Vote' (Suffrage Atelier poster, c. 1911)	181
11.1	J. M. W. Turner, 'The Northampton Election, 6 December 1830' (watercolour, c. 1830–31)	185

List of tables

1.1　Habermas's public sphere　　　　　　　　　　　　　23

Acknowledgements

This book has its origins in a course of the same name that I have taught at the University of Northampton for over a decade. I would therefore like to thank the students who took the module, since I learned a lot from them and many of their ideas doubtless made their way into the text. I would like to thank my colleagues at Northampton too, especially Martyn Green, Tim Reinke-Williams and Mark Rothery who read portions of the manuscript. Some sections of the book were informed by other courses and other institutions: Chapters 5 and 7 had their origins in lectures I gave at Sheffield and Chapter 9 is a love letter to my time at Manchester. I originally discussed ideas for such a book with my doctoral supervisor Frank O'Gorman, who – as the writer of a key textbook himself – offered useful tips on the process. Francis Dodsworth, Ben Griffin and Matt Roberts kindly offered comments on chapters, and Amy McCormack and Emma McCormack gave advice and encouragement. I would also like to thank everybody at Routledge involved in producing the book, especially Laura Pilsworth and Morwenna Scott. Any errors or misinterpretations are of course my own.

Introduction
What is citizenship?

Citizenship is a vital issue in Britain today. Issues such as political engagement, national identity, civil rights and immigration are perennially in the news, and become even more prominent during general election or referendum campaigns. On the one hand, this preoccupation with citizenship is a recent phenomenon. Successive Conservative and Labour governments since the 1990s have emphasised the rights and responsibilities of the ordinary citizen, from John Major's 'Citizen's Charter' to David Cameron's 'Big Society', via Tony Blair's introduction of citizenship classes for schoolchildren and citizenship tests for immigrants. On the other hand, these are issues with a long heritage. This book explores the period 1688 to 1928, and argues that this was the crucial phase in the development of notions of citizenship in Britain. Although the book has many themes, the key focus is on gender, since I will argue that the debate around citizenship was fundamentally concerned with the position of men and women in politics and society.

So what is citizenship? It is not an easy word to pin down: two recent commentators noted that it is 'one of the most porous concepts in contemporary academic parlance'.[1] Citizenship is the condition of being a citizen, and a citizen is a member of a larger body: originally a city, but now more usually a wider community such as a nation or a polity. Citizenship involves status, which not all inhabitants of a community will necessarily possess, so in a sense citizenship involves full membership of that community. The most potent symbol of membership today is the passport. In countries such as the UK that do not have identity cards, the passport is the closest you get to documentary proof of citizenship. As with other documents that are used in this way in practice (such as the driving licence or the National Insurance card), this was not its intended function. Originally, a 'pass port' was a signed letter permitting a specific journey. It is still essentially a travel document, signifying that the ruler of one state is requesting that its bearer be given safe passage into another: as the wording of the passport still relates, 'Her Britannic Majesty's Secretary of State Requests and requires in the Name of Her Majesty all those whom it may concern to allow the bearer to pass freely without let or hindrance, and to afford the bearer such assistance and protection as may be necessary'. This includes rights, such as the ability to cross borders and consular protection when abroad.

2 What is citizenship?

In a more fundamental way, membership of the citizenry comes with rights. The precise nature of these rights and who gets to enjoy them depends upon time and context – hence the importance of a historical perspective when discussing citizenship – but, broadly speaking, they fall under the categories of political, civil and social rights.[2] Political rights usually involve the ability of the citizen to participate in the decision-making of the community. In modern democratic polities, the most important of these is the right to vote in elections, but we will also consider a range of other forms of political action including petitioning, publication and protest. Civil rights include freedom of speech, conscience and religious worship, and also certain protections within the legal system. Finally, citizens today enjoy certain social entitlements such as pensions, unemployment benefits and disability benefits although, as we will see, these are more recent and often controversial.

Although nowadays these rights are enjoyed automatically by citizens, historically the rights of citizenship have often been paired with its responsibilities. Citizenship is a reciprocal business and non-citizens in particular have commonly had to demonstrate that they have earned their inclusion by performing certain duties. On the one hand, citizens have to live for the state. In some political traditions, this involves renouncing suicide, which was illegal in Britain until 1961. Citizens have to obey the laws of the community, and pay tax and social insurance. Citizens should be politically active and aware, demonstrating public spirit and being vigilant towards threats to the community, from within or without. They can also contribute to the life of the community in other ways, through public service and voluntary action. Commentators on the political right tend to emphasise responsibilities over rights: Cameron's 'Big Society' proposed that citizens should perform voluntary service to replace functions formerly provided by the big state, and Margaret Thatcher argued that, 'the sense of being self-reliant, of playing a role within the family, of owning one's own property, of paying one's own way are all part of the spiritual ballast which maintains responsible citizenship'.[3]

As well as living for the community, citizens can be required to die for it. The most fundamental contribution that a citizen can make to a community is to fight for its very existence. There have been many examples in history of political communities requiring military service as a precondition of citizenship, most famously ancient Rome. In more recent British history the link has not been quite so direct, although we will see how military service was often discussed in terms of citizenship and voting rights in the seventeenth and eighteenth centuries, often in explicitly classical terms: in particular, since fighting was the business of men, this was commonly an argument for aligning citizenship with masculinity in an exclusive way. In times of military emergency, states can require military service of their citizens through conscription, but Britain's military tradition has largely been voluntarist and conscription has usually been regarded as a breach of the citizen's civil rights. Britain avoided conscription throughout the French Wars, despite facing an enemy with huge armies of conscripted citizens, and continued to do so until 1916. The award of the vote to all men and some women at the close of the First World War has commonly been linked to their war service, and we will explore the extent to which this was the case in Chapter 10.

There is more to citizenship, however, than just rights and responsibilities. Although citizenship is usually considered in legalistic terms, it can also be thought about as a lived condition. Citizens are expected to hold certain values and emotional attachments. They are expected to see themselves as part of a community and to identify with it in a personal way. Many political cultures require citizens to declare their loyalty to their flag, their constitution or their governors in a formal way. At a practical level too, historians like Kathryn Gleadle have drawn our attention to the 'micro-level' of day-to-day political interactions.[4] This can shed light on a deeper and more subtle engagement with politics, particularly from groups such as women who may have been excluded from more legalistic models of citizenship.

Nevertheless, the question of who is included in citizenship and who is excluded is a crucial one. Nowadays, citizenship in Britain is relatively inclusive: it is granted to people for whom it is the country of their birth or parentage. It can subsequently be applied for, commonly on the basis of marriage or residence, and in recent years the application process has involved a citizenship test. Indeed, this book may well be read by people seeking to prepare for it. To a certain extent, this test is concerned with the formal rights and responsibilities of citizenship, but questions on the history and culture of Britain (such as which admiral was killed in battle in 1805, or who Morecambe and Wise are) suggest that our third category of citizenship as a lived experience is currently regarded as being important. Of course, a significant minority of people living and working in the UK – whether legally or otherwise – are foreign nationals who do not enjoy the full rights of citizens, such as the ability to vote in parliamentary elections. Other exclusions exist as well. The queen and members of the House of Lords cannot vote, nor can prisoners. The political status of prisoners has been notably controversial in recent years, as Britain's stance is at odds with the implementation of human rights legislation elsewhere in the European Union. This serves to highlight the extent to which citizenship is regarded as being reciprocal in Britain, since one has to obey the laws in order to have a say in how they are framed.

Once granted, citizens today enjoy full rights after the age of 18. This is the age at which Britons can vote in parliamentary elections: it is sometimes debated whether this should be lowered to 16 (as it was for the Scottish independence referendum in 2014). For the period covered by this book, the age of majority was 21 and this remained the voting age until 1969. The linkage of citizenship to adulthood is significant, since it suggests that the performance of functions like voting requires a certain level of responsibility and independence. We will see how the contrast between adults and children was often used as an analogy in debates about whether women should be given the vote, for example.

If citizenship is relatively inclusive in Britain today, this was not the case before the Equal Franchise Act of 1928, which is the end date of this book. Prior to this, not all adult nationals enjoyed the same rights and the key factor here was gender. No women could vote in parliamentary elections before 1918 and,

4   *What is citizenship?*

before the late nineteenth century, nor could most men. Voting was based upon qualifications, which related to property ownership and residence, and which were highly exclusive and geographically haphazard in practice. In the eighteenth century, growing calls to reform the system focused upon the supposedly masculine qualities that citizens should possess, and the debate continued to be conducted in these terms throughout the nineteenth century as the Reform Acts extended qualifications further down the social scale. Citizenship was also unequal in other senses. Men and women did not enjoy the same legal or property rights in the nineteenth century, and when a woman got married she effectively ceased to exist in civil and economic terms. *Citizenship and Gender in Britain* therefore focuses on the fundamental role of gender in the theory and practice of citizenship between 1688 and 1928.

Citizenship and history

As we have seen, we need a historical perspective when discussing citizenship, not least because the nature of citizenship changes so hugely according to time and context. History, however, is also vital in other senses. If citizenship is partly about how the individual conceives of their identity within their political community, then the history of that community is very important. In particular, how we tell the story of the national past informs our sense of our values, our political traditions, and our emotional attachment to our community. When Britons today are asked what 'British values' consist of, the same answers tend to recur: tolerance, the rule of law, fair play, liberty and so on. (Indeed, these are the types of answers that are required by the citizenship test.) But these values are based on a particular telling of Britain's history, whereas it is perfectly possible to find examples of intolerance, illegality, unfairness and oppression in the historical record. Equally, if you asked the same question of a Dutch or a Canadian citizen – to take two random examples – they would probably name very similar 'national' values.

Nevertheless, knowing your nation's history has long been regarded as a fundamental part of citizenship, and has informed how history has been taught in schools. For the Victorians, learning history *was* learning citizenship, and this attitude has been very enduring. John Tosh notes that the reason history teachers were not more involved in the citizenship curriculum was because 'their own subject is still regarded as a course in citizenship in all but name'. This may explain why the debates in the 1980s about the content of the National Curriculum were so heated where history was concerned. Should the story of the eighteenth and nineteenth centuries be one of technological achievement and military success, or smoking chimneys and imperial oppression? In a way, the question of whether we should tell a right-wing or a left-wing version of British history is beside the point. Prescribing a particular vision of the past and requiring students to identify with it is politically problematic, not to mention a turn-off for the students themselves. Tosh has argued that we need to move beyond this and instead to focus on political skills that can be enhanced by the study of history.

There is much talk of 'transferable skills' in higher education – most of which are common to a range of subjects – but the study of history fosters particular knowledge and abilities in the citizen:

> Historical perspective enhances the citizen's capacity to make informed judgments about the issues of the day, and to make intelligent use of the vote – in short, to exercise his or her active membership of the body politic. Thinking historically – or 'thinking with history' – means employing historical perspective to illuminate current issues.[5]

The study of history can therefore foster the kinds of critical skills that are essential to good citizenship in Britain today.

Citizenship also raises interesting questions about how we study history. The issue of citizenship cuts across the histories of politics, society, the law, gender and nationalism. It requires an interdisciplinary approach and therefore has the potential to tell the familiar story of modern Britain in a new way. As well as telling a different story, it also informs the methods that we use to tell it. Citizenship is a political topic but *Citizenship and Gender in Britain* is not a conventional political history. Traditional political history focuses on the structures of politics – the politicians, parties and institutions – without questioning why these things exist. By contrast, recent writing on the cultural history of politics has emphasised that politics is not a natural thing to do, but is a cultural activity that takes place within a specific historical context. Rather than regarding 'political culture' as something that accompanies 'real' politics, cultural historians are interested in the subtle ways in which power operates *through* culture. As we will see, politics is fundamentally a cultural activity, centrally concerned with questions of communication, representation, performance and identity.

Identity is a big theme of this book. The citizen is the political individual, and we are concerned with the identity of that individual in two senses. First, in terms of self-identity: how that individual sees themselves and how they locate their identity within a wider collectivity. Second, in terms of social identity: how others regard them and how the 'political individual' is characterised. Identity is a central concern of cultural history. The 'cultural turn' in historical studies in the late twentieth century shifted historical attention from the objective (the study of 'facts') to the subjective (the perspectives of past actors). Whereas many historians expressed alarm at this approach, even wondering out loud whether it threatened the very existence of history as a discipline, it has proved to be very productive. It is arguably more honest about what a historian can accomplish with their flawed source material and also offers fascinating new perspectives on the past. Historical sources can be used to reconstruct how individuals in the past viewed their world and their place within it, and can therefore offer insights into why they acted the way that they did. This can help us to understand how citizenship was an identity and a lived condition, rather than just a legal fiction. It can therefore offer a much richer understanding of what politics is and how it is done.

6 *What is citizenship?*

Citizenship is a political issue, but in order to understand how the citizen is defined we need to engage with social and cultural history. Social and cultural historians tend to categorise individuals in terms of the 'holy trinity' of gender, class and race (or nation). None of these categorisations are set in stone: rather, historians tend to emphasise that all three are cultural constructions, which have historically helped to construct each other. For example, feminist women's historians have tended to emphasise how notions of gender are often informed by class, and vice versa.[6] Throughout the period 1688–1928, we will see that gender, class and national identity figured prominently in discussions of citizenship, and how these three categories were used together to define who should be included and excluded in the political nation. Of the three categories, however, gender was arguably the most important. The rest of this introduction will explain why, by sketching out the argument of this book by way of its contents of its chapters.

Citizenship and gender, 1688–1928

The period covered by this book is bounded by two major political events. It begins with the Glorious Revolution of 1688–89 – which defined the political order thereafter and enshrined key aspects of citizenship in the Bill of Rights – and concludes with the Equal Franchise Act in 1928. It is therefore a political chronology, charting the development of the British political system and focusing in particular on the movement to widen the franchise. This movement begins in earnest in the 1760s, but draws upon opposition critiques from previous decades, and continues throughout the nineteenth and early twentieth centuries, as men and women who are excluded from the franchise campaign for their inclusion. The histories of (men's) parliamentary reform and women's suffrage are usually regarded as being entirely separate – and are usually studied by very different types of historians – so this book is unusual in treating them as part of the same continuum. The debate on the franchise concerned who should be included in electoral citizenship, and this was largely conducted in terms of gender: what sorts of men – and subsequently women – should be given the vote, and what qualities of masculinity or femininity should the citizen possess?

The focus on the vote requires some justification. We have already seen how citizenship involves much more than just voting and this book will consider the full range of political, social, cultural and military activities involved in citizenship. Prioritising the electoral system could also be criticised for marginalising women from a narrative about this period, although we will see that women engaged extensively in the electoral process even before they obtained the vote itself. Nevertheless, voting was an activity of peculiar importance in this period, when it was arguably viewed in a different way to how it is today. In a practical sense, people believed that the vote could achieve real change: this was the means to change the laws, which they believed would have a direct practical impact on their lives. It is notable how often reformers expressed faith in the political system and the constitution, even as they sought to change it. It is easy to lose sight of this nowadays, when general election turnouts fell to a low of 59 per cent in 2001 and when people commonly express the view that their vote does not matter. This may be the result of the 'first past the post' voting system (explained in Chapter 3), where only votes in closely contested 'marginal' constituencies are likely to effect a different outcome, and where voters elsewhere often feel disenfranchised. Some voters got a shock after the EU Referendum in 2016, when every vote *did* count equally: one such voter lodged a protest vote as 'I didn't think my vote was going to matter too much', and later regretted it.[7]

As well as having a practical impact, the vote also was also of huge symbolic importance. This was especially the case for people who did not have it: indeed, the history of women's suffrage tells us a great deal about how the vote was valued in this regard. Possessing the vote was the marker of full citizenship, a sign of human dignity and full belonging. If you did not have the vote, obtaining it was the holy grail. And once you did have it, the act of participating in a parliamentary election was the ordinary citizen's most concrete and emotive experience of the national political system. The vote was therefore a moral and emotional issue, as well as a straightforwardly electoral one.

The structure of the book is broadly chronological, with chapters alternating between surveys of periods and of themes. Chapter 1 considers the origins of modern British politics. It sets out the structures of politics – the monarchy, the House of Lords and the House of Commons – as they were redefined at the end of the seventeenth century. Politics in the following century, however, is arguably less significant for its official structures than it is for what was happening outside of them. The 'long' eighteenth century was hugely important for the growth of extra-parliamentary politics, and scholars have often linked this to wider changes in social, cultural and intellectual life. We will explore Jürgen Habermas's theory that this period witnessed the birth of the 'public sphere', and we will think about how gender historians have used this concept to explain men's dominance of these new political arenas. Men in politics is the focus of Chapter 2. What sorts of qualities were demanded of men in the political arena, and how did this change over the course of the Georgian period? In focusing on masculinity, this chapter links political change to social change, by exploring how shifts in the nature of politics related to those in ideas about masculinity, and vice versa.

Chapter 3 focuses on the electoral system. The eighteenth century was a period when very few men and no women could vote, when electoral qualifications varied hugely according to where you happened to live, and when elections were notoriously corrupt and barely even competitive. Whereas historians traditionally took a dim view of this, the chapter will evaluate more recent work that has rehabilitated the Hanoverian electoral system. Although few people could vote, elections in this period were huge public festivities where the participation of non-voters was arguably just as important. In particular, women had key roles to play in the sociable and commercial aspects of elections, and women of the elite could further get involved as canvassers, hostesses and organisers. The roles that men were required to play in the electoral theatre also tell us more about the nature of political masculinities.

In Chapter 4 we shift our focus to citizenship as an aspect of national belonging. Love of country has frequently been regarded as a key attribute of citizenship but in the mid-eighteenth century patriotism had political connotations that we may not recognise today. The 'patriots' were those who were critical of the establishment and patriotism was often espoused by those who claimed to stand up for the rights of 'the people' against a supposedly foreign ruling class. The 'Age of Revolutions' posed a problem for this line of argument, however: it was difficult for reformers in Britain to sympathise with revolutionaries in America and later France while claiming to be patriots. We will see how the 1790s was a key decade in British politics and ideas about citizenship. On one side of the political spectrum, radicalism became distinctively working class and writers like Thomas Paine and Richard Price claimed to be 'citizens of the world'. On the other, loyalist politics claimed patriotism for the establishment and, in an era of invasion scares, volunteering initiatives reaffirmed the link between citizenship and military service. This might appear to be the beginning of the connection between nationalism and the political right, with which we are familiar today. The reality, however, was not so simple: we will see how patriotism remained contested terrain, and how loyalist patriotism retained much of its former democratic potential.

As well as being important for notions of patriotism, historians have long argued that the period of the French Revolution was crucial for notions of gender in Britain. Loyalists and Evangelicals preached a very conservative vision of the family and of women's role: some historians identify in this decade the origins of the Victorian notion of 'separate spheres' for men and women.[8] Radicals too tended to emphasise the rights of men at the expense of women, but for different reasons: citizenship had formerly been associated with property and rank, so radicals emphasised that it should instead be organised along gender lines in order to make a case for giving the vote to men. Chapter 6 will show how there was an enduring association of citizenship with male domesticity in the nineteenth century. When the Whig party took power on a platform of parliamentary reform in 1830, they emphasised that the vote should be given to 'married men and the fathers of families': they identified responsible voters in the propertied patriarchs of the middle classes, and the First Reform Act of 1832 passed a steep property qualification that excluded working men. This gave rise to Chartism, a nationwide movement of working people dedicated to obtaining the vote. They too, however, were committed to a gendered notion of political entitlement: Chartists sought the vote for men and presented a vision of family life where the breadwinner would bring home a wage sufficient for the whole family. As was often the way with the British left, the rights of the male worker trumped those of women, who were relegated to auxiliary roles in the movement.

In Chapters 5 and 7, we pause the chronological story to think about women's roles in British politics. We begin by surveying the numerous ways in which women of all classes were able to participate in politics in the eighteenth and nineteenth centuries. This highlights the value of approaching politics through the lens of social and cultural history, since conventional approaches to political history have been unwilling to look beyond the traditional structures where men predominate. This approach challenges the preconception that women were excluded from the public sphere in this period – although, as we will see, women's political action came with certain conditions and boundaries if it was not to threaten the status quo. By contrast, in Chapter 7 we will concentrate on women who were prepared to critique the society in which they lived. In the era of the French Revolution, feminists such as Mary Wollstonecraft challenged women's subjugation and suggested for the first time that women should have the vote. Although feminism in the Victorian period can seem socially and politically conservative by comparison, they won crucial victories in their campaigns for women's rights to divorce, property and an education. As well as being urgent in themselves, these campaigns settled key questions around women's civil and political status: it would be difficult to imagine women as independent citizens without them, so they were a precondition of the later campaigns for the suffrage.

The Second Reform Act of 1867 was a pivotal moment in the relationship between citizenship and gender in Britain, and we will see in Chapter 8 how much of the pioneering work on this topic focused on it. Disraeli sought to give the vote to the British working man, but the debates around the Bill reveal that this was as much an exclusive measure as an inclusive one: non-Britons, paupers and women did not meet the criteria for political responsibility. Nevertheless, the Act created an unprecedentedly large electorate and political parties realised that they needed to change what they stood for and how they communicated if they were to appeal to this new constituency. The Conservative and Liberal parties were both remarkably successful at this, but went about it in quite different ways and projected competing models of masculinity that voters could identify with. This golden age of popular politics created a vibrant political culture in which these new citizens could participate.

Chapter 9 continues the story into the later nineteenth century and thinks about citizenship in a more social way. Prior to this, the state had little involvement in society, and classical liberals in the age of Gladstone sought to minimise it further. They believed that state intervention was a moral and economic evil, since it removed the impetus for individuals to improve their own condition. The citizen should be self-governing and self-supporting, so the freeing of the citizen was accompanied by a range of new arm's-length techniques in order to foster this. At the end of the century, however, this prescription of *laissez-faire* was widely felt to be insufficient to the dire social challenges of the day. Given widespread poverty and unemployment, some Liberals started to propose more interventionist solutions and a bigger role for the state. This was the origin of modern Britain's 'welfare state', which involves very different ideas about the citizen's rights and obligations, and a broader conception of what citizenship *is* and how it is lived from day to day.

The final chapter focuses on women's suffrage. The story of the suffragettes and their militant campaign is well known, and it is usually told as a beginning. In traditional political studies, women's suffrage is the first time that gender becomes a consideration: men are not ascribed a gender, and given political history's focus on state structures, women only become visible when they seek to participate in them. Similarly, in histories of the women's movement, suffragism is the 'first wave' of British feminism rather than something that was drawing on older campaigns or political traditions. By contrast, this book will seek to place suffragism within a broader historical perspective: it argues that the debate about citizenship in Britain had revolved around gender for two centuries, and it only ceased to be a consideration when men and women were granted the vote on an equal basis in 1928. Women's suffrage is, therefore, the end to this story rather than a beginning.

Many of the topics covered by this book – parliamentary reform, women's suffrage, the labour movement, the rise of party – are very familiar to British historians. This book seeks to create a new synthesis and to trace the themes of citizenship and gender through this crucial period in British history. In so doing, the story it will tell will diverge from conventional 'Whig' narratives about democratisation and constitutional progress. In common with other works on the 'new political history',[9] this is as much a story about exclusion as it is about inclusion, and as much about power as it is about freedom. This is not just about adding gender to political history, or vice versa. Hopefully this perspective has the potential to change both histories, by helping us to think about what politics consists of and how it is lived and managed, as well as deepening our understanding of what it means to be a man or a woman.

Notes

1 K. Canning and S. Rose, 'Introduction: Gender, citizenship and subjectivity: Some historical and theoretical considerations', *Gender and History*, 13:3, 2001, 427–43 (p. 427).
2 T. H. Marshall, *Citizenship and Social Class and Other Essays*, Cambridge: Cambridge University Press, 1950, p. 10.
3 *The Independent on Sunday*, 6 May 1990.
4 K. Gleadle, *Borderline Citizens: Women, Gender and Political Culture in Britain, 1815–1867*, Oxford: Oxford University Press, 2009, p. 11.
5 J. Tosh, *Why History Matters*, Basingstoke: Palgrave, 2008, pp. 125, 120–1.
6 L. Davidoff and C. Hall, *Family Fortunes: Men and Women of the English Middle Class 1780–1850*, revised edn, London: Routledge, 2002.
7 L. Dearden, 'Anger over "Bregret" as Leave voters say they thought UK would stay in EU', *The Independent*, 25 June 2016, www.independent.co.uk/news/uk/politics/brexit-anger-bregret-leave-voters-protest-vote-thought-uk-stay-in-eu-remain-win-a7102516.html [accessed 22 June 2017].
8 C. Hall, 'The early formation of Victorian domestic ideology', in S. Burman (ed.), *Fit Work for Women*, London: Croom Helm, 1979, pp. 15–32.
9 James Vernon coined the phrase in *Politics and the People: A Study in English Political Culture, 1815–1867*, Cambridge: Cambridge University Press, 1993, p. 1.

Recommended reading

Bock, G. and Janes, S. (eds.), *Beyond Equality and Difference: Citizenship, Feminist Politics and Female Subjectivity*, Routledge: London, 1992.

Canning, K. and Rose, S. (eds.), special issue on 'Gender, citizenship and subjectivity', *Gender & History*, 13:3, 2001.

Dudink, S., Hagemann K. and Clark, A. (eds.), *Representing Masculinity: Male Citizenship in Modern Western Culture*, Basingstoke: Palgrave, 2007.

Gleadle, K., *Borderline Citizens: Women, Gender and Political Culture in Britain, 1815–1867*, Oxford: Oxford University Press, 2009.

Tosh, J., *Why History Matters*, Basingstoke: Palgrave, 2008.

Wahrman, D., 'The new political history: A review essay', *Social History*, 21:3, 1996, 343–53.

1 The state and the public sphere

A citizen is a member of a political community. This chapter will outline the nature of that community, in order to provide a context for the discussion of citizenship in the chapters that follow. It will begin by thinking about the formal structure of politics, including the state and key offices within it. The starting point for this discussion is the Glorious Revolution of 1688, which codified some of the citizen's rights and defined the political order thereafter. The chapter will then consider the nature of the political community in a more informal way by exploring the new phenomenon of the 'public sphere', an arena outside of the official structure of politics in which political activity was increasingly taking place. Although this concept has been widely debated by historians, we will see how it can provide a useful framework for thinking about what politics is and how it is experienced, as well as linking it to changes in social and cultural life. Gender historians in particular have debated the extent to which this public sphere was a male arena, and we will see throughout this chapter how gender had an important influence on the shape of the political world.

The Glorious Revolution and the making of Britain

The 1680s was a politically fraught decade in the four nations that would later make up the United Kingdom. Since 1603, England and Wales had a joint monarchy with Scotland, and the issue of the succession had become hugely contentious. Charles II's heir was his brother James – who was to become James II of England and James VII of Scotland – but many people opposed his succession because he was a Catholic. England and Scotland were Protestant countries that were proudly independent of Rome and of Catholic powers on the continent, and Catholics were a persecuted minority who did not possess the full range of rights enjoyed by members of the state church. James was a threat to all this. After he took the throne in 1685 he put pressure on parliament to overturn Catholic disabilities and purged any officials of the Crown who opposed him

This contention over the succession created the 'first age of party', which drew the political battle-lines for the following century and even gave us one of the party labels that we still use to this day. The 'Tories' (named after Irish, and therefore papist, outlaws) were those who upheld the divine right of kings and the legitimate succession. Their loyalty to the monarch and his successors even trumped their commitment to a Protestant Church of England. By contrast, the 'Whigs' (also named after criminals, tellingly, but this time Scottish and therefore Protestant ones) were committed to Protestantism and the rights of parliament. They attempted to exclude James from the succession and, when this failed, they sought an alternative line of succession. They opened negotiations with the Dutch Stadtholder, William of Orange, who was married to James's daughter, Mary. In November 1688, William landed with a Dutch army in the West Country. Amid widespread anti-Catholic rioting, James's regime collapsed and he fled to France. After a struggle between the Commons and the Lords, parliament declared that James had 'abdicated' his throne and that William and Mary would rule instead in a unique joint arrangement.

The events of 1688–89 acquired the label 'the Glorious Revolution' and it long had pride of place in Whig histories, which told a rather self-congratulatory story of Britain's unique path to liberty and greatness. One reason it was 'glorious' was its supposed bloodlessness, but that was hardly true. William's military invasion of England was resisted, and it set in motion three years of brutal civil war in Ireland, which left thousands dead and established the 'Protestant ascendancy' over a predominantly Catholic island. The battles and sieges of this war are etched in the consciousness of Protestant and Catholic communities in Northern Ireland, where the political ramifications of this period are still felt to this day. In eighteenth-century England, however, the revolution was widely celebrated as the foundation of the nation's liberties. Kathleen Wilson has shown how this was not merely an aspect of elite political discourse, but that it permeated popular political culture. The Glorious Revolution was at the centre of popular understandings of representative institutions, political liberties and the role of 'the people' in politics.[1] It is therefore an appropriate place to start a survey of the history of citizenship.

The Glorious Revolution changed the political game. The monarch remained the head of state and was still divinely appointed, albeit now a Protestant God's instrument of deliverance rather than an all-mighty patriarch with an indefeasible succession. But the monarch could no longer impose its arbitrary will on the people: the primacy of parliament was established and the new joint monarchs and their successors were shackled. A new coronation oath required monarchs to swear that they would govern 'according to the statutes in parliament agreed on, and the laws and customs of the same'.[2] The revolution was codified in the Bill of Rights of 1689, which listed the misdemeanours of James II, declared the throne 'vacant' and settled the succession thereafter. More importantly, it also asserted certain 'ancient right and liberties'. Some of these concerned the rights of parliament, asserting that monarchs could not interfere in the laws or collect taxation without their approval, but around half of its provisions concerned the rights of the individual. The Bill of Rights used the term 'subject' rather than 'citizen', but we would recognise them as citizenship rights. These included political rights such as the right to petition and the right to free and frequent elections, as well as civil rights such as the right to bear arms, freedom of speech and due process under the law.[3]

Strikingly, the political debate around the Glorious Revolution was often conducted by means of a family analogy, so it has attracted the attention of feminist scholars. Sir John Filmer had presented the case for absolute monarchy and Divine Right in his *Patriarcha, Or the Natural Power of Kings* (1680). He argued that the king's power in a state was equivalent to that of a father in a family, so his opponents had to engage with the position of men, women and children in society. In response to Filmer, John Locke wrote his *Two Treatises of Government* (1689), which is often regarded as the key philosophical justification for the revolution. In the first treatise he took *Patriarcha* apart line by line, contesting the view that absolute monarchy had a biblical basis, and refuting Filmer's familial model of the state by arguing that the patriarch's power is contractual rather than total. Modern feminists have debated the implications of this: on the one hand, Locke presented marriage as consensual; on the other, his separation of state (public) and family (private) arguably rendered women invisible and reinforced domestic patriarchy.[4] In the second treatise Locke developed his vision of government. He used history in a different way to Filmer: rather than tracing a line of kings back to the Old Testament, Locke argued that man had existed in a 'state of nature' before the institution of society. In his natural state, man had rights to life, liberty and property, and he only agreed to be governed in order to protect those rights. Government is therefore contractual, and citizens reserve the right to have a revolution if the government fails to act in their interests. We will see how Locke's ideas proved to be hugely influential among radicals, reformers and feminists in the century that followed.

The direction that government took in the 1690s had a similarly lasting impact. In terms of foreign policy, William III was committed to the defence of European Protestantism, so he hugely expanded the army and commenced a century of almost continuous war with France. In order to pay for this, he imported financial innovations from Holland in the form of the Bank of England and the National Debt. War finance could now be quickly and reliably acquired and some military historians have argued that this 'fiscal-military state' was at the root of Britain's spectacular military success in the eighteenth century.[5] Ironically, William was now able to raise more tax for war and have larger standing armies than his predecessors had done, and was less reliant on parliament to do this. William's critics perceived the growth of the state with alarm, arguing that this led to a multiplication of paid functionaries who consumed taxation and had to do the government's will. Increasingly this was perceived to be a threat to liberty itself since it unbalanced the constitution and corrupted public morals. From this period, critics of government positioned themselves as 'independent men', who were able to speak truth to power because they had not been bought off.[6]

A key military threat after 1689 was James himself, since he and his successors did not give up their claim to the throne. The Jacobites set up an alternative court in France, which gave them financial and military assistance for decades and helped them to mount two significant rebellions. They had high hopes of a successful return, since they enjoyed support among many Catholics, Tories and Scots. The Whig establishment were terrified at this prospect and Jacobitism was ruthlessly put down, so it largely existed as a secret underground movement. Jacobitism was long derided by historians as an anachronistic and cranky movement, but scholarship in recent decades has rehabilitated it as a potent and relevant political force. Historians such as Paul Monod have highlighted its rich political culture of songs, toasts and tokens, and the intense emotional loyalty of its followers to 'the king over the water'.[7] Far from being backward-looking, Jacobitism was commonly a focus for critiques of the ruling establishment and the emerging fiscal-military state, so should form part of our understanding of the development of modern opposition politics.

The extent of support for the Jacobites in Scotland also had an important bearing on the creation of the British state. The Act of Union of 1707 that created Great Britain is a hugely contentious issue in Scottish historiography in particular. Although England and Scotland had been drawing closer together for years in economic and political terms, security considerations were to the fore. Scotland represented England's only land border, and had a long history of cooperation with England's enemy France that predated the Jacobite threat. The Union itself was a political fudge: the Scottish ruling class were bought off and Scotland retained its legal and religious independence. Nor was it popular: the Union was greeted with rioting on the streets of Scottish towns and cities, and the beginning of the Hanoverian dynasty with the coronation of George I in 1714 met with a similar response. As Linda Colley has argued, Britain was a state but it was not yet a nation: it was an administrative entity but it was not yet a cultural body that its people identified with or felt committed to.[8] The process by which Britain came to be a nation is an important theme of this book, since it is a key context for the developing notion of citizenship.

The structure of politics

Another important context for the study of citizenship is the political system itself. Much of the British political system of the eighteenth and nineteenth centuries would be familiar to Britons today. Many of its institutions, offices and conventions still exist. But it is not safe to assume that, because we are dealing with something that appears the same, we have to approach it the same way. Although we have seen the dangers of Whig history, it is nevertheless true that much of the story of British political development is of gradual adaptation without existing arrangements. There are very few watersheds or efforts to redefine practices in a 'modern' way: even political settlements that might appear to do this – such as the First Reform Act of 1832 – turn out on closer inspection to be partly about continuity or compromise.

The nature of the British constitution typifies this. In most countries, the 'constitution' is a single written document setting out the nature of their political system and the rights of citizens within it. Citizens of the United States of America, for example, have a very clear idea of what their constitution is, and current political issues such as free speech or the right to bear arms are commonly discussed in relation to it. The constitution of the United States dates from the period of the American Revolution, when they were establishing a new political system and needed to define it. Having never had such a revolution, Britain has no such document: the nearest we get is probably the Bill of Rights, from the quasi-revolution of 1688–89. Because Britain's political arrangements have developed gradually over the centuries, the constitution is the agglomeration of successive settlements, pronouncements and practices. Documents such as the Magna Carta, legal precedents embodied in the common law and the established procedures of government all collectively comprise the constitution.

Given the lack of clarity about what the British constitution is, a striking feature of politics in the eighteenth and nineteenth centuries is that everybody was talking about it. Speeches at the hustings and in parliament pledged to uphold the constitution, Whigs and Tories alike warned that the constitution was in danger, and politicians and their critics all claimed to be acting in a constitutional way. Even most radicals had faith in the perfectibility of the constitution, and sought to restore it to its former glory rather than replace it with a new one. Constitutionalism was the central political discourse of the day, partly because of its very adaptability. Because the constitution was unwritten, its legacy was up for debate and all sides could claim to uphold it: conservatives could claim to protect tradition, whereas radicals could identify the 'true' meaning of the constitution in the progress of popular liberties. Since the British constitution is essentially a question of historical precedent, political argument often involved historical argument. This was the purpose of the great Whig constitutional histories. The huge, multi-volume histories of English political development by Macaulay, Maitland and Stubbs all sought to fix a particular interpretation of the constitution in line with their political beliefs.[9] Even today, talking about the constitution requires historical knowledge and skills. The essentially historical nature of the British constitution is another reason why historians make good citizens.

Part of the meaning of 'constitution' is things as they are constituted so, in a sense, the structure of government *was* the constitution. Britain had an unusual form of government known as a limited monarchy, which combined democratic and undemocratic elements recognisable from other political systems. On the one hand, parliament was elected by the people, who were free to criticise their government and whose rights were protected by the law. On the other, many aspects of the system were elitist, hereditary or autocratic. At the heart of the political system lay the three central institutions of the monarchy, the Lords and the Commons. Power was divided between them but not equally, epitomising this tension between the democratic and the undemocratic. In the eighteenth century, many Britons and commentators from abroad regarded this political system as the best in the world, combining the elements of autocracy, aristocracy and democracy more perfectly than the best republican constitutions, ancient or modern. The French commentator Jean-Louis de Lolme noted in 1771 that, in the English political system, 'Liberty has at last been able to erect herself a temple'.[10]

The key to a successful governmental structure was balance: as in classical republics, the idea was that each element should be able to check the other, ensuring that good government was carried out in the interest of all. This balance of power between the monarch, Lords and Commons had shifted over the centuries. Conservative wisdom was that this had occurred in an almost-magical and peaceful way, which is a key reason why anti-reformers were so reluctant to tamper with the constitution. Originally the monarch was sovereign – the root of the system's power and legitimacy, as granted by God – and parliament had been called into existence purely to grant revenue. But gradually the representative chamber had grown in power, both in terms of its practical importance in the business of government and as the basis of the political system's legitimacy. By the 1830s, the Commons was the most important part of the constitution, and the government's power rested on its ability to command a majority in the elected chamber rather than on the monarch's favour. A form of representative democracy had arrived, but this was not the Commons' original function and many anomalies and anachronisms exist to this day. It is worth thinking about each of these three institutions in turn and how their functioning altered over the course of the eighteenth and nineteenth centuries.

The monarchy

In Britain, the monarch is the head of state. They exercise the executive power: they have the final say, sign off legislation and approve the appointment of ministers. In contrast with France, which followed Salic law, in Britain the office could be held in its own right by a woman. For about a third of the period covered by this book, a woman held the most powerful office in the British political system. We will see how, at the time and since, queens were often evaluated in terms of their gender. Queen Anne (r. 1702–14) was long regarded by historians as a weak woman, beset by illness and easily manipulated: more recently, her reputation has been re-evaluated and she is now generally regarded as a determined and skilled political operator.[11] Kings, too, were judged in terms of their masculinity: in Chapter 5 we will see how the chequered record of George IV (r. 1820–30) as a husband and a father, and his reputation as a spendthrift and a debauchee, raised questions about his ability to rule.

In a sense, the position of the monarch in the political is analogous to a president in a republican system like the USA or France, but whereas presidents are implicated in party politics, monarchs today are supposed to remain scrupulously above it. Nowadays the power of the monarch is mostly symbolic: they are a figurehead with a largely ceremonial role. In 1867, Walter Bagehot distinguished between the 'dignified' and 'efficient' roles of the monarchy: on the one hand, the monarch was there to 'excite and preserve the reverence of the population'; on the other, they carried out important functions and exercised real power.[12] The Glorious Revolution may have asserted that monarchs are there at the behest of parliament, but they were still appointed by God. In the eighteenth century it was treason to criticise the monarch directly, so opposition politicians had to tread very carefully, criticising instead the 'wicked ministers' who were misleading their ruler. A common opposition tactic in this period was to rally around the heir in the hope that a change of monarch would improve their fortunes. The court of the Prince of Wales often became a rival power base for party politics, helped by the fact that monarchs rarely got on with their eldest sons in this period. This serves to remind us that we are still dealing with what was essentially a dynastic political system well into the nineteenth century.

The monarchy exercised a direct influence over political affairs. They chose the prime minister and appointed government ministers. A 'minister' is literally someone who ministers to – or serves – the monarch. Even today, ministers are royal appointments and the monarch performs the ceremony of 'kissing hands'. If the parties in Westminster are unable to form a government, the monarch is the constitutional backstop (as we saw in 2010 and 2017, when there was no clear majority in parliament and the palace liaised with 10 Downing Street about the process for forming a government). The monarch also has a role in the day-to-day running of politics, such as their role signing legislation into law. In periods when the monarch was indisposed, the machinery of government ground to a halt. George III (r. 1760–1820) suffered bouts of mental illness from the 1780s, which caused great political uncertainty until his son was appointed regent in 1811. And after the death of her husband Albert in 1861, Victoria (r. 1837–1901) went into a long period of profound mourning and spent much time away from London, refusing to perform her public duties. As well as creating practical problems for government, this gave strength to anti-monarchism and even republicanism.

Victoria also intervened more directly into party politics. Early in her reign she was devoted to the Whig prime minister, Lord Melbourne. He acted as a mentor to the young queen and they became personally very close. So when in 1839 the Whigs were too weak to keep power and Melbourne was forced to resign, Victoria refused to allow changes to appointments in the royal household. In this period, household roles such as ladies in waiting were party appointments, and the Conservative leader Sir Robert Peel refused to take office while Whigs retained influential personnel at court. Melbourne therefore struggled on without the confidence of the Commons. Victoria's actions during the 'Bedchamber Crisis' damaged him, his party and the reputation of the monarchy. Her devotion to individual politicians also proved a problem later on, when she clearly favoured the Tory Benjamin Disraeli over his Liberal rival William Gladstone, whom she detested. When the Liberals won an election in 1880 she tried to offer the premiership to other people, and she undermined Gladstone in office, showing his correspondence to opponents and blocking his appointments to cabinet. These instances illustrate that the queen had real power and was unwilling to give it up, but the fact that she was deemed to have acted improperly also shows that the 'efficient' role of the monarchy had decisively declined by the nineteenth century.

The House of Lords

The House of Lords was also much more important and powerful in the eighteenth and nineteenth centuries than it is today. Originally a body of nobles assembled to advise the monarch, in more recent times the House of Lords has acted as a second chamber to scrutinise the Commons. Its members are 'peers', or members of the nobility. Today, hereditary peers have largely been abolished and peers sit for life, having been granted their position based on their ability and experience, but in the eighteenth and nineteenth centuries it comprised men of the aristocratic elite. Women were not allowed to sit in the Lords. Margaret Haig Thomas was the only child and heir of Viscount Rhondda, and wished to take up his seat after he died in 1918 but was prevented from doing so. A former suffragette, she campaigned for decades for this to be overturned and, although she lived to see women included in the Life Peerages Act of 1958, she died before hereditary women peers were admitted in 1963.

In terms of procedure, the Lords functions in a similar way today as to how it did in the eighteenth century. New legislation (a 'Bill') has to be read, debated and voted upon in the Commons, then it is sent up to the Lords. The Lords will scrutinise and debate the Bill, and can reject it or send it back with amendments. Only once a Bill has passed both houses three times does it receives royal assent and become an Act, passing into law. New peers are appointed by the monarch, but these are party nominees and governments seek to bolster their position in the Lords by appointing their supporters. The Lords tend to be conservative with a small 'c' – acting as a break on the less conservative suggestions of the Commons – but in the nineteenth century they were often Conservative as well. Reformist legislation was often blocked, so Whigs and Liberals attempted to create more peers when in office. The most famous example of this was the Reform Bill Crisis of 1830–32 when the Lords kept rejecting the Whig proposal to change the electoral system. The king was eventually persuaded that the Reform Bill had to pass, so created a large number of Whig peers to win the crucial votes. Tellingly, this is an example of working within existing structures rather than abolishing them, and it was only done with great reluctance. Nevertheless, the 1832 Reform Act reduced the clout of the Lords at the same time as it reinforced the legitimacy of the Commons.

The Victorian House of Lords, however, was much more important than it is today. For example, many prime ministers and prominent cabinet members were drawn from the Lords. Most Victorian prime ministers were drawn from the Lords rather than the Commons; Russell and Disraeli had separate terms as prime minister in both houses. Characteristically, Gladstone – committed Liberal and 'the People's William' – refused a peerage and remained in the Commons throughout his career.

The House of Commons

The commons is the democratic element of the British constitution. We will evaluate just how 'democratic' it was in practice when we examine the electoral system in Chapter 3, but for now we will focus on what happens within Westminster. By the nineteenth century, the Commons was the most important part of the constitution. It was revered around the world as a model of working democracy. On the other hand, visitors were shocked at incivility and combativeness of MPs. As today, jeering, cheering and heckling were the norm, and the atmosphere was that of a gentleman's club. The two ranks of banked seating, in contrast to the more consensual semicircle in representative assemblies abroad, fosters this gladiatorial culture, pitting government and opposition against one another. This boisterous, masculine culture changed little with the arrival of the first female MPs from 1919. Even today, studies cite the masculine culture of the Commons as a reason why women are put off running for political office (along with practical issues such as its anti-social sitting hours).[13] The 2017 general election returned a record number of female MPs – 208 out of 650 – but this is still less than a third.

The principle was gradually established that governments were chosen according to their ability to command a majority in the Commons. A party without a majority cannot get their business passed and, crucially, cannot win votes of confidence. By the nineteenth century, getting into power was a question of 'winning' a general election by obtaining the most seats. After the Septennial Act of 1715, these elections took place at least every seven years, but governments could call them more often – usually when they thought they could win, or if they needed public support – so in practice they were more frequent. Elections for individual seats, or by-elections, would be occasioned by the seat becoming vacant.

The party system as we know it did not come into being until the Victorian period. In the eighteenth century, MPs could identify as Whigs and Tories, but these denoted attitudes towards the monarchy and executive power rather than parties as we would recognise them. Party groupings were very loose, often relying on familial connection, and parties were not national bodies with developed infrastructure in the country at large. There was little connection between Westminster and the localities, and campaigns in the constituencies would barely reference party membership at all. It is arguably more meaningful to talk about 'court' versus 'country': those who supported the king's government (or held a paid post, or had otherwise been bought off) versus those who stood for the interests of 'the people'. In this period, party itself was suspect: it was associated with faction and could be seen to compromise individual conscience. As we have seen, political opposition was problematic in a monarchical system, and factional behaviour against the monarch's government was technically treasonable and politically unsavoury. Most members were 'independents', who would support the king's government except when they could not conscientiously do so.

It was not until the mid-nineteenth century that the House (and the nation) was divided into two parties, led by two distinctive leaders, standing for different ideals and legislative programmes. Whichever party won the election would get into power and its leader would become prime minister, whereas the second largest party would become the official opposition. Parties were becoming more disciplined, with party whips to ensure voting discipline and party clubs acting as power bases, but they were still not all-powerful like they are today. There were still independents in parliament and party loyalties were more provisional: 'crossing the floor' was more common than it is today, and the Whig group ceased to be a party in its own right as its members drifted to the Liberals and the Conservatives. Politicians were also 'independent' in a financial sense: politicians did not receive a salary until 1911, so politics was necessarily the vocation of the elite. Supporting themselves by their own means was presented as a positive good, since it supposedly ensured that their consciences could not be compromised. Not only did MPs not receive a salary, but they had to pass a landed property qualification: 'a Law, which was intended to confine the Election to such Persons as are *independent in their Circumstances*; have a valuable Stake in the *Land*; and must therefore be the most strongly engaged to consult the *publick Good*, and least liable to *Corruption*'.[14] These were obvious bars to the participation of working men in parliament, which generations of radicals, Chartists and Labour activists sought to overturn. Even in the Commons, therefore, we can see the tension between democratic and undemocratic elements that pervaded the British constitution as a whole.

In conclusion, then, the structure of British politics in the eighteenth and nineteenth centuries is superficially similar to today's, but it operated in a different way, which was appropriate to its time. We can see this in the new Palace of Westminster, which was constructed after a fire destroyed the old parliament buildings in 1834. Given that this was immediately after the Great Reform Act, one might have expected a bold architectural statement in a classical style to project democracy and openness. Instead, Charles Barry's 'palace' is in the style of a gothic cathedral, evoking the feudal and confessional past rather than equality. The plain and cramped Commons chamber contrasts with the opulent Lords, where the symbolic power lay. Like many civic buildings, the Palace of Westminster had a clear sense of history, and this should remind us that Georgians and Victorians had a very historical perspective on their political system. They were acutely aware that it had developed over the centuries and that, in order to understand the constitution, they had to understand history. Then as now, the writings of historians were political statements, so we should be alive to the political importance of how we tell the story of British politics.

The emergence of the public sphere?

The formal structure of the state is an important context for the study of citizenship, but citizenship as an activity largely takes place outside of it. In the rest of this chapter we will therefore think about politics in a broader way, thinking about what it consists of in cultural terms. We will focus on the physical spaces, networks and media through which politics is conducted, and we will also explore the ways in which people in the eighteenth and nineteenth centuries thought about politics as a sphere of activity. The concept of 'the public' is crucial here and became fundamental to the ways in which the political world beyond Westminster was conceived of and granted a role in the political process. Today, we take the idea of a 'public' for granted. The term recurs in our political discourse and we all claim to belong to 'the public': a body of people with opinions, who can express their will and exert pressure on those who govern us. If the citizen is the political individual, then the public is a key way in which we think about aggregates of citizens and how we have a collective identity as a member of a political community.

This has not always been the case, since 'the public' is a characteristically modern phenomenon. In the early modern world, people beyond Westminster clearly did have political opinions, but this body of opinions was not yet comprehended in a collective way, nor granted a legitimate way in which it could be expressed. Up to the seventeenth century, political power was located in the court: this is where much of politics was conducted and discussed, and much of what happened beyond the court was dependent on its patronage. Nor was political opinion entirely free, since to criticise the monarch or the conduct of their government was potentially a treasonous activity. The monarch and the court possessed political authority, and there was little sense that the body of people and opinions in the world outside underwrote it. The public was therefore a new phenomenon of the eighteenth century, in two senses. First, there were new forums in which people beyond Westminster and the traditional political classes could participate in national political life. Second, the public was a new idea, a new way of thinking about collective opinion and a new player in political life. Historians have tended to assume that the latter reflected the existence of the former: in the following section we will explore both facets and the causal relationship between them.

When academic historians discuss this subject, they usually use the concept of the 'public sphere', coined by the German scholar Jürgen Habermas in his 1962 work *The Structural Transformation of the Public Sphere: An Inquiry into a Category of Bourgeois Society*. The subtitle is significant, since Habermas links the emergence of the public sphere to that of the bourgeoisie, the middle class. His work therefore fits a broadly Marxist chronology about the rise of capitalism and the class system, but unlike Marxists he had an optimistic view of the middle class, projecting them as private, educated and reasoning individuals, and therefore promising material for citizenship. Habermas argues that, prior to the eighteenth century, politics took place in the realm of the court and the state, and beyond this was the apolitical world of the family and economic life. In the eighteenth century, however, private individuals come to occupy a new space between the private realm and the formal sphere of public authority (Table 1.1). This public sphere is created when private citizens associate outside of the private realm and discuss political questions. Increasingly, this becomes a recognised space where citizens can discuss matters of mutual interest and oversee the operations of the state. This makes the political and administrative actions of the state accountable and provides a forum that can put pressure on the state, therefore creating a new relationship between governors and the governed.

Habermas depicts a European phenomenon: as with the Enlightenment (of which this was a part) this was happening simultaneously in many countries. But it happened earliest and most comprehensively in Britain: as with accounts of the rise of a class society, or of industrial revolution, Britain is the ideal type. Despite this, it was only after *Structural Transformation of the Public Sphere* was

Table 1.1 Habermas's public sphere

Private realm	Public sphere in the political realm	Sphere of public authority
Civil society (realm of commodity exchange and social labour) Conjugal family's internal space	Public sphere in the world of letters (clubs, press)	State Court (courtly noble society)

Adapted from Jürgen Habermas, *The Structural Transformation of the Public Sphere: An Inquiry into a Category of Bourgeois Society* (1962) trans. Thomas Burger, Cambridge: Polity, 1989, p. 30.

translated into English in 1989 that it became influential in British studies. Historians in the growing field of popular politics found it a useful way to talk about the growth of extra-parliamentary politics, and it has helped literary scholars to look beyond textual analysis and engage with questions of readership, the circulation of reading materials and the social bases of Enlightenment. It has probably been most influential within gender studies, since it fitted the existing narrative within women's history about the rise of 'separate spheres'. It has long been argued within academic feminism that women were confined to the private sphere of the home and the family from the eighteenth century: we will explore this interpretation in greater depth in Chapter 5 as it has major implications for how we interpret women's access to politics. The corollary of this was the public sphere of politics, economics and the law, which was increasingly monopolised by men. Although Habermas had little to say about gender, his account has helped historians to flesh out the latter, which had previously often been assumed rather than fully explained. His account has the same periodisation, focuses on spaces both within the home and beyond it, and similarly identifies the new middle class as the drivers of the process.

Like all structural models, Habermas's public sphere has come in for its fair share of criticism. By the time it was translated into English it was already slightly old-fashioned, in focusing on class and arguing that economics determined cultural change. At the time, the idea of separate spheres was being critiqued as the new gender history was reassessing the methods of women's history.[15] Nevertheless, the public sphere remains a useful concept, as political life was changing in important ways in the eighteenth century, and in ways that related to changes in social and intellectual life. New forums of political life were emerging and we will now turn out attention to four of them: extra-parliamentary politics, public spaces, political institutions and the press.

The electorate

A key aspect of the public sphere was the creation of a vibrant extra-parliamentary political culture. We will examine the mechanics and the culture of Georgian elections in Chapter 3, but it is worth pausing here to note the remarkable politicisation of the electorate that took place in this period. In the seventeenth century, elections took place infrequently: if a monarch did not need to raise money for war then they could avoid calling a new parliament, as Charles I did in the 1630s. As we have seen, however, the post-1688 constitutional settlements changed the political landscape. After the Triennial Act of 1694, elections had to be held at least every three years (later changed to seven). Regular elections kept issues on the political agenda at the local level and required electoral interests to develop electoral machinery like election agents and canvassers. Political causes now had continuity from election to election, and keeping political issues in the memory made candidates increasingly accountable for their promises.

On the side of the voters, they were becoming more assertive and independent. Large constituencies became increasingly difficult to control and voters protested when powerful patrons sought to control the representation. Cities and boroughs in this period typically had two MPs, so local elites would commonly come to an arrangement prior to the election to only field two candidates, thus avoiding a contest. Voters, however, liked to be asked their opinion so would sometimes put up an additional candidate to force a contest and focus attention on populist issues. Frank O'Gorman argues that these 'independence' protests offered a basic critique of parliamentary representation, and were a forerunner of radicalism and reform.[16] Even before the parliamentary reforms of the nineteenth century, however, the electorate was growing. Electoral qualifications were usually based around property and the eighteenth century was a period of inflation, when prices more than doubled, so more people were meeting the qualifications. O'Gorman estimates that the electorate of England and Wales grew from 240,000 in 1689 to 439,200 in 1831. It should be noted that this was not keeping pace with population, which grew from 5.4 million to 13.9 million in the same period. Only men could vote in this period and only 14.4 per cent of them had the vote in the last election before the Reform Act.[17]

As we will see in Chapter 3, however, elections in the eighteenth century were not necessarily about the voters. In this period, elections developed into huge festive events where the whole community got involved. These festivities included public events such as processions, speeches, music and rituals, where non-voters could participate just as much as voters. There were also numerous opportunities for women to influence – and profit from – the proceedings. Electoral participation should not therefore be equated with voting in this period: for those who partook of the rich communal culture of an election, it was probably their most tangible experience of national political life.

Public spaces

The terms 'public' and 'sphere' both suggest space, and Habermas's account has helped historians to think about the new ways that space could be used to political ends in this period. The eighteenth century was a time of change for Britain's towns. The urban population trebled over the course of the century and the design and function of towns significantly altered. Formerly, towns had been rough places of trade and the urban had been criticised as the seat of vice, corruption and disease. Over the course of the eighteenth century, however, the town was increasingly celebrated as the centre for all that was progressive and sociable. This 'urban renaissance' involved a redesign of the cityscape. Many of the densely packed and unsanitary old buildings were cleared away – a process helped by a number of great fires in the late seventeenth and early eighteenth centuries – and were replaced by well-proportioned buildings and wide streets. New public venues such as assembly rooms made the city the destination for refined leisure.

These new urban spaces provided forums for political interaction. The quintessential venue of the public sphere was the coffeehouse. The man-about-town James Boswell recorded his many visits to coffeehouses in his famous diary. For example, on 27 November 1762 he went to Child's coffeehouse in St Paul's Yard, 'read the political papers, and had some chat with the citizens'.[18] One did not just go to a coffeehouse for the fashionable new caffeinated beverage although, in contrast with the alcohol served in taverns, it did lend itself to a refined and rational sort of conviviality. The coffeehouse was conducive to the 'polite' conduct celebrated in the pages of *Tatler* and *The Spectator*: it was an arena where citizens could meet as equals and discuss elevated matters in a non-violent atmosphere. The standard greeting at a coffeehouse was 'what news?', whereupon one could talk to a complete stranger about the public questions of the day. It was also fairly accessible in social terms, since for the price of a drink you could peruse the newspapers and gain admittance to political discussions. It was, however, a specifically male space, which lent itself to the performance of a masculine type of urban political citizenship.

Other spaces of the eighteenth-century town could be used for political ends in unintended ways. The urban renaissance created large open spaces such as squares, parks and promenades. These were intended to promote polite interaction, but their very openness could be appropriated to subversive political ends. Crowd demonstrations were a common feature of eighteenth-century popular politics. George Rudé cautioned decades ago that we should not call them a 'mob', since they were in fact politically articulate and had defined goals. The crowd would often come out if it felt that the moral code of the community had been broken in some way, with regard to issues such as food prices, enclosure or military conscription. In the early nineteenth century, the radical movement often used the tactic of the mass demonstration both to demonstrate their strength in numbers and their moral worthiness for citizenship: a demonstration that was peaceful, respectable and well-organised spoke volumes about its participants. Steve Poole notes how in certain cities, specific sites were 'invested with particular resonances and power'. In Bristol, for example, Queen Square had formerly been common land but had been transformed into a fashionable space for the merchant elite and the site of key civic buildings. Radical and Chartist demonstrations therefore sought to occupy this space in order to lay a claim to political inclusion. As Poole argues, citizenship in Bristol involved 'active, visible and unrestricted access to the public and civic domain, symbolically represented ... in social conflicts over particularly resonant topographies and spaces'.[19] The politics of the crowd should not just be read in symbolic terms, however: a demonstration or a procession should be considered as a lived experience, involving physical effort, potential danger and emotive sensory experiences.[20] The study of space can therefore help us to think about citizenship as a lived condition, both as an individual and as a part of a larger body of people.

Political institutions

The eighteenth century was a golden age of associational life. Eighteenth-century towns were notable for the number of societies devoted to such diverse intellectual activities as antiquarianism, literature, philosophy and statistics, or for more practical activities like trade or policing. What they had in common was a sense of civic pride, of voluntary service and of masculine sociability. Karen Harvey has drawn our attention to their drinking rituals, which can shed light on the emotional (and chemical) ways in which bonds are created between men. At punch parties, these men would gather to drink from a large bowl, which was commonly decorated with the insignia of their association. The material form of the bowl was significant in another sense: 'circular and open bowls enable sharing and coming together', as did the practice of passing the bowl from man to man.[21]

Some institutions had an expressly political purpose. Westminster's political parties had their preferred gentleman's clubs, with Whigs frequenting Brooks's whereas Tories went to Boodle's or White's. Clubs were the site of informal party power bases in the eighteenth century, but became more formally associated with party infrastructure in the nineteenth. Lower down the social scale, debating clubs were a popular feature of eighteenth-century towns and especially in London. In the early eighteenth century they often met in pubs, highlighting the crossover between politics and sociability. Although not as 'polite' as the discussion in a coffeehouse, debates were nevertheless very structured and controlled, and would cover such topics as current affairs, religion, foreign policy and social questions. By the 1780s, these societies had grown to the extent that they were moving from taverns into larger venues. Alcohol was replaced with tea and an admission fee was charged, which ensured the respectability of the gathering but remained fairly accessible. Donna Andrew argues that this was the high water mark of female participation in these societies: some were sexually mixed whereas others like La Belle Assemblee were women-only, and debated contentious topics such as the state of marriage and gender relations.[22] This flourishing of public debate came to an end in the 1790s, when the French Revolution made the radicalism and social mixing of the debating clubs seem too threatening. A cartoon of 1795 depicts a rowdy scene, where the plebeian audience are not respecting the rules of rational debate (Figure 1.1). The chair demands 'Silence, Gentlemen! Only Ten Speak at a Time!' while a donkey in the window mirrors their braying. By mocking their roughness and their intellectual pretensions, the artist is countering the radicals' claims that men of this class were fit to be citizens.

The model of the association was also used to pursue political causes. An association was a like-minded, voluntary group who would pledge to pursue a

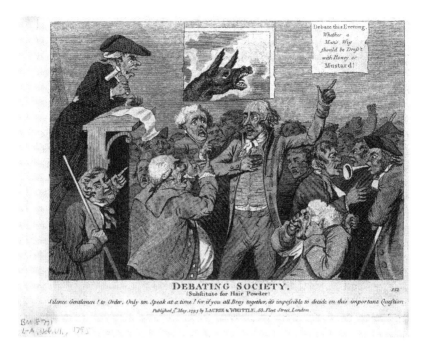

Figure 1.1 Isaac Cruikshank, 'Debating Society. (Substitute for Hair Powder)' (1795). Courtesy of the Lewis Walpole Library, Yale University.

specific cause, and would not disband until it had been achieved. Causes pursued by eighteenth-century associations included moral reform, anti-Catholicism, religious observance and military defence, among others. In the 1780s, the Reverend Christopher Wyvill set up the Association Movement to press for parliamentary reform. This grew out of the structures of electoral politics, whereby large county meetings would be held and resolutions passed. Wyvill sought to establish an association in every county, to throw their weight behind pro-reform candidates and to use their collective power to put pressure on parliament. Pressure groups were also a common feature of nineteenth-century politics. They would typically pursue humanitarian causes such as prison reform or anti-slavery, or economic causes like opposing the Corn Laws. As we will see in Chapter 5, causes with a moral dimension were often dominated by women, so the pressure group offered them an avenue into politics at a time when many other avenues were closed.

The press

The growing availability of print in the eighteenth century is central to Habermas's notion of a public sphere. The print industry boomed in this period and printed works became available in new forms, reaching new audiences. One such invention of the eighteenth century is the novel, a genre that was increasingly dominated by women both as readers and writers – so this was an aspect of the public sphere from which they were decidedly not excluded. By contrast, genres such as history, politics, philosophy and economics were seen as masculine. The division of gendered 'natures' implicit in separate spheres – between public and private, rational and emotional, practical and frivolous – was certainly perceptible in the eighteenth-century publishing industry.

Another printed form that is synonymous with the eighteenth century is the satirical print. Political cartoons from the period are often used by historians since they comment on political and social questions in a highly topical way, and often convey their point very forcefully and amusingly. We should be careful about assuming that they 'reflect' public opinion,[23] however, since they were often created to intervene in political events and artists could be in the pay of politicians (or in the case of Sir George Townshend be a politician themselves). Nor should we assume that they had a wide social reach. Although they were a visual medium, they usually contained a lot of text that would have been lost on the illiterate, and understanding their complex symbolic language requires a high degree of visual literacy. They were also more expensive and less widely circulated than historians often assume.[24] With these qualifications in mind, however, we will be using examples of political prints throughout this book, since they tell us a great deal both about politics and about gender.

The most significant aspect of the printing industry for eighteenth-century politics, however, was the newspaper. After the Printing Act lapsed in 1695, we see an exponential growth in circulation and the numbers of titles. Newspaper circulations increased twenty-fold between 1700 and 1850. London led the way with a handful of titles at the beginning of the century, but by the mid-century it had six weeklies, six tri-weeklies and six dailies. Provincial newspapers also exploded from nothing at the beginning of the century to 70 weeklies by its end.[25] There were no national newspapers in this period and people outside of the capital tended to read the title published in their nearest provincial centre, such as the *Northampton Mercury* or *Jackson's Oxford Journal*. Provincial newspapers often reproduced much of their copy from London papers, however, so in practice there was consistent coverage of national and international affairs.

The question of how newspapers were consumed is complex. Newspapers were expensive articles by today's standards and before the 1830s the government was keen to keep it that way, given fears about political information circulating among the working classes. All legal newspapers carried a government stamp, which represented most of the value of the purchase, and in times of political tension the Stamp Tax was raised to make newspapers less accessible: in 1815 the tax was four pence, pushing the cost of a newspaper to six pence or more. One did not necessarily have to buy a newspaper in order to read it, however. As we have seen, newspapers were often available to read in coffee shops or taverns, and they were also carried by subscription libraries and private reading rooms. A single newspaper would pass through many hands – so circulation did not equate to readership in this period – and newspapers were often read aloud. Reading practices were much more oral and communal than they are today, making written material available even to the illiterate. Calculating literacy rates is a complex business, since more people could read than write, and being able to sign one's name is not a reliable measure of the latter, but broadly speaking 60 per cent of men and fewer women were literate in the mid-eighteenth century.

However Georgians accessed their contents, newspapers were consumed voraciously. Looking at a Georgian newspaper today, it is perhaps difficult to understand why: a single sheet of paper folded in two, with tiny text, no headlines, no illustrations and frequently dry or obscure content, they can seem unappealing to modern readers. Historians generally now access newspaper content from this period electronically and go straight to the article they require by means of a keyword search, so we are more detached than ever from the reading practices that Georgians developed in order to navigate them. Nevertheless, the importance of newspapers to politics in this period cannot be overstated. Newspapers had a key role to play in many political conflicts of the time. For example, we will see in the following chapter how the radical John Wilkes was persecuted for criticising the government in his paper *The North Briton* in the 1760s, and this case served to cement important rights regarding the press and freedom of speech. Wilkes also helped to secure the right of newspapers to print parliamentary debates. Thereafter, the appearance of the proceedings of parliament in the press became a fundamental aspect of politics, since parliament became ever-more visible and accountable to the public. Politicians came to appreciate the importance of this and their awareness of the wider audience outside of the chamber began to affect what was said within it. The process by which debates were reported in the press was somewhat haphazard: parliamentary reporters were not permitted to take notes, so relied on prodigious feats of memory to record what was said.[26] Some MPs therefore made corrected versions of their speeches available to newspapers in an effort to gain some control over how their words were reported.

Given the importance of the press to political life, the freedom of the press came to be regarded as a fundamental liberty and something that was key to the functioning of the constitution. Freedom to speak one's mind became an important facet of the British self-identity and, in particular, related to masculine values such as independence and candour. Any restrictions on the freedom of the press were met with hysterical accusations of 'enslavement' or 'tyranny'. The Stamp Tax was therefore the focus of radical ire and in the post-war period radicals published underground 'unstamped' newspapers, which had the double benefit of being cheap and not sending money to the Treasury. As one such paper, *The Gorgon*, noted in 1818:

> CORRUPTION has not yet encountered a more formidable and dangerous enemy, than in the circulation of cheap, weekly publications; and the malignant, but abortive attempts, that have been made to suppress the lights to the poor, prove with what detestation and alarm their progress has been viewed by the tools of power.[27]

As we approach the Victorian period, however, we can see a change in attitude towards the press. Stamp duty was reduced to a penny in 1836 and abolished altogether in 1855. The government's attitude shifted from keeping the press as expensive and inaccessible as possible to positively encouraging it. There were several reasons behind this. It removed a key radical complaint at a stroke and arguably made the press easier to regulate, since the underground press was beyond government control. With respectable publications now affordable, market forces killed off less respectable and more radical types of literature. More generally, there was a change in attitude towards political citizenship itself. Some commentators like James Mill argued that the press was a useful 'safety valve', allowing the lower orders a legitimate avenue to criticise the government that was much safer than the alternatives.[28] James Vernon has argued that this was part of an effort to reform the culture of politics by encouraging self-education and participation in a rational and private political activity. As one commentator noted in 1836, 'he would rather that the poor man should have the newspaper in his cottage than he should be sent to the public house to read it'.[29] The liberalisation of the press may therefore have been intended to control people rather than free them, by turning them into self-governing citizens.

Conclusion

The eighteenth century therefore witnessed the birth of new political forums, outside of the formal state, which allowed citizens to come together and express their collective will. Another striking feature of Georgian politics is that contemporaries realised this was happening. Georgians recognised that 'the public' was a new and powerful actor in political life. A newspaper that launched in 1801 addressed its first editorial 'TO THE PUBLIC' and added that it looked up to 'that generous Public, as a patron, whose merit is to be gained by favour alone'.[30] Politicians came to acknowledge 'public opinion' as an important part of political life: a tribunal for national questions, where the people could express their views, and to which their representatives should be mindful when deciding on a course of action. Because it was new, people debated what form it took and what its role should be. In cartoons of the day, a range of devices were used to represent public opinion, including weathervanes, clocks and pendulums: this suggests that ideas about the phenomenon were still experimental and provisional. A cartoon entitled 'March 1829' portrayed the debate on Catholic emancipation (Figure 1.2). It depicted 'public opinion' as a pair of scales, balancing the forces of 'liberality' (progressive newspapers, the Irish interest and 'rats' in the Tory party) against those of 'prudence' (conservative newspapers, the state church and the monarchy). As an artistic production, the cartoon is crude, suggesting that it was dashed off in order to comment on current events, but it is telling that the artists chose a representation of 'public opinion' in order to visualise the political state of play.

There is also the question of who was included in 'the public'. We might assume today that the public includes everybody, but this was not the case in the eighteenth century. Lord Cockburn noted that, 'The *public* was the word for

Figure 1.2 Anon., 'March 1829' (1829). © Trustees of the British Museum.

the middle ranks, and all below this was the *populace* or the *mob*'. This might appear to tally with Habermas's concept of a 'bourgeois' public sphere. Anna Clark argues that, after 1815, radicals sought to replace this exclusive category of 'the public' with 'the people'. As well as being more inclusive in social terms, some radicals included women within this definition.[31] Even 'the people' could be exclusive, however. When elections 'took the sense of the people', they asked the opinion of propertied male householders, and 'the people' is also exclusive in national and racial terms.

Terms like this were not necessarily used to refer to social groups, however. The term 'public' was more usually used in a moral way to discuss personal virtues. 'Public life' was the vocation for virtuous men of a certain rank and 'public spirit' suggested a manly, disinterested and patriotic commitment to the common good. Private interest, by contrast, was everything that was secretive, factious and selfish, the opposite of the manly openness that was prided in political life. 'Public' and 'private' was therefore a gendered binary, which could refer to personal ideals and models of behaviour. We will see in the following chapter how appropriate political behaviour was assessed in gendered terms: one had to be 'manly' to participate in political life, and any hints of slovenliness, self-interest, vice or effeminacy could undermine an attempt to be taken seriously as a public figure.

As we will see throughout this book, mapping the public sphere onto men and the private sphere onto women is much more problematic. We will return to this issue in Chapter 5 when we explore women's roles in more detail, but we have already seen numerous examples of women participating in the political world and of men being excluded from it. Even social class is not necessarily the dividing line here. Although working people may not have been included in some notions of the 'public', there were both formal and informal ways in which they could access it. Many working men had the vote, were literate or could participate in street politics. Habermas's public sphere is therefore too strict a sociological structure, which does not reflect gender or class in a comprehensive way. What it does help us to understand is the way that politics was changing in this period. In the eighteenth century, new arenas were developing that fundamentally changed the nature of political life, and Habermas helps us to understand the social and cultural conditions for this shift. We should not see the new ideas about this 'public' as a direct reflection of this change, but they do tell us that people at the time perceived that the political world was changing and that they were trying to comprehend it. The notion of 'public opinion' was one of the defining ideas of the eighteenth century and has shaped British politics ever since.

In this chapter we have seen a story of change between the seventeenth and the nineteenth centuries, and this is the backdrop for the chapters that follow. The transformation of the informal political sphere was more rapid than that of the formal state structures, which remained relatively settled and resistant to reform. It was not a one-way process of the public putting pressure on the state, since we have seen various ways in which the institutions of the state tried to influence popular politics or alter its very form. Citizenship as an activity involves both formal and informal political participation, and is inseparable from the wider society and culture in which it takes place. In the next chapter, we will see how politics in the eighteenth and nineteenth centuries was bound up with particular ideas about masculinity, and that changing ideas about gender can therefore help us to understand the changing nature of the political world.

Notes

1 K. Wilson, 'Inventing revolution: 1688 and eighteenth-century popular politics', *Journal of British Studies*, 28, 1989, 349–85.
2 Coronation Oath, 1689, in E. N. Williams, *The Eighteenth-Century Constitution: Documents and Commentary*, Cambridge: Cambridge University Press, 1965, p. 37.
3 The Bill of Rights, 1689, in Williams, *Eighteenth-Century Constitution*, pp. 26–33.
4 C. Pateman, *The Sexual Contract: Aspects of Contractual Liberalism*, Stanford: Stanford University Press, 1988.
5 J. Brewer, *The Sinews of Power: War, Money and the English State, 1688–1783*, London: Unwin, 1989.
6 M. McCormack, *The Independent Man: Citizenship and Gender Politics in Georgian England*, Manchester: Manchester University Press, 2005, p. 64.
7 P. Monod, *Jacobitism and the English People*, Cambridge: Cambridge University Press, 1999.
8 L. Colley, *Britons: Forging the Nation, 1707–1837*, New Haven: Yale University Press, 1992.
9 J. Vernon, 'Narrating the constitution: the discourse of "the real" and the fantasies of nineteenth-century constitutional history', in J. Vernon (ed.), *Re-Reading the*

Constitution: New Narratives in the Political History of England's Long Nineteenth Century, Cambridge: Cambridge University Press, 1996, pp. 204–38.
10 J.-L. de Lolme, *The Constitution of England; Or, An Account of the English Government* (1784 edn), ed. D. Lieberman, Indianapolis: Liberty Fund, 2007, p. 342.
11 E. Gregg, *Queen Anne*, London: Routledge, 1980.
12 W. Bagehot, *The English Constitution*, London, 1867, p. 5.
13 House of Commons, *Speaker's Conference (on Parliamentary Representation)*, London: HMSO, 2010, p. 47.
14 *The Craftsman* 375, 8 September 1733, emphasis in the original.
15 See for example: A. Vickery, 'Golden age to separate spheres? A review of the categories and chronology of English women's history', *The Historical Journal*, 36:2, 1993, 383–414.
16 F. O'Gorman, *Voters, Patrons and Parties: The Unreformed Electorate of Hanoverian England*, Oxford: Oxford University Press, 1989, pp. 259–85.
17 O'Gorman, *Voters, Patrons and Parties*, p. 179.
18 J. Boswell, *Boswell's London Journal*, ed. Frederick Pottle, London: Yale University Press, 1950, p. 51.
19 S. Poole, '"Till our liberties be secure": Popular sovereignty and public space in Bristol, 1780–1850', *Urban History*, 26:1, 1999, 40–54 (pp. 40, 54).
20 I am indebted to Katrina Navickas for this observation.
21 K. Harvey, 'Ritual encounters: Punch parties and masculinity in the eighteenth century', *Past and Present*, 214, 2012, 165–202 (p. 197).
22 D. Andrew, 'Popular culture and public debate: London 1780', *The Historical Journal*, 39, 1996, 405–23.
23 T. Hunt, *Defining John Bull: Political Caricature and National Identity in Late Georgian England*, Aldershot: Ashgate, 2003, p. 2.
24 E. Nicolson, 'Consumers and spectators: The public of the political print in eighteenth-century England', *History*, 81, 1996, 5–21.
25 H. Barker, *Newspapers and English Society, 1695–1855*, London: Longman, 1999, p. 29.
26 D. Wahrman, 'Virtual representation: Parliamentary reporting and languages of class in the 1790s', *Past and Present*, 136:1, 1992, 83–113.
27 *The Gorgon*, 23 May 1818.
28 Quoted in Barker, *Newspapers*, p. 21.
29 Quoted in J. Vernon, *Politics and the People: A Study in English Political Culture c. 1815–1867*, Cambridge: Cambridge University Press, 1993, p. 142.
30 *The Weekly Dispatch*, 27 September 1801.
31 A. Clark, *The Struggle for the Breeches: Gender and the Making of the British Working Class*, Berkeley: University of California Press, 1995, pp. 141, 158, emphasis in original.

Recommended reading

Andrew, D., 'Popular culture and public debate: London 1780', *The Historical Journal*, 39, 1996, 405–23.

Barker, H., 'England, 1760–1820', in H. Barker and S. Burrows (eds.), *Press, Politics and the Public Sphere in Europe and North America*, Cambridge: Cambridge University Press, 2002.

Colley, L., *Britons: Forging the Nation, 1707–1837*, New Haven: Yale University Press, 1992.

Donald, D., *The Age of Caricature: Satirical Prints in the Reign of George III*, New Haven: Yale University Press, 1998.

Habermas, J., *The Structural Transformation of the Public Sphere: An Inquiry into a Category of Bourgeois Society* (1962), trans. Thomas Burger, Cambridge: Polity, 1989.

Harling, P., *The Modern British State: An Historical Introduction*, Cambridge: Polity, 2001.

McCormack, M. (ed.), *Public Men: Political Masculinities in Modern Britain*, Basingstoke: Palgrave, 2007.

Vernon, J. (ed.), *Re-Reading the Constitution: New Narratives in the Political History of England's Long Nineteenth Century*, Cambridge: Cambridge University Press, 1996.

Weil, R., *Political Passions: Gender, the Family and Political Argument in England, 1680–1714*, Manchester: Manchester University Press, 1999.

2 Political masculinities, 1688–1837

In the previous chapter we explored the 'public sphere', a new political domain in the eighteenth century that historians have often regarded as being male. In this period, however, there was a lot more to masculinity and politics than just men inhabiting the public sphere. This chapter will show how gender was central to political life in the eighteenth century and would continue to be so into the nineteenth. Political virtue, political conduct and political legitimacy were all commonly thought about in terms of masculinity. In a society where only a minority of men were full citizens, and when other men were trying to establish their moral claim to it, citizenship was a very qualitative business. A man's capacity for citizenship was evaluated in very personal and moral terms, and gender was among the most important ways of talking about individual virtue. This chapter, then, will focus on political masculinities. We will begin by thinking about masculinity and politics as a historical field, thinking about how it emerged and its wider implications for the study of history. We will then focus on some case studies from the Georgian period, including the notorious rake and radical John Wilkes. Wilkes is significant both for his masculinity and his politics, but the masculine image that he projected in the 1760s would have been entirely inappropriate only two decades later. Like the political world, masculinity changes over time, and shifts in either one of these areas can influence the other. We will therefore think about how masculinities changed over the course of the Georgian and Victorian periods, and what this tells us about the nature of citizenship. This is not a descriptive exercise, asking 'what is masculine in political situations?' Gender norms are bound up with questions of power, so we need to think about how masculinity is used in a political way and the far-reaching effects that this can have.

The history of masculinity

The histories of women, gender and masculinity are relatively recent fields of study, so it is worth pausing here to think about how and why they emerged. Women's history has existed since the 1970s in Britain. Inspired by second-wave feminism and the new social history, women's historians sought to rescue women from historical invisibility by studying their social lives and their experiences of oppression. Much pioneering work was done in this tradition, some of which we will explore in Chapter 5. Over the course of the 1980s, some feminist historians turned away from social-structural explanations and instead engaged with the new cultural history. Instead of focusing on the social experience of a single group ('women'), they emphasised the diversity and contingency of female experience, and the necessity of viewing gender in a relational way ('masculinity' and 'femininity'). This involved a move away from explanations based upon social structure, such as class and separate spheres, towards more cultural explanations of power.

At the same time, there was growing interest in men's lives and welfare. Historians involved in this movement emphasised that men's roles and their patriarchal relationships with women are not fixed but are defined by their time and culture. They argued that the expectations that society placed upon men were damaging to both men and women, so understanding and critiquing these roles was a pro-feminist endeavour. Their focus was on 'masculinity' rather than men as a social group: unlike women, men did not need reinstating in the historical record, but their very dominance was so taken for granted that the question of *what it means to be a man* had generally been overlooked. The history of masculinity as it became established in the 1990s was therefore a cultural history, concerned with subjective issues such as representation, emotion and sexuality.

Given that men are commonly regarded as dominating the public sphere, it is perhaps surprising that little of this early work on masculinity focused on politics. Political histories of the eighteenth and nineteenth centuries showed little interest in masculinity. Men dominate the subject matter of political history – they were the politicians, the voters, the civil servants, the 'men of letters' – and political history was content to describe them without questioning *why* they were dominant. Political history tends to focus on the official structures of politics, so only regards women as being worth studying when they sought to participate in them, principally with the suffrage movement. In this tradition, the gendered nature of politics is taken for granted rather than critiqued. The universal actor of political history is the (male) public, rational citizen, whereas women are relegated to the invisible private realm. Women's history partly came about in reaction to this type of history and did much to critique it. They ended the invisibility of the private realm and extended our definition of the political to encompass sex and gender as questions of power. In focusing on women as a social group, however, much of the focus was on the private sphere: the role of men in the public was often assumed rather than directly studied. Even the early history of masculinity had little to say about politics. As part of the gender history project, historians of masculinity sought to challenge 'separate spheres' by highlighting the private aspects of male experience, such as fatherhood, domesticity or relationships. For example, the first major book on masculinity in Britain was John Tosh's *A Man's Place: Masculinity and the Middle-Class Home in Victorian England* (1999).

It was not until the twenty-first century, then, that a history of political masculinities really developed in Britain. To this day, the field remains surprisingly compact and we will survey much of it in this book. There are several possible reasons for this. As well as the rather protracted story of its emergence, it remains a controversial topic. Political historians might wonder what an apparently frivolous consideration may have to offer to an august and rigorous historical field. Gender historians might equally argue that it is hardly offering something new, given that historians have always studied men doing traditional things like politics: is this, at best, a distraction and, at worst, a takeover bid? Men in politics is indeed a familiar topic, but this chapter will argue that there is much to be gained from looking at this in a new way, and shedding critical light on *why* it is familiar.

Georgian political personae

The history of political masculinities promises to shed new light both on politics and also on the nature of masculinity. This section will argue that eighteenth-century Britain is a case in point. Not only was the political culture of the day influenced by changing ideas about gender, but competing models of masculinity need to be viewed in a political perspective. As with other periods of history, there was no single model of how to be a man: historians tend to use the plural 'masculinities' to suggest that gender identities were fluid and multiple. The sociologist R. W. Connell argues that masculinities are plural: in a given society, there is a dominant (or 'hegemonic') masculinity that is bound up with the power of the state and the social order, and other forms of masculinity are in a subordinate, complicit or marginalised relationship with it.[1] This interpretation is useful in helping us to understand the ways in which masculinity is bound up with social power, but we will see that it is not necessarily the best characterisation of Britain in this period, since it is the anti-establishment model of masculinity that arguably becomes the dominant one.

Georgian masculinities were bound up with a critique of the ruling class, which focused on their personal virtues, or supposed lack thereof. The establishment in the early eighteenth century tended to subscribe to a very formal code of masculine behaviour, epitomised by the courtier. The courtier possessed the breeding and rank of the international ancient nobility and the image they sought to project was one of refinement, formality and high fashion. This very studied and mannered masculinity was codified in courtly conduct manuals like Castliglione's *Book of the Courtier* (1528). Beyond the world of the court, aristocratic politicians similarly subscribed to a very showy model of masculinity. Paul Langford argues that they subscribed to a 'if you've got it, flaunt it' attitude, noting that portraits of the prime minister Sir Robert Walpole present him in all his glory, 'robed, ribboned, decorated'.[2] Their very status and wealth were bound up with their claim to rule, since ruling was seen as a duty of rank and their broad acres supposedly ensured their disinterestedness. The Georgian political order was *their* political order: they even rather looked down on the Hanoverian monarchs who had, after all, been installed at their behest.

Politics was therefore dominated by a narrow elite. They were increasingly under attack, however, from those who were excluded from political power. Criticisms tended to focus on their moral worthiness for office, with a view both to undermining their right to rule and to emphasise that those who sought power were more deserving of it. Strikingly, this critique was based around gender and nationalism. In masculine terms, the court and their hangers-on were portrayed as being degenerate and effeminate. 'Effeminacy' can connote men taking on characteristics associated with femininity, but in the eighteenth century the term was also used in a moral way, to suggest a failure of the qualities associated with manliness. Critics of the elite portrayed them as lacking moral fibre and being addicted to luxury and refined manners. In this way, criticisms of effeminacy were linked to those of foreignness. Courtiers and aristocrats were criticised for their attachment to foreign tastes, such as French food, Italian opera and oriental luxury goods. Self-styled patriots characterised their opponents as being 'Frenchified'. This line of argument could also be powerfully applied to Britain's German monarchs after 1715: the first two Georges spoke German, installed Germans at court, spent much of their time there and allegedly conducted foreign policy in the interests of Hanover rather than Britain. The political 'outs' – opposition politicians, Jacobites, critics of the status quo and those with frustrated ambitions – therefore had a rich symbolic language with which to attack the political 'ins'.

This came to a head during the Seven Years' War of 1756–63, which proved to be a turbulent time in British politics. Britain tended to start wars badly, since concerns about a 'standing army' meant that the military had to be built up from a small base, and the Seven Years' War was no exception. Britain endured numerous defeats to its great rival France, and the fall of Minorca in particular typified the stuttering war effort. At Minorca, Admiral Byng failed to engage a larger French fleet, and became a symbol of the unmanly and unpatriotic ruling class. The government attempted to scapegoat Byng, court-martialling him for cowardice and executing him, but this did not head off the wider critique. Meanwhile, the deployment of troops abroad left Britain vulnerable to French invasion, so the government brought over troops from their allies Hanover and Hesse-Cassel to guard the coasts. This was common military practice at the time, but the presence of German troops in Kent caused a xenophobic outcry: critics of the government alleged that this was a conspiracy by the Hanoverian government to oppress the English people, and did it not also cast aspersions on Englishmen that they were unable to defend their own homes, wives and children?[3]

A stage play from the time shows how critics of the establishment were able to mobilise arguments based upon nationalism and gender. *The Fall of Public Spirit* (1757) tells the story of Old Time and Ancient Spirit, who travel from Britain's glorious past to the present day. Old Time declares, 'Good Heaven, what a *Pygmy Race* of Mortals dance before my eyes! Certainly these can never be *Britons*'. In particular, they encounter a character called Effeminacy:

EFFEMINACY.
I was a Foot-boy to a Man of considerable Quality here in England; but he having always an antipathy to his Lady (whom he married to increase his Fortune) they agreed to part; and some time afterwards his Grace was pleased to confer more than ordinary Favours on me; – my Livery was taken off, and I was admitted to the caresses of his Grace in the Room of his Lady, who has now gone to Bath with an Irishman that used to look after his Grace's Horses.

ANCIENT COURAGE.
O then I find you are his Minion, an Incubus to his Grace.

EFFEMINACY.
Whatever you please to call me, that is any Way connected with good Quality and Politeness.

ANCIENT COURAGE.
Why then I call thee an unnatural Existence, which having no Respect to the Order of Nature, lives in the continual Inversion of her Laws – Art thou ashamed of thy filthy Crime? – Crimes which even the vilest Brutes despise, and scorn to be guilty of.[4]

The characters of Old Time and Ancient Courage embody the sense in opposition argument that things were better in the past, and that Britons in the present had been degenerated by luxury and corruption, rendering them amenable to oppression. Today we would regard this passage as being homophobic: Effeminacy is guilty of an unnamed 'filthy Crime' with his master, who has himself rejected conjugal heterosexuality and is being cuckolded by his wife. In part this source is a criticism of the sexual morals of the ruling elite, designed to flatter a middling audience who prided themselves on their domestic morality and godliness. It also hints at the dangers of refined manners – and of polite resorts such as Bath – which threatened to tip male behaviour into effeminacy.

The insinuation of sexual relations between men, however, needs to be regarded in its proper context. Georgians did not understand sexuality in the way we do today: the notion of a 'homosexual', who exclusively has relationships with men and is defined that way in social and psychological terms, was not coined until the later nineteenth century. Sexual preferences did not define you as a person to the same extent in the eighteenth century, when attention was instead focused on bodily acts. Sodomy was a capital offence and a crime against God, which had long been associated with religious deviance and the occult, and was often regarded as a foreign practice. It also had a political significance. As with so many things in eighteenth-century Britain, this referenced ancient Rome, where the power of the male citizen related to his sexual dominance of women, slaves and younger or less powerful men. To take the passive role in sodomy was to lose manhood, self-ownership and even citizenship. In *The Fall of Public Spirit*, this signifies the existence of corruption and illegitimate influence in high places: men like Effeminacy are 'minions' to the establishment, who are corrupting the political world to the detriment of general liberty.

In response to this supposed effeminacy and foreignness, opposition critics asserted their superior virtue with a culture that was manly and patriotic. Once again, their ideas were partly drawn from the classical world. Britons in the eighteenth century were quick to draw comparisons between themselves and Rome in particular, asserting that they too were a great civilisation with a powerful military and a huge empire. The republican political thought of Greece and Rome was a standard reference point, to highlight either the comparable symmetry of the British constitution, or its deficiencies. Critics of the establishment were drawn to the democratic implications of classical thought, arguing that power and legitimacy in the state rested in the citizenry rather than the elite. This citizenry needed to be virtuous and vigilant, proving their worthiness through military service, property ownership and domestic patriarchy. Their virtue was evaluated in terms of obligation: only 'independent' persons could have a free and conscientious voice in the polity, whereas dependent persons were necessarily unfree so should not be involved in politics. This evaluation was fundamentally gendered, since only men could be 'independent' by situation and by nature, whereas women were domestically dependent, and any men who were not in this independent situation were not fully manly.

As well as linking citizenship to gender in a fundamental way, this line of argument developed into a thorough critique of the ruling class and the patronage system that lasted well into the nineteenth century. Anyone who depended on a patron was unfree, lacked manly virtue and had no conscience of their own. The patronage system therefore created armies of 'yes men', which dangerously increased the power of Britain's rulers and unbalanced the constitution. These criticisms were targeted at the government's system of patronage under Walpole and his successors. The use of grants, contracts and paid posts was apparently a dangerous attempt to create 'dependents' in positions of authority, who would do the government's will rather than work for the general good. This hostility to the state is difficult to relate to today, when it is, of course, reasonable that someone should receive a salary for performing a government office. Particular ire was reserved for 'pensions': not the social support for the elderly with which we are familiar, but a recurring payment to an individual from government, which was a favourite way of securing reliable votes in parliament before the advent of party discipline. As we have seen, MPs were supposed to be self-supporting, as guaranteed by steep property qualifications. The opposition vaunted their 'independence' as they criticised the courtiers, placemen and pensioners who were bleeding the nation dry and subverting the political system. They argued that only independent men, who were uncontaminated by the government's networks of patronage, had the free will to speak out against the corrupt ruling oligarchy.

This political ideology came to be known as 'Country patriotism'. Its proponents argued for the rights of the 'the Country' and 'the people' against the court, the government and the establishment. In so doing, the implication was that they were more indigenous and virtuous, and therefore more deserving of office: it was an ideology of the political 'outs', but was often used by people who themselves had ambitions to be political 'ins'. This Court/Country division did not correspond to party lines: instead, politics was a circular continuum, where opposition Whigs and Country Tories had much in common and used much the same language (Figure 2.1). This was an intensely patriotic ideology, which regarded England as an elect nation, whose unique path was smiled upon by God. Country thought revelled in the rights of the 'freeborn Englishman', who enjoyed unrivalled liberty, prosperity and legal protection: it was therefore an ideology that focused heavily on the rights of the citizen, albeit in a very exclusive sense. Rather than being an abstract political theory, Country writers believed that England really did possess a citizenry of propertied householders who were committed to preserving liberty. Historians such as J. G. A. Pocock have shown how thoroughly this neo-classical vision of the political system was superimposed onto English social conditions, for which it was apparently a good fit.[5] Indeed, there was a sense that the constitution had developed over the centuries around the Englishman's national character in an organic way. Given his predisposition to liberty and assertiveness, the sturdy freeman provided a bulwark against oppression.

As well as being a patriotic ideology, Country thought was also highly gendered. As we have seen, it offered a critique of luxury, immorality and degeneracy of the court in particular, and urban modernity in general. Against this, it contrasted an image of bracing rural virtue, which celebrated straightforward and hearty manliness. This celebration of the rural was a strong current in English cultural life, which came to a head with the Romantic movement at the end of the century. An enduring manifestation of this is the figure of 'John Bull', the personification of Britain – or often, more specifically, England. Invented by John Arbuthnot in 1712 as a satire of Whig politics, John Bull later became a heroic representation of all that was admirable about the straightforward Englishman. His name references the beef that is his preferred dish, a sign both of prosperity and masculine strength, which he washes down with a tankard of

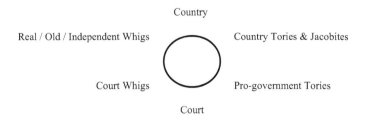

Figure 2.1 Early Georgian political ideologies.

frothy beer. He is instantly recognisable by his stocky build, his assertive demeanour and the simple attire of a country squire: usually top boots, a blue frock coat and breeches, with a brimmed hat. In the nineteenth century he acquired a Union Jack waistcoat but, to this day, his dress is that of the eighteenth. John Bull was immortalised in satirical prints from the eighteenth century, where he was commonly portrayed as being in conflict with characters such as Frenchmen, Scots and fops. Although he would later become a pro-establishment, nationalist figure – he often appeared in First World War recruiting posters, for example – in the eighteenth century he was more usually depicted as being put-upon, demonstrating how Englishmen were weighed down by taxes or oppressive laws.[6]

In the mid-eighteenth century, the politician who played the Country role most successfully was William Pitt the Elder. Pitt came from a modest background, so had to rely on his own talents to get on in the political world. A formidable speaker, he projected a masculine image of patriotism, independence and sincerity. He capitalised on the disastrous start to the Seven Years' War, lambasting the government for its handling of the conflict and putting his weight behind causes like militia reform: 'patriots' argued that home defence should be carried out by a citizen militia rather than by standing armies or foreign 'mercenaries'. Eventually, George II was forced to call upon him, whereupon he became the first truly popular prime minister, who was there because of a popular mandate rather than royal favour. When the year of victories came in 1759, the public gave Pitt the credit. Tellingly, his image remained that of a man who was above party politics and its blandishments: his refusal of a peerage gained him the nickname 'The Great Commoner' (until he accepted one in 1766). Even when used in power, Country politics remained the politics of the outsider.

John Wilkes and radical masculinity

The accession of George III in 1760 prompted a big change in political life, and several gender historians have noted its effects in that arena too: political events can therefore drive gender change. George broke with his predecessors, ejecting the Whigs and bringing Tories into government. He also installed his former tutor, the Earl of Bute, as prime minister, which prompted a howl of protest about 'royal favourites' and illegitimate influence. In opposition, the Whigs became more assertive in their criticisms of executive power, and some of their number, such as John Wilkes, started to deploy the old 'Country patriot' arguments in ever-more radical ways. At the same time, Marilyn Morris argues that the arrival of George III anticipated the way that political morality was to go in later decades. 'Young, British-born and chaste, the king raised expectations of national moral regeneration.' Unlike his predecessors, he projected an image of virtuous domesticity and martial fidelity – considerations that, Morris notes, would hardly have been relevant to a monarch or statesman in the early eighteenth century.[7]

It is worth focusing on Wilkes, both because of his political significance, but also because his colourful masculine image was inseparable from his politics.

John Wilkes did not start out as a radical. He was the son of a brewer but had loftier social ambitions. He married for money and the marriage promptly broke down after he had spent it all. Much of it went on running for parliament in Aylesbury, where he employed the distinctly un-radical method of bribing voters: 'I will give two guineas per man, with the promise of whatever more offers. If you think two guineas not enough I will offer three or five.'[8] The arrival of George III frustrated Wilkes's ambition of a lucrative position in government, so he turned to journalism, courting the favour outside of parliament that Whigs no longer enjoyed within it. His set up a paper called *The North Briton* in opposition to the paper *The Briton*, which was written by the Scot Tobias Smollett who was in the pay of the government. Smollett's paper reflected George III's desire to promote an inclusive, British patriotism: he famously declared at the opening of his first session of parliament, 'Born and educated in this country, I glory in the name of Briton'.[9] In contrast to his predecessors, George III saw himself as indigenous, and we will see how his patriotic image became an asset in later years. In the 1760s, however, Wilkes objected to the notion of Britishness, since he was specifically an English patriot. In Wilkes's xenophobic rhetoric, the Scots were as much an enemy as the French or the Spanish, and were all the more threatening for being closer to home. The 1745 Jacobite rebellion was a recent memory and Wilkes saw the favour now shown to Scots in Westminster, such as Bute, as an obstacle to his own ambitions.

Wilkes's Scottophobia tells us a great deal about his national identity and also his masculinity. For Wilkes, the Scots were an 'other'. This concept is used in cultural studies to suggest that self-identity is located in a binary relationship of opposites: an 'other' emphasises both their difference from you and shores up your own sense of self. Therefore when Wilkes called the Scots dependent, easily oppressed, poor and disloyal, he was emphasising that the English were independent, free, prosperous and loyal. An exaggerated version of Englishness was central to Wilkes's masculine persona. He declared that 'the spirit of liberty and independence ... constitutes the true character of an Englishman', and he approached politics in a spirit of manly directness. Wilkes's speeches reveal a chauvinist version of English history, revelling in its national pre-eminence. He supported Pitt's vigorous prosecution of the Seven Years' War and bitterly attacked the government's conduct during the Peace of Paris (1763), where the victorious British returned conquered territories to France and Spain.

Matters came to a head with issue 45 of *The North Briton*, where his criticism of the Peace was judged to have come too close to attacking the king himself. He was charged with a seditious libel and a general warrant was issued to arrest Wilkes and dozens of other individuals connected with the paper. Wilkes won his release on the grounds that, as an MP, he enjoyed parliamentary privilege against prosecution, but he was also adept at turning his personal travails into wider constitutional issues. As he put it: 'The rights of this free kingdom, gentlemen, have often been violated in my person.'[10] General warrants were unpopular and Wilkes argued that they were unconstitutional: this case therefore helped to establish legal due process, press freedom and freedom of speech as key citizenship rights in Britain. This victory made Wilkes a popular hero: '45' became a radical symbol and London's streets redounded to the cry of 'Wilkes and liberty'. The Wilkeite phenomenon became Britain's first radical political movement, turning the popular politics that we explored in the previous chapter into an anti-establishment force for the first time. Historians such as George Rudé and John Brewer have demonstrated the extent of popular involvement in Wilkeite politics, which provided a political outlet for the urban middling sorts in particular. It is also an early example of how politics was becoming commercialised, since his supporters could express their commitment through acquiring material objects such as plates, prints or medals bearing Wilkes's image and slogans.[11]

The government needed a pretext to expel him from the Commons, and unfortunately for Wilkes, he provided one. He had privately printed a pornographic poem entitled 'An Essay on Woman', which the government declared an obscene libel, so he was forced to flee to France before the government could expel him. The instrument of his downfall was oddly fitting, given Wilkes's sexuality. Wilkes was a famous libertine who devoted himself to the pursuit of pleasure. Having abandoned his wife, he had numerous mistresses and was a member of the notorious Hellfire Club, at which he indulged in heavy drinking, blasphemy and lewdness. In the 1760s, Wilkes's libertine lifestyle was actively celebrated by many of his supporters. The song 'Wilkes and Liberty' employed a typically priapic pun:

> When Scottish Oppression rear'd up its d–n'd Head
> And *Old English* Liberty nearly was dead;
> Brave WILKES like a true *English* Member arose,
> And thunder'd Defiance against *England's* foes.[12]

Vigorous masculinity was an asset in 'Country' politics and Wilkes further underlined his heterosexual virility with homophobic attacks on Bute and the court, insinuating that inappropriate influence was being exercised in high places. Rakish masculinity went further than this, however, since libertinism was a philosophical statement. In the age of the Enlightenment, libertinism involved throwing off all of the social, religious and political restrictions of the old world.

Wilkes's hyper-masculinity was therefore part of his claim to embody liberty in all its forms. He was keen to emphasise his martial attributes, often challenging his social betters to a duel, both to defend his masculine honour and to enhance his claim to social status: duelling was a key gentlemanly accomplishment and a way of claiming that he was socially the peer of his antagonist. In common with other 'patriots', Wilkes was an enthusiastic supporter of the militia, since it emphasised the power and the activism of the citizenry, and was an alternative to a permanent army that a ruler could use to oppress the people. He rose to the rank of colonel in the Buckinghamshire Militia: he was doubtless seeking to cement his status in the county, since commissions in the militia were supposed to reflect social rank, but by all accounts he served conscientiously. Even after the king ordered that he be dismissed after the 45 affair, he continued to wear a red coat to advertise his patriotic and military credentials.[13] Wilkes saw himself as a classical warrior citizen, vaunting his classical learning and identifying himself with Roman opponents of tyranny. His belief in masculine independence and the dangers of corruption were symptomatic of Georgian opposition thought's debt to the classics.

When Wilkes returned from French exile in 1768 he sought the safety of a parliamentary seat. His decision to stand for the county of Middlesex was a good one: its two seats were traditionally shared between a Whig and a Tory, denying the electors a choice, so Wilkes stood as an independent on a platform of popular rights. It also capitalised on his popularity among the metropolitan middling sorts, who duly placed him at the top of the poll. Notoriously, the Commons voted to expel him and another election was held, which he also won. He was repeatedly expelled and re-elected until the government declared him 'incapable of being elected'. As Wilkes argued, this undermined the principle of free election:

> If ministers can once usurp the power of declaring who *shall not* be your representatives, the next step is very easy, and will follow speedily. It is that of telling you, whom you *shall* send to parliament, and then the boasted constitution of England will entirely be torn up by the roots.[14]

Eventually the ruling was overturned and Wilkes was able to take up his seat, partly due to the efforts of a campaigning group set up in his support, the Society of Supporters of the Bill of Rights.

Wilkes remained committed to the rights of electors and he holds the distinction of tabling the first motion for parliamentary reform, on 21 March 1776. Wilkes sympathised with the American colonists who were protesting at their lack of representation, and argued that parliament's coercive attitude towards them was a sign that it did not represent the views of the English people. He therefore proposed a sweeping reform to the electoral system:

> I wish, Sir, an English parliament to speak the free, unbiased sense of the body of the English people, and of every man amongst us, of each individual, who may be justly supposed to be comprehended in a fair majority. The meanest mechanic, the poorest peasant and day-labourer, has important rights respecting his personal liberty, that of his wife and children, his property, however inconsiderable, his wages ... Some share therefore in the power of making those laws, which deeply interest them, and to which they are expected to pay obedience, should be reserved even to this inferior, but most useful set of men in the community.[15]

Wilkes's handling of gender and class in this passage is telling. His proposed change to the franchise was strikingly inclusive in class terms – 'every man' – but was exclusive in terms of gender. Men deserve a say in the framing of the laws because of their property ('however inconsiderable'), their labour and their position in the family. Women and children do not require political rights in their own right, but men do in order to protect them. We will see how this familial model of an independent male citizen and dependent non-citizens was to recur in reformist political argument over the coming century: radicals often used arguments based on gender in order to overturn the association of citizenship with property and rank. Wilkes's views on masculinity, therefore, do not just tell us about his political personality, but shed light on wider contemporary understandings of political citizenship.

Changing values

In the 1760s, John Wilkes was a man of his time. Up to this period, one's external masculinity was not necessarily a reflection of one's inner being. We have seen how Wilkes adopted a range of masculine identities, and even the ones that today might be disadvantageous to a serious politician did not appear to impugn his political integrity. This was a period when gender identities were relatively flexible: as Philip Carter has shown, James Boswell flitted between a range of masculinities when he was exploring London as a young man, performing the role of a polite man, a rake, a scholar or a *homo religiosus* as required.[16]

The period of the American War, however, prompted a change in Britain's moral atmosphere. The conflict itself was hugely troubling, pitting fellow countrymen against one another on one side of the Atlantic and dividing public opinion on the other. The eventual loss of the colonies plunged Britons into a period of soul-searching: losing a key part of the empire – and being beaten by Britain's traditional enemies France and Spain into the bargain – punctured the complacent sense of national superiority. Some argued that this was a sign of God's disfavour and urged a moral reformation. The historian Dror Wahrman goes further, and argues that the later eighteenth century witnessed a crisis of identity for Britons. He characterises this period as one of 'gender panic', when the fluid and playful identities of the early modern world were closed down and replaced with modern notions of self: your social being was expected to reflect who you actually were in terms of gender, race and class.[17] Wahrman's account of change is consistent with wider chronologies in the histories of gender, medicine and sexuality, which suggest that the later eighteenth century saw a shift towards modern binary notions of gender difference, whereby men were superior and domestic heterosexuality was the norm. Men's dominance was no longer the rest of tradition and biblical precept, but was declared 'natural' by the new science of the Enlightenment.

From the 1770s, therefore, public men were expected to be virtuous in both their public and their private lives. Even Wilkes had to reinvent himself as a 'reformed rake' in order to appeal to the sober merchants and dissenters of London. His tenure as lord mayor was marked with the utmost propriety and he even contrived to present himself as a family man: he could not claim to be a good husband, but he doted on his daughter Polly and she became his consort for official functions, bestowing an image of sentimental fatherhood upon the former hell-raiser. By the 1790s, the private lives of public figures were ever-more important. Women's historians have long identified the period of the French Revolution as having a lasting impact upon gender codes. George III responded to the Revolution's assault on traditional hierarchies by 'endorsing a model of manliness based on familial responsibility': the royal family presented an almost-bourgeois image of domesticity and godliness, quite at odds with their royal predecessors and many of their aristocratic contemporaries.[18] At the same time, the Tory counter-revolution combined with evangelical Christianity to imbue the new middle classes with an ideology based upon domestic virtue, industry and godliness. Only a virtuous nation that protected its womenfolk could hope to prevail against the atheists: 'separate spheres' was therefore a highly political ideology rather than a social structure as such. Nor was it just reactionary, since it was also a way for the middle classes to trumpet their moral superiority to those socially above and below them, and thence to push for political rights to match their newfound economic power.

The end of the eighteenth century was therefore a pivotal period in gender relations and for political masculinities in particular. It is worth concluding this chapter by surveying how ideas about masculine virtue shifted over the course of the eighteenth and nineteenth centuries, since this transition forms the backdrop for much of what we discuss in this book. Tosh argues that that Georgian masculinities were characterised by 'gentlemanly politeness' whereas Victorians lauded 'manly simplicity'. Polite masculinity focused on outer refinement – of dress, speech and manners – which only a man of means would have the time and money to cultivate. This was therefore a refined masculinity that was only available to gentlemen. The Victorians were suspicious of politeness, since they were concerned that it was a façade that concealed the real man: they therefore preferred simple to refined manners. Indeed, the meaning of the term 'gentleman' shifts over this period from meaning someone who is genteel to any man who is worthy of respect.

Instead, the Victorians were concerned with 'manliness'. Manliness is a word that is rarely used nowadays but up until about the mid-twentieth century, a man who acted honourably or bravely might be commended for being 'manly'. It was a way of evaluating what it meant to be a man, but was less neutral than the psychological term 'masculinity'. Manliness focused on the moral and physical qualities possessed by a good man. In contrast with politeness, manliness concerned the inner man rather than outer refinement. It was therefore more socially accessible, since any man could achieve manliness. As Tosh notes, moral manliness was more important than birth, breeding or education: 'Manliness had to be earned, by mastering the circumstances of life and thus securing the respect of one's peers.'[19] Probably the key statement of this ideal is Samuel Smiles's *Self-Help* (1859), where the author argued that helping oneself is good both for the individual and society, whereas the recipient of help loses the impetus to do this. A key arena for self-help was the world of work, which the Victorians regarded as a sphere for moral as well as economic improvement. Work was an arena of struggle and competition, where one would learn moral lessons and acquire 'character'. This particularly spoke to the Victorian middle-class man, who prided himself on being self-made and for whom occupation was a key social identity.

The ideals associated with virtuous masculinity therefore travelled further down the social scale over the course of the eighteenth and nineteenth centuries. We can see this shift in relation to the term 'independence', which was a key marker of masculine virtue in this period. In the eighteenth century, an 'independent man' was someone who did not have to work, due to inherited wealth and station. In the nineteenth, on the other hand, independence was achieved *through* work: it meant supporting oneself and family through one's own endeavours. Crucially, 'independence' was often taken to be the marker of political citizenship and helps us to understand why citizenship was so gendered in the masculine for such a long time. A voter needed to be independent from undue influence and able to exercise his conscience in a free way: a dependent person such as a wife, a child, a servant or a pauper was apparently unable to do this. We will see in later chapters how reformers made the case for extending the franchise by emphasising that 'independent' people were fit to exercise it, and how the Reform Acts of the nineteenth century made this criterion official and successively lowered the benchmark down through the social scale.

A key marker of the male citizen's independence and respectability was his position within his household. The man's status as a husband and a father was therefore vital in the nineteenth century. Thanks to Tosh's pioneering work, our primary image of Victorian masculinity is a domestic one. He argues that in the mid-nineteenth century, the home was of profound importance to men's lives. Although the man's place in the home was riven with tensions, home and family were of immense emotional significance, and were central to men's sense of masculinity and humanity. It also had an important religious dimension, since the family was a sacred institution and Evangelicals emphasised the importance of a godly home life. This was above all the father's responsibility, for it was he who led family prayers and kept family members on the right path: his authority came from God, in whose place he stood within the house.[20] While on the face of it this may suggest a rather apolitical vision of the Victorian man, Tosh always insisted that home, work and politics were fundamentally linked in this period.[21] Men's familial stations and relationships underwrote their standing in the political world, and we will see how politics often involved domestic and personal dimensions. Later chapters will explore how masculinity underwent further changes through the nineteenth and twentieth centuries.

Conclusion

As we have seen in this chapter, the study of masculinity can tell us a great deal about the political world and how it relates to the wider society. It can help us to understand the political values of the day and what was considered to be virtuous or otherwise in the political arena. It can also shed light on the political ideas of the time and how people understood politics as an activity. Citizenship concerns the role of the individual in politics, and we have seen how gender was a key way of thinking about the individual and their position in society. In particular, the links between masculinity and political citizenship were strong in the Georgian and Victorian periods, to the extent that one's fitness for citizenship could be evaluated in terms of 'manliness'. This has to be fundamental to our understanding of politics in the eighteenth and nineteenth centuries – and of why it took until the twentieth for women to be granted the parliamentary franchise.

Notes

1 R. W. Connell, *Masculinities*, Cambridge: Polity Press, 1995.
2 P. Langford, 'Politics and manners from Sir Robert Walpole to Sir Robert Peel', *Proceedings of the British Academy*, 94, 1997, 103–25 (p. 109).
3 M. McCormack, 'Citizenship, nationhood and masculinity in the affair of the Hanoverian soldier', *The Historical Journal* 49:4, 2006, 971–93.
4 *The Fall of Public Spirit: A Dramatic Satire in Two Acts*, London, 1757, pp. 6–7, emphasis in original.
5 J. G. A. Pocock, *The Machiavellian Moment: Florentine Political Thought and the Atlantic Republican Tradition*, Princeton: Princeton University Press, 1975.
6 M. Taylor, 'John Bull and the iconography of public opinion in England c. 1712–1929', *Past and Present*, 134:1, 1992, 93–128.
7 M. Morris, *Sex, Money and Personal Character in Eighteenth-Century British Politics*, New Haven: Yale, 2014, p. 59.
8 Quoted in G. Rudé, *Wilkes and Liberty: A Social Study of 1763 to 1774*, Oxford: Oxford University Press, 1962, p. 18.
9 18 November 1760: *The Parliamentary History of England*, London, 1813, vol. XV, p. 982.
10 *English Liberty: Being a Collection of Interesting Tracts, From the Year 1762 to 1769, Containing the Private Correspondence, Public Letters, Speeches and Addresses of John Wilkes, Esq.*, London, n.d., pp. 318, 291.
11 Rudé, *Wilkes and Liberty*; J. Brewer, 'Commercialisation and politics', in J. Brewer, N. McKendrick and J. Plumb, *The Birth of a Consumer Society* (London: Europa, 1982), pp. 231–62.
12 'Wilkes and Liberty. A New Song', handbill, May 1763.
13 M. McCormack, *Embodying the Militia in Georgian England*, Oxford: Oxford University Press, 2015, p. 177.
14 *English Liberty*, pp. 243–4, emphasis in original.
15 *Parliamentary History*, vol. XVIII, pp. 1295–6.
16 P. Carter, 'James Boswell's manliness', in T. Hitchcock and M. Cohen (eds.), *English Masculinities, 1660–1800*, London: Longman, 1999, pp. 111–30.
17 D. Wahrman, *The Making of the Modern Self: Identity and Culture in Eighteenth-Century England*, New Haven: Yale University Press, 2004.
18 Morris, *Sex*, p. 59.
19 J. Tosh, 'Gentlemanly politeness and manly simplicity in Victorian England', *Transactions of the Royal Historical Society*, 12, 2002, 455–72.
20 J. Tosh, *A Man's Place: Masculinity and the Middle-Class Home in Victorian England*, New Haven: Yale University Press, 1999, p. 36.
21 J. Tosh, 'What should historians do with masculinity? Reflections on nineteenth-century Britain', *Historical Workshop Journal*, 38, 1994, 179–202.

Recommended reading

Collini, S., 'The idea of 'character' in Victorian political thought', *Transactions of the Royal Historical Society*, 35, 1985, 29–50.
Downs, L., *Writing Gender History*, London: Arnold, 2004.

Dudink, S., Hagemann, S. and Tosh, J. (eds.), *Masculinities in Politics and War: Gendering Modern History*, Manchester: Manchester University Press, 2004.

Hitchcock, T. and Cohen, M. (eds.), *English Masculinities, 1660–1800*, London: Longman, 1999.

Langford, P., 'Politics and manners from Sir Robert Walpole to Sir Robert Peel', *Proceedings of the British Academy*, 94, 1997, 103–25.

McCormack, M., *The Independent Man: Citizenship and Gender Politics in Georgian England*, Manchester: Manchester University Press, 2005.

Morris, M., *Sex, Money and Personal Character in Eighteenth-Century British Politics*, New Haven: Yale University Press, 2014.

Sainsbury, J., *John Wilkes: The Lives of a Libertine*, Farnham: Ashgate, 2006.

Skinner, Q., *Liberty Before Liberalism*, Cambridge: Cambridge University Press, 1997.

Tosh, J., 'Gentlemanly politeness and manly simplicity in Victorian England', *Transactions of the Royal Historical Society*, 12, 2002, 455–72.

Tosh, J., 'What should historians do with masculinity? Reflections on nineteenth-century Britain', *Historical Workshop Journal*, 38, 1994, 179–202.

3 The British electoral tradition

So far we have thought about citizenship in two senses. In the Introduction we explored citizenship as a legal condition that comes with rights and responsibilities. Subsequently we have thought about citizenship in more cultural terms, as a collective identity (being a member of a polity and a 'public') and as an individual identity (based upon gender, nation and class). In this chapter we will look at citizenship in arguably its most concrete sense: being a voter and participating in an election. In the Georgian period, an election was an individual's most direct experience of the national political system, when being a citizen was an immediate activity with tangible consequences.

Traditionally, the eighteenth-century electoral system had a very poor reputation among historians. For the Victorian Whig historians, it epitomised the corruption and disorder of the previous century that their more enlightened contemporaries were busy reforming. Wealthy elites apparently dominated tiny electorates by means of bribery and intimidation, while the common people drank and rioted. This stereotype persists to this day, encapsulated by the episode 'Dish and Dishonesty' of the 1987 TV comedy *Blackadder the Third*. Here, the Prince Regent needs to win a crucial parliamentary vote, so his butler Blackadder plots to win a by-election in the fictional rotten borough Dunny-on-the-Wold with Baldrick as a puppet candidate: bribery, murder and corruption ensue (along with a nice satire of BBC election coverage). Ironically, it was around this time that historians were revising the dominant interpretation of the Hanoverian electoral system, presenting a wholly more positive picture of a vibrant and participatory political culture.[1] A key lesson of this work was the importance of the non-voters: elections in this period were huge community festivities where everybody got involved, including groups such as women and the poor. Getting involved in an election therefore meant much more than voting: approaching politics in this more social and cultural way entails a much broader definition of what constitutes 'political participation'.

As such, this new work helped to create a space for the history of women in elections, both as participants in the street theatre and more elite women who were integral to the process. This chapter will survey this work and will conclude with a case study of probably the century's most famous example of female electioneering, Georgiana Duchess of Devonshire at the Westminster election of

1784. We will also think about the role of masculinity at election time, since the ideals and models of behaviour that were expected of men in the electoral drama were highly gendered. Gender should be central to our understanding of electoral citizenship in the long eighteenth century, and we will see that the electoral tradition established in this period endured into later ones.

The electoral system

Britain today has an unusual electoral system, known as 'first past the post'. Deriving its title from a horse race, what this means in practice is that an election is held in every district, known as a 'constituency'. The candidate with the most votes wins the constituency and becomes a member of parliament. The party with the most MPs then forms a government: as we saw in Chapter 1, it is important that a party has a majority so that it can win votes in the Commons and get its business through. As a system, first past the post has advantages and disadvantages. On the plus side, it is easy to understand, delivers a clear representative for each community who can speak to both local and national issues, and tends to produce stable governments with clear majorities. (The recent experience of the 2010 and 2017 elections, which failed to deliver a clear winner, is historically unusual.) As it is a 'winner takes all' system at the local level, it tends to favour big parties with a strong nationwide profile and squeezes out small parties: this is a key reason why extremists of left and right have failed to gain a foothold in British politics. This very unrepresentativeness is the key disadvantage of the current British system, since the ruling party typically only receives around 40 per cent of the popular vote. Elsewhere in the world, variations on the system of proportional representation are more common, where the proportions of the popular vote are more accurately represented in the number of members in the assembly. Governments are typically coalitions as it would be unusual for a single party to obtain a clear majority of the popular vote. Some smaller parties today such as the Liberal Democrats and the Greens – who do badly out of first past the post – argue that Britain should adopt proportional representation.

Although the British political system has some advantages over its alternatives, if one was designing a political system today, it would unlikely be first past the post. In order to understand how Britons ended up with this system, it is necessary to explore its history. It is possible to trace the origins of parliament to the institutions of Anglo-Saxon government, but parliament began to be formalised in the thirteenth century. The Magna Carta of 1215 asserted that laws apply to kings as well as subjects, and insisted that barons be involved in royal decision-making. From the mid-century, representatives from the localities were assembled when the king needed their agreement to raise taxes: in the eighteenth and nineteenth centuries, these 'knights of the shire' continued to represent the counties in the House of Commons. Members representing the boroughs and cities were created over the following centuries. During late medieval and early modern periods, towns that were populous or economically significant were granted Royal Charters that gave them two MPs. This process halted well before the eighteenth century, however, and by the nineteenth century the electoral map was very out of date. Before the system started to be reformed in 1832, the English and Welsh constituencies represented in parliament were heavily weighted towards the agricultural south, and grossly underrepresented the north, which had grown in population and prosperity during the Industrial Revolution. Formerly prosperous areas such as Cornwall were overrepresented, whereas new economic powerhouses such as Manchester and Leeds had no MPs at all. The situation in Scotland was of more recent provenance, since the 45 MPs it sent to Westminster were defined as part of the 1707 Act of Union, but a much smaller proportion of the adult population were eligible to vote north of the border, and electorates were usually tiny.

The system was therefore not representative of population, but a key argument against making it so was that it was not supposed to be. In the political theory of the time, the system provided 'virtual representation': MPs represented the nation and those who did have power exercised it on behalf of those who did not. So in a 'somewhat mysterious but ultimately satisfying way', everybody was represented in Westminster, even if they did not happen to live in a constituency that was directly represented by an MP.[2] The First Reform Act of 1832 made little attempt to make the electoral map more reflective of where people actually lived in a mathematical way, even though by this period there were census returns that would have allowed them to do this. In this period, MPs were generally not regarded as the direct delegate of those who voted for them, and the electors were not seen as the source of sovereign power that gave the system its legitimacy.

Nor was entry into parliament necessarily competitive. For much of the early modern period, choosing an MP was more a matter of 'selection' than election, whereby people would approve their local leaders rather than choose them.[3] Each constituency returned two members, so it was usually possible to arrange a compromise whereby the political interests in the area would get one each, often along Whig/Tory lines. Far from seeking a contest, local elites sought to avoid 'disturbing the peace of the county'. Harmony was the goal, so decisions would be made behind the scenes prior to the election, rather than in public at the election itself. The situation began to change from the late seventeenth century, with the rise of party and the growth of a politicised public sphere. As we saw in Chapter 1, the new legal requirement that elections be held regularly contributed to the development of a continuous and partisan political culture in the constituencies.

The nature of elections was changing by the eighteenth century and we will shortly explore the rich electoral culture that emerged in this period. The medieval structure of the system largely remained fixed, however, and its key features persisted. The system still promoted consensus rather than conflict: the two-member constituencies remained, compromises were common and around two-thirds of elections were uncontested.[4] 'Virtual representation' remained an important consideration: this was a powerful argument against changing the system, but it also tells us that elections were about the nation and the wider community rather than just the people doing the voting. Finally, this was a *local* system: it was intended to select community leaders – rather than just party representatives – and the electoral process needs to be regarded as a communal one. In order to understand the first past the post system that we have today, it is necessary to approach it in this historical way.

The electorate

Who could vote in the eighteenth century? The short answer is that it depended on where you lived. Before the Reform Act of 1832 created a nationally uniform system, each borough had its own qualification, which could involve owning property, living in a certain area, paying local taxes or being a 'freeman' or a member of a corporation. Broadly speaking, these franchises sought to create an electorate of local propertied men. The amount of property owned by voters varied hugely and it would be a mistake to say that voters were wealthy. In freeman boroughs, where you had to have completed an apprenticeship, there were large electorates of skilled working men, whereas the middling sorts did not qualify. The 'property' in question usually related to one's house, since the voter was supposed to be the head of a household with a fixed abode. Bizarre qualifications like the 'potwalloper' franchise, where voters had to be able to boil a pot, are comprehensible in this context: this proved that voters had a house with a hearth and therefore a sufficiently substantial dwelling.

It is difficult to find explicit justifications from the time for this electorate of propertied male householders, since it was based on traditional practice rather than constitutional pronouncement, and was apparently taken for granted. One such attempt to do so was the *Commentaries on the Laws of England* (1765–69) by the judge Sir William Blackstone. In this multi-volume work, Blackstone sought to bring together centuries of statutes and precedents in order to make a single statement about the nature of the English law and constitution. It became a standard reference work about the English law in the eighteenth century (and in America is still used when referring to legal precedents that predate the Revolution of 1776). Blackstone explained electoral qualifications as follows:

> The true reason of requiring any qualifications, with regard to property, in voters, is to exclude such persons as are in so mean a situation that they are esteemed to have no will of their own. If these persons had votes, they would be tempted to dispose of them under some undue influence or other. This would give a great, an artful, or a wealthy man, a larger share in elections than is consistent with general liberty. [For this reason] all popular states have been obliged to establish certain qualifications; whereby some, who are suspected to have no will of their own, are excluded from voting, in order to set other individuals, whose wills may be supposed independent, more thoroughly on a level with each other.

The reason for requiring voters to possess property was not because they wanted voters to be wealthy, but rather because they wanted voters to be independent. A voter in 'a mean situation' has 'no will of their own' because they depend on others, or are susceptible to bribery or intimidation. Giving the vote to more such people would therefore undermine the principle of liberty, since it would just be giving more power to the people who could corrupt them. Blackstone then went on to describe the system of elections for the counties, which were based on a 40 shilling freeholder qualification that restricted the vote to owners of substantial landed property. Blackstone explained that this property had to be freehold, since copyholders were 'little better than villeins, absolutely dependent on their lord'. A voter who has the means to support himself without threat of eviction has a free conscience: this would 'render the freeholder, if he pleased, an independent man'.[5]

Blackstone talks about the voter in male terms and at no point does he discuss women's exclusion from the vote. Women were not legally excluded from the voting until 1832, so their exclusion in cases where they otherwise met the qualifications was an anomaly. Widows with property, in particular, were the cause of some debate since in other respects a widow retained the legal and economic status of her deceased husband. Derek Hirst has found examples from the seventeenth century of women being allowed to vote in elections that were subsequently disputed,[6] but there is no evidence of this in the eighteenth century, where propriety and local custom seem to have prevented it. Depending on the local franchise, it was sometimes possible for a woman to confer a vote on a man by choosing a proxy, taking in a lodger or even getting married for the purpose.[7] It is likely that such arrangements gave the woman a say in how these votes were cast – as well as money from the recipient of the vote – but women were not able to vote in their own right.

Fundamentally, women were not considered to be independent. By their nature and their relationship to others in the family, they were apparently dependent, and they were thus excluded from the key criterion for citizenship in this period. 'Independence' had several elements, all of which help us to understand how citizenship was inextricable from gender. First, it involved the freedom to act conscientiously. Before the rise of liberal understandings of liberty in the nineteenth century, freedom was commonly thought about in terms of obligation: someone in a position of obligation – even if they were not being directly coerced – was fundamentally unfree and had no will of their own. The precondition of a free conscience was therefore independence. Within the household, only the (male) household head was held to be in this situation, whereas wives and daughters were necessarily dependent upon them. Second, independence involved the ownership of property, or the means to acquire it, since being able to live without dependence on others potentially placed one above undue influence. Property was largely a male category in this period. Under the law of *coverture*, a woman lost her property and her right to own any on getting married: as with her legal and civil identity, her economic status was subsumed in that of her husband. Third, independence was bound up with manliness. As we saw in Chapter 2, 'independence' connoted character traits such as boldness, straightforwardness and courage. As well as being admirable in themselves, such qualities were highly necessary at election time, when one was expected to endure the rough-and-tumble of street politics and to stand by decisions that could have a material impact upon your life.

Women therefore lacked direct representation but, once again, the theory of 'virtual representation' maintained that this did not matter. Those who had power exercised it on behalf of those who did not, so husbands or fathers would look after the political interests of those who depended upon them and would vote on their behalf. In a sense, the vote did not pertain to an individual at all, but to the household: in theory, the husband could consult his wife over how the family's vote was to be cast, and it is possible that this happened in practice. Such women were in no worse a position than the vast majority of adult men, who could not vote either. Blackstone's argument that it was in the interests of liberty that unfree and unfit persons should be excluded from voting persisted well into the nineteenth century, when the Reform Acts only extended this right to men further down the social scale on a very gradual basis. Finally, elections were not just about voting: as we will now see, women and men of all social classes were involved in their rich communal culture.

The culture of elections

British elections in the Georgian period were very unlike those of today. Although some features such as the canvass and the declaration are familiar to us, we have to approach elections from this period in a completely different way. Whereas general elections today are national events that are concluded in a day, Georgian elections were focused on the local community and could last weeks. During this period, the usual social rules did not apply and the community engaged in festive activities such as drinking and feasting, while participating in public rituals and ceremonies. Whereas commentators on today's elections are very focused on who people vote for, this is arguably the least interesting aspect of Georgian elections, where the process is much more significant than the result. It is therefore worth approaching elections from the perspective of an anthropologist rather than that of a political historian, by thinking about the social meaning of human behaviour. Frank O'Gorman pioneered this 'social' approach to English elections, where he demonstrated that elections up until about 1860 had a common sequence of rituals, which tell us a great deal about the social and political order.[8]

Before an election took place, there would be a run-up consisting of behind-the-scenes negotiations and addresses in the local press. The election proper began with the ceremonial entry of the candidates into the town. Modelled on a royal progress, these could be grand occasions. Large crowds followed the procession and the horses would be unhitched from the candidate's carriage at the edge of the town so that the people could pull it along, symbolically welcoming their champion into the community. The arrival of the popular candidate Sir John Edgerton at Chester for the 1818 election was greeted by 'two or three thousand respectable citizens': 'the Champion of the Independence of the City, alighted from his carriage, amidst the congratulatory shouts of the assembled crowd'.[9]

Throughout the election, voters in the town would be canvassed to ask for their support. As today, the process of a candidate coming to a house and requesting a vote is a highly ritualised affair, but there was more at stake in this period. Elections took place in small, face-to-face communities where the candidate was typically in a position of social and economic power. A candidate could be one's employer or landlord, a wealthy aristocrat, a justice of the peace or even your commanding officer in the militia. Moreover, voting in this period was open rather than secret, so votes had consequences. Candidates could extract promises from voters in return for promised rewards, whereas voters who defied the wishes of a candidate would have to bear the consequences. Votes were often printed in a 'poll book': this data is of immense interest to historians but was also useful at the time, since election agents used the poll book from the previous contest to track down voters and ascertain their polling intentions. Nevertheless, during the canvass it was the voter who had the power, turning conventional social relations on their head. In the cartoon 'Candidates Canvassing for Seats in Parliament' (Figure 3.1), an aristocratic candidate and his agent approach a rat catcher. Here, the candidate has to bow and scrape to the voter, requesting his suffrage in the most polite terms. The voter proudly rebuffs his request, reminding him 'how your Worships committed me to the County Jail for a Month … so your Worships may if you please call again tomorrow'. The symbolism of the 'rat catcher' is obvious: as his sign proclaims, 'all sorts of vermin destroyed'.

Figure 3.1 'Candidates Canvassing for Seats in Parliament' (1818). Courtesy of the Lewis Walpole Library, Yale University.

As well as canvassing voters, canvassers also sought their favour indirectly. Women were commonly canvassed, not least because the canvass often took place when their menfolk were out at work, and canvassers recognised the influence that a wife could have on her husband's vote. The canvass would commonly be accompanied by promises of free food and drink, since candidates were expected to 'treat' the voters. Elections were sociable occasions and political parties commonly set up their campaign headquarters in pubs. Candidates had to be careful not to be seen to be bribing the voters, since evidence of bribery could result in them losing the seat if there was subsequently an enquiry, so 'treating' had to be couched in legitimate forms and cash bribes were rare. The provision of food and drink was acceptable since it fell within the remit of hospitality. Perhaps for this reason, Northampton voters were given golden guineas in sandwiches at the 1768 election, which was notorious for being the most expensive and corrupt election of the century.[10]

The candidates would be formally nominated at a large civic occasion. They would typically deliver heroic speeches where they would flatter the voters and set out their political principles. In the manner of a weigh-in at a boxing match, they would also attack their rivals and spur on the crowd for the contest ahead. It was at the nomination where the candidates who were to take the field would be decided, and if there were not more candidates than seats then they would be declared elected there and then. If no one else came forward – or if local elites had been successful in sewing up the election in advance – there would be no contest. If there were more candidates, then this was the point at which they had to demonstrate that they had sufficient support to proceed to a poll. The non-voters had an important role to play here, since this was a public event from which they could not be excluded. If the nomination was held indoors, the non-voters could pack the hall to squeeze out supporters of candidates they disliked. Either way, they could vocally express their views and influence proceedings. An account of the Durham election in 1830 records the interjections of the crowd as a local gentleman attempts to nominate an unpopular candidate:

> (*Great disapprobation.*) Gentlemen, I would scorn to say a thing behind a man's back that I would not say to his face, and that is the reason why I have brought it before him on this day – (*Hisses*) – that I may justify myself, and that I may shew if I have been free on former occasions, I am still as independent as I ever was. (*The whole Hall was unanimous in its disapprobation.*)[11]

If the nomination produced a contest then the election would proceed to a poll. The process of polling was very different to today. Before the 1832 Reform Act limited the duration of the poll and established voter registration, the process of polling voters was very slow and could take weeks. Polling would continue until the losing side ran out of voters, so 'first past the post' was originally an endurance race rather than a sprint. Every night the running totals would be announced at the hustings, so parties would be able to gauge their position and locals would join in the excitement of following the unfolding event. These announcements would often be followed by processions, commonly with marching bands that would play the candidate's signature tune (often a popular song from the day, with new words written for the occasion). At Chester in 1826, Lord Grosvenor's band were in 'open mutiny' at his haggling over their fee, so 'they offered to play (and *vote* into the bargain) for the INDEPENDENT party for *half price!*'[12]

The process of voting could be complex and intimidating. One reason why there was such an emphasis on the manly moral qualities of the voter was that voting was an ordeal, and was arguably supposed to be. Before the Ballot Act of 1872, voting was open and the record of your vote was made public, so voters were aware that they had to bear the consequences of their choice. The process of voting would have gone something like this. First, a voter would have to make his way to the poll, sometimes running the gauntlet of hostile crowds and hired thugs who were trying to stop him. He would then endure a long wait because the process was very slow. Prior registration on an electoral roll was only introduced in 1832: before this, one had to claim your right to vote at the poll itself, which could include proving that you met the property or residence qualifications with suitable documents. A lawyer from the opposing party could then try to throw out the claim and oaths would be administered, often in a tactical way in an attempt to trip up the voter or intimidate him. Only when the vote was accepted as valid would the voter declare his vote. This was a public act, which could well get a reaction from the surrounding crowds, as at Poole in 1835: 'cheers being given by the populace for every vote to Sir JOHN BYNG and Mr TULK, and disapprobation for every one to Messrs IRVING and BONAR'.[13]

Polling would continue until all the voters had been polled or the trailing side conceded the contest. Although the result would be widely known, it would be formally announced at the declaration. This would be a public event at the hustings and would have a very different tone to the nomination. The concluding speeches were supposed to be gracious and consoling, where winners would be magnanimous and losers would be complimentary to the victor. After the conflict and misrule of the election, this was the point at which harmony and order was to return. As a report on the conclusion of the York contest in 1830 put it, 'we hope the acerbity of party strife will die away, and that the blue and the orange and the pink, will mingle together in society as friends'.[14] There was one ceremony still to perform, however. The victorious candidate would be 'chaired': seated in a richly decorated chair, the community would literally raise up their choice and parade them through the streets. William Hogarth famously depicted a chairing in his series of prints that depicted the riotous 1754 election for Oxfordshire (Figure 3.2). The bewigged MP does not look comfortable in his situation: in a metaphor for the whole social order, the power of the elite rests on the mob and they are in constant danger of being toppled. Some MPs were understandably keen to avoid being chaired and were relieved if the ceremony was cancelled on safety grounds. Not all chairings were so riotous, since some were well-organised civic processions with a clear order of precedence, thus highlighting the political and social hierarchy that they sought to restore after an election.

Figure 3.2 William Hogarth, 'Chairing the Member' (1754–55). Courtesy of the Lewis Walpole Library, Yale University.

The meaning of these rituals has been interpreted in different ways by various historians. O'Gorman makes an analogy with carnival: in some Catholic countries, carnival is a period of feasting and public revelry, where the world is temporarily turned upside-down.[15] Did the inversion of the existing order just serve to reinforce it once it had been restored? Or did this period of misrule serve as a 'safety valve', to allow people to let off steam in a controlled way before resuming their lowly place in the hierarchy? Interpretations like these emphasise the conservative significance of elections, but James Vernon argues that the official meanings of events such as the chairing could be subverted. He argues that the election was 'a story complete with a central cast of characters, and a sequence of events which built an epic narrative full of suspense and excitement'. Ordinary people were encouraged to see themselves as part of that narrative and attempted to impose themselves upon it.[16] Sources from the time present a heightened story of the election, emphasising the grand constitutional issues at stake and the vital role of the humble citizen at this critical juncture. A gendered perspective is useful here, since men in particular were expected to live up to particular roles at election time. We have seen how the predominant behavioural ideal during an election was 'the independent man': being able to act conscientiously, owning property and being physically 'manly' were important considerations in an open voting system where voters were vulnerable to bribery and intimidation.

Some aspects of this electoral culture were remarkably enduring. When the 1832 Reform Act gave MPs to towns like Manchester – so symbolic of urban modernity and industrial progress – they adopted the old electoral culture and its rituals wholesale. There are records of chairing ceremonies as late as the 1960s and other aspects of the Georgian system persist in a modified form to this day. Nevertheless, the carnivalesque culture of elections declined over the course of the nineteenth century as it came to be at odds with a changed political culture and new expectations of manly behaviour. Political reform in the nineteenth century served to modify the electoral process. The First Reform Act made elections shorter, by establishing prior registration and limiting the duration of the poll: while this undoubtedly made the voting process more efficient, it also limited opportunities for political street theatre and informal political expression. Other new regulations such as the introduction of multiple polling places served to disperse the crowd by removing their single focal point. The effect of this was to make elections more about voting and less about the kinds of activities that included the non-voters: the line between citizens and non-citizens was drawn more starkly. The introduction of the Secret Ballot in 1872 and the Corrupt Practices Act in 1883 (which sought to put an end to activities like treating) had a similar effect: while they brought the system closer to our modern standards of democracy, they made elections a private act for citizens rather than public events for everybody. Vernon links these developments to a wider shift in the culture of politics in the nineteenth century, whereby politics was taken off the streets and was made rational and domestic. This is bound up with the shift towards a print-based political culture that we saw in Chapter 1, and the change from 'outer' to 'inner' manifestations of masculinity that we saw in Chapter 2. If electoral manliness in the eighteenth century was all about public defiance, by the end of the nineteenth it was more concerned with private conscience.

Women and elections: the Duchess of Devonshire

Georgian elections were not just about men. Women of all classes participated at election time. Women got involved in the public events and were canvassed by the candidates. One election leaflet from Shropshire in 1796 urged candidates to desist from canvassing 'Freemen's WIVES at so late an hour, when *their Husbands* are from home' and also from encouraging maidservants to kiss their master in an attempt to influence his vote: despite its bawdy tone, it gives us a hint that canvassers engaged with women of lowly stations.[17] Some women made a lot of money at election time, including providers of food and drink, and also landladies. Given that some borough franchises concerned one's place of residence, women with rooms to let could take in multiple lodgers at election time, each of whom had a valuable vote that she would expect to profit from. Activities like this suggest that ordinary women could possess a great deal of knowledge about the nature of the political process.

Women of the elite had more direct opportunities to exert a political influence. The political elite in this period consisted of a small number of titled families, who were connected by familial and social ties. Women had an important part to play in this network and looking after the 'family interest' was an expected female pursuit, even if it extended to politics. Electoral politics was a family business, since the local power bases that fought elections tended to be the dominant families in the community. Fighting elections was a family effort, since wives and daughters would be expected to contribute to the campaigns of their husbands and fathers, often in very public ways. As Elaine Chalus argues, 'the familial and factional nature of politics' required that elite women were politically interested, aware and active at election time.[18]

Women could not stand for election but sometimes they had a significant influence over who did. Powerful local families commonly selected which candidates were to stand and, in an era when two-thirds of elections were uncontested, this was often where the MP was effectively chosen. Women had key roles behind the scenes as facilitators and go-betweens in these kinds of negotiations. In some cases they made the choice themselves. In Weymouth, Lady Johnstone managed the family's electoral interest between the death of her husband and the heir reaching his majority: the family owned much of the property in the town so had a decisive influence over the election of its MPs. By a historical quirk, Weymouth and Melcombe Regis had four MPs until 1832, so this was a significant bloc of MPs and it was effectively managed by a woman.

As well as working behind the scenes, elite women had public roles at election time. The family had a significant role in the canvass, so women would accompany canvassing parties and would attempt to persuade voters to support their relative. Elite women were highly visible at the set-piece election events, often riding in richly decorated carriages or appearing in prominent locations wearing dresses, ribbons and rosettes in party colours:

> The windows of the Albion Hotel and News Room, and all of the surrounding houses, were filled with ladies, wearing the colours of the party at their breasts, and among whom was *Lady Broughton*, completely attired in *crimson*, in compliment to the cause of Independence.[19]

Women were also involved in an organisational capacity. We have seen how the sociable side to elections was very important, at least until the Corrupt Practices Act. The role of the hostess fell within women's traditional remit so they organised the election breakfasts, dinners and 'treats'. Electioneering was therefore a legitimate way into the public sphere for elite women, arguably because it represented an extension of the familial role for women of their class.

Some elite women were involved in high politics at the national level. Even into the twentieth century, Westminster politics revolved around networks of family and personal connection, and women had prominent roles in this world as hostesses, intermediaries and political fixers. The most famous of these in the Georgian period was Georgiana Cavendish, Duchess of Devonshire. Georgiana has recently received a great deal of historical and public attention, being the subject of a bestselling biography and a 2008 feature film, *The Duchess*. This interest is partly because, as a Spencer, she was an ancestor of Diana, Princess of Wales, and the parallels between their lives are striking. Both were determined women who were trapped in loveless marriages, were plagued by the media after becoming prominent celebrities, and who took on high-profile political causes. Georgiana was born into high society and, a great beauty, was the sensation of her coming-out season. She married the Duke of Devonshire, one of the wealthiest men in Britain and a powerful figure in the Whig party, if a rather ineffectual one. The relationship was not a happy one and there was infidelity on both sides, but Georgiana took a keen interest in her husband's politics, first campaigning on his behalf and then taking a more autonomous role in leading Whig circles. She was friends with the party leader, Charles James Fox, who saw that the Whig party could take advantage of her great popularity as a celebrity and a leader of fashion.

Matters came to a head in 1784. Fox had been in power in coalition with Lord North, but the government fell at the end of 1783 and George III asked Pitt the Younger to form a government. Pitt called a general election and the Whigs were determined to make a stand at the seat of Westminster, the most populous and prestigious constituency in the country. Fox was standing against two ministerial candidates, Sir Cecil Wray and the admiral Samuel Hood, and the government poured money into the contest in an attempt to defeat Fox and demoralise the opposition. Prominent Whigs mobilised in Westminster in an attempt to save Fox and Georgiana took a leading role. She threw herself into electioneering and proved popular with the crowds and an effective canvasser. One newspaper proclaimed: 'She is the candidate to all intents and purposes.' The election was a particularly gruelling and bitter one and lasted for 40 days, a record for the period. Fox was eventually declared elected alongside Hood, due in large part to Georgiana's efforts, and managed to keep his seat even after the controversial result was subject to a lengthy scrutiny.

Georgiana's role in this election has received a lot of attention from gender scholars, due to the hostile coverage that she received. Her participation drew much negative comment from journalists, pamphlet writers and caricaturists, many of whom were in the pay of the government. These attacks tended to focus on her gender, highlighting her sexuality and morality, and suggesting that she was taking on roles that were inappropriate for a woman. One of the most common stories of the election suggested that she kissed a butcher while canvassing his vote: this prompted a slew of satirical cartoons, many of which were obscene and suggested that she was trading other sexual favours for votes. Cartoons such as these played on the sexual connotations of the 'public woman', likening Georgiana to a prostitute. Her attackers also alleged that she was having an affair with Fox (wrongly, as it turned out: she was instead having an affair with his Whig colleague Charles Grey). As one lewd ditty put it:

> SAYS Fox to House, 'tis ten to one;
>   At Westminster I am undone;
>   But I still have one County clear –
>   I can come in for Devonshire.'[20]

One of the more sophisticated prints of the election, 'The Devonshire Amusement' (Figure 3.3), brings together the various criticisms that were made of Georgiana on the basis of her gender. The print is divided in two (the 'contrast' was a common format for eighteenth-century prints), depicting the public and the private, and making it clear that the duke and the duchess are in the wrong respective spheres. The duke is indoors tending to an infant: he appears effeminate and miserable, declaring 'This work does not suit my Fancy. Ah William every one must be cursed that like thee takes a Politic Mad Wife.' His portrait on the wall has the horns of a cuckold, referring to the allegation that his wife is having an affair: cuckoldry is as much a criticism of the man as the woman, as he has failed to master his wife. By contrast, Georgiana is in the public sphere, but the depiction of her body suggests that she does not belong there: her huge breasts and hips underline her femininity, and her wild hair and dishevelled clothes suggest an out-of-control sexuality. The Whigs attempted to counter these hostile representations with propaganda of their own. These too focused on gender, portraying her as a 'female patriot' or a goddess-like figure alongside classical abstractions like Liberty and Fame. These positive portrayals, however, were notably less effective than the hostile ones: where women in politics was concerned, the negative symbolic repertoire was much more extensive than the positive.

The significance of Georgiana's reception in the 1784 election has been much debated among historians. It might appear that the backlash against her electioneering was part of a wider closing off of the political world for women: it parallels

Figure 3.3 'The Devonshire Amusement' (1784). Courtesy of the Lewis Walpole Library, Yale University.

the chronology that we saw in Chapter 1 regarding female debating societies, or in Chapter 2 regarding the 'gender panic' of this decade. Certainly there were misogynistic themes in the 1784 election that are perceptible elsewhere in late eighteenth-century politics and society. On the other hand, female electioneering was far from unusual, and continued unabated throughout the nineteenth century. What made Georgiana's participation problematic was not the fact she was a woman, but because she was campaigning on behalf of a non-relative. Campaigning for a husband or father was perfectly acceptable, but a man with whom one was widely rumoured to be having an affair was not. Georgiana was also vulnerable to this kind of attack given her status as a socialite, gambler and leader of fashion: in the 1780s atmosphere of national and military crisis, moral reformers focused on these kinds of activities among the elite and their effect on the spiritual health of the nation.

Conclusion

What the 1784 Westminster election does tell us is that gender needs to be central to our understanding of the British electoral process. Participating in the official capacity of a candidate or a voter was limited to men, and the roles that these men were expected to play were articulated in terms of masculinity. Women may have been excluded from these official manifestations of citizenship, but there were nevertheless numerous ways that they could get involved in electoral politics, which related in fundamental ways to their social position as women. Women's domestic and familial roles could have political aspects, providing legitimate avenues into the public sphere: in a sense, the hostility to Georgiana was a sign that she was no longer acting in this domestic and familial capacity. Nevertheless, a key lesson of this 'social' approach to elections is that the informal manifestations of politics are every bit as important as the formal ones. An electoral system that was as much about the non-voters as the voters, and where the social meaning of the process was as important as the actual result, requires this kind of approach. Historians of women in politics have been particularly attentive to these informal and often hidden interactions, and have helped to nuance historians' definition of 'politics' as a result. The electoral system should therefore be central to our understanding of the connections between gender and citizenship in the eighteenth and nineteenth centuries.

Notes

1 J. Phillips, *Electoral Behaviour in Unreformed England: Plumpers, Splitters and Straights*, Princeton: Princeton University Press, 1982; F. O'Gorman, *Voters, Patrons and Parties: The Unreformed Electorate of Hanoverian England, 1734–1832*, Oxford: Oxford University Press, 1989.
2 P. Langford, 'Property and "virtual representation" in eighteenth-century England', *The Historical Journal*, 31:1, 1988, 83–115 (p. 114).
3 M. Kishlansky, *Parliamentary Selection: Social and Political Choice in Early Modern England*, Manchester: Manchester University Press, 1995.

66 *The British electoral tradition*

4 O'Gorman, *Voters*, p. 13.
5 Sir W. Blackstone, *Commentaries on the Laws of England*, London, 1765–69, vol. 1, p. 166. 'Villein' is medieval term for a feudal tenant who is legally tied to the lord of the manor.
6 D. Hirst, *Representative of the People? Voters and Voting in England Under the Early Stuarts*, Cambridge: Cambridge University Press, 1975, pp. 18–19.
7 E. Chalus, *Elite Women in English Political Life, c. 1754–1790*, Oxford: Oxford University Press, 2005, pp. 35–9.
8 F. O'Gorman, 'Campaign rituals and ceremonies: The social meaning of elections in England, 1780–1860', *Past and Present*, 135, 1992, 79–115.
9 *History of the Contested Election in Chester 1818*, Chester, n.d., p. 29.
10 Z. Dyndor, 'The political culture of elections in Northampton, 1768–1868', PhD thesis, University of Northampton, 2010, p. 184.
11 *Proceedings and Addresses, at the Durham City Election*, Durham, 1830, p. 6.
12 *A Narrative of the Proceedings at the Memorable Contest for the Representation of Chester in 1826*, Chester, 1826, p. 11.
13 *Account of the Election of Two Representatives in Parliament for the Borough of Poole*, Poole, 1835, p. 27.
14 *The Poll for Members of Parliament, to Represent the City of York*, York, 1830, p. xi.
15 O'Gorman, 'Campaign rituals', p. 112.
16 J. Vernon, *Politics and the People: A Study in English Political Culture, c. 1815–1867*, Cambridge: Cambridge University Press, 1993, p. 99.
17 'Advertisement Extraordinary' (election broadside, Shropshire, 13 February, 1796).
18 E. Chalus, '"That epidemical madness": Women and electoral politics in the late eighteenth century', in H. Barker and E. Chalus (eds.), *Gender in Eighteenth-Century England: Roles, Representations and Responsibilities*, London: Longman, 1997, pp. 152–78 (p. 152).
19 *Narrative*, p. 103.
20 *History of the Westminster Election, Containing Every Material Occurrence*, London, 1785, pp. 254, 248.

Recommended reading

Chalus, E., *Elite Women in English Political Life, 1754–1790*, Oxford: Oxford University Press, 2005.
Foreman, A., 'A politician's politician: Georgiana, Duchess of Devonshire and the Whig party', in H. Barker and E. Chalus (eds.), *Gender in Eighteenth-Century England: Roles, Representations and Responsibilities*, London: Longman, 1997, pp. 179–204.
Langford, P., *Public Life and the Propertied Englishman, 1689–1798*, Oxford: Oxford University Press, 1994.
Lawrence, J., *Electing Our Masters: The Hustings in British Politics from Hogarth to Blair*, Oxford: Oxford University Press, 2009.
O'Gorman, F., *Voters, Patrons and Parties: The Unreformed Electorate of Hanoverian England, 1734–1832*, Oxford: Oxford University Press, 1989.
O'Gorman, F., 'Campaign rituals and ceremonies: The social meaning of elections in England, 1780–1860', *Past and Present*, 135, 1992, 79–115.
Phillips, J., *Electoral Behaviour in Unreformed England: Plumpers, Splitters and Straights*, Princeton: Princeton University Press, 1982.
Stott, A., '"Female patriotism": Georgiana, Duchess of Devonshire, and the Westminster election of 1784', *Eighteenth-Century Life*, 17, 1993, 60–84.
Vernon, J., *Politics and the People: A Study in English Political Culture, c. 1815–1867*, Cambridge: Cambridge University Press, 1993.

4 Patriotism and revolution, 1776–1819

As we have seen, citizenship involves being a member of a national community. Love of country is often regarded as a citizen's key attachment and an important way of thinking about their identity, as well as informing the kinds of obligations that are required of them. This chapter focuses on a period when this issue came into sharp focus: the 'Age of Revolutions', encompassing those in America and France. Revolution did not spread to Britain, but many people at the time thought that it could, and the political situation overseas had a profound effect within Britain itself. Moreover, both revolutions drew Britain into major wars that involved huge efforts on the part of the state and the civilian population, further polarised the political situation, and had far-reaching social and cultural consequences.

The relationship between patriotism and citizenship is a complex one. Today we tend to align nationalism with the political right: in the twentieth century, nationalism was associated with fascism and right-wing political parties, whereas the left tended to be less comfortable with it and instead emphasised internationalism. As we saw in Chapter 2, however, this has not historically always been the case: 'patriotism' was the stance of those who stood up for the people against the establishment, and early radicals like John Wilkes had a very nationalistic political style. Historians such as Hugh Cunningham have drawn on the eighteenth century in order to demonstrate that patriotism is politically contested territory, since a vision of citizenship based on love of country could be used either to support or to critique the status quo.[1] The political implications of patriotism became more pressing and complicated during the Age of Revolutions. British radicals commonly identified with revolutionaries in America and France, but once Britain was at war with them it was difficult to do this and to claim to be patriotic. War often has a polarising effect on politics and the side doing the fighting tends to lay an exclusive claim to patriotism. In the 1790s, those who opposed the French Revolution and its ideals, and supported king and country, made patriotic appeals as never before.

It might appear that patriotism shifted from the left to the right in this period, but this chapter will explore the complexities of this phenomenon. We will begin by thinking about the origins of radical patriotism and how radicals used patriotism in the light of revolution abroad: did they abandon it and appeal to other commitments, or were they able to rework it? The chapter will then shift its focus to the 'loyalists' who opposed radicalism and revolution. They may have appropriated patriotism from the radicals, but arguably they were not able to do this without retaining some of its radical connotations. Indeed, requiring people to be active and vigilant in a time of war suggests a model of citizenship that is far from conservative. The threat of French invasion necessitated a nationwide drive to get civilian men involved in military defence, and we have seen how military service has historically been a key duty of citizenship and a means to earn citizenship rights. This period of British history therefore presents an opportunity to explore the relationship between citizenship and patriotism.

Patriotism

Questions of national identity and patriotism are nowadays at the forefront of historical discussion about Britain's eighteenth century. As we saw in Chapter 1, the British state was created in 1707 with the Act of Union. It was not yet a nation: at the beginning of the century, the peoples of England, Scotland, Wales and Ireland identified with those nations instead. A 'nation' suggests a coherent body, where land, people and culture are unified in an organic way, and which provides a focus for collective affection and identity. Whereas a state can be created with the stroke of a pen, a nation can only be the product of a long cultural process. One can be the citizen of a state in an administrative sense (in terms of rights, laws, finance, and so on) but the subjective aspects of citizenship (such as identity or loyalty) concern the nation.

Linda Colley famously argued in her book *Britons: Forging the Nation, 1707–1837* that, over the course of the eighteenth century, the peoples of the British state came to see themselves as members of a British nation. The process by which this came about was war: between 1689 and 1815, Britain was repeatedly at war with France. This was not strictly the 'Second Hundred Years' War' that some historians have termed it but, even during periods of peace, France was Britain's rival in a commercial, imperial and cultural sense. Colley argues that France became Britain's 'other', enabling it to define its identity in both negative and positive terms: 'Britain' was the opposite of France, and conflict with an external enemy encouraged the English, Scottish and Welsh to emphasise what they had in common.

The British Isles provided promising material for nation-building. First, they had a shared geography. The archipelago of 6,000 islands off the northwest coast of mainland Europe was by no means a unified entity, but it did provide a coherent cluster and a sense of separateness from the continent. (This remains prominent in many Britons' identities to this day.) Although many languages were spoken across the British Isles, the English language was dominant and served as a *lingua franca*: Britain in the eighteenth century was more linguistically unified than France, for example. English, Welsh and Scots were also linked by religion, since the official religion was Protestantism and Catholics were a minority with limited rights. The British were self-congratulatory about their brand of Christianity, which they contrasted with France's superstitious Catholicism (and, after 1789, their apparent atheism). Britons also congratulated themselves on their political system, a unique combination of monarchy and representative democracy, which preserved their special liberties. The monarchy itself eventually became the focus of national affection: whereas the first two Georges identified as German and were regarded that way by an indifferent public, George III saw himself as British. After the party struggles of the 1760s, he became a widely popular monarch, known for his approachable manner, simple tastes and love of domesticity. Colley argues that he became a rallying point for patriotic affection during the French Wars at the end of the century.[2]

Other factors encouraged the British to see themselves as superior to the French. Britons congratulated themselves on their relative prosperity, a theme that recurred in satirical prints that commonly portrayed a plump John Bull enjoying beef and plum pudding, to the envy of scrawny French peasants. Britons saw themselves as a trading nation, and historians such as Kathleen Wilson have argued that the empire came to be culturally dominant in the eighteenth century, informing ideas about gender in particular.[3] The empire was a shared focus for a British identity, providing a sense of global superiority and national mission: Britons told themselves that this was an empire based upon common interest and the spread of religion and civilisation. In a practical sense, it also provided many job opportunities: the Scots and Irish in particular, who faced barriers to getting on at home, staffed the empire in disproportionate numbers. They also served in large numbers in the armed forces, which became both a melting pot of personnel and a means to incorporate national martial traditions (such as the wearing of tartan) into the wider British project. The navy, in particular, became a focus for national affection. As an island nation, it was the 'wooden walls' of the navy that kept Britain safe from invaders, protecting its liberties from foreign tyrants, while at the same time expanding the beloved empire. The common sailor, 'Jack Tar', became a British hero. He became a popular stock character in the theatre, where he was instantly recognisable for his salty lingo, his bravery and his instinctive patriotism.

Since its publication in 1992, *Britons* has been hugely influential but also very controversial. Historians of Scotland, Ireland and Wales have queried the extent to which these identities were supplanted by 'Britishness'. England has historically tended to dominate its neighbours, and arguably the features that Colley identifies as Britishness are really forms of Englishness: the terms are often (and incorrectly) used interchangeably to this day. More seriously, Ireland does not feature in Colley's account: it probably should have done, since the Union of 1800 sits within her chronology, but it is understandable why it is excluded from an account that relies upon a clear distinction between a unified Britain and its 'other'. Subsequent scholars have thought about how Colley's interpretation relates to the Irish experience. Catriona Kennedy, for example, considered wartime culture in Britain and Ireland, and the experiences of Irishmen in the armed forces. She argues that Irish and Scottish soldier writers appeal to 'Britishness' more frequently than their English counterparts, suggesting that 'the idea of Britishness resonated most at the margins, rather than at the centre of the Union'.[4]

This chapter will show how the political implications of nationalism changed over the course of our period. Samuel Johnson defined 'patriot' as 'One whose ruling passion is the love of his country' in his 1755 *Dictionary of the English Language*. By the fourth edition of 1777, however, he added: 'It is sometimes used for a factious disturber of the government.'[5] In Johnson's day, patriotism could indeed be an anti-government stance. We saw in Chapter 2 how 'Country patriotism' was a critique of the establishment, which emphasised that the ruling class and the Hanoverian dynasty were culturally foreign and did not have the interests of the nation at heart. At the same time, the 'patriots' claimed to be more committed to the interests of the nation and the people. They drew on the classical associations of the concept – such as manly virtue, public spirit and disinterestedness – and juxtaposed this with the alleged effeminacy, factiousness and corruption of their enemies. Early radicalism emerged out of this patriotic political critique.

There is a further sense in which patriotism could be radical. Radicals could appeal to a version of English history that emphasised a story of struggles to preserve liberty. Key events in English history such as Agincourt or the defeat of the Spanish Armada could be presented as battles against foreigners who were trying to take their precious liberties away. Eighteenth-century Britons saw themselves as having a unique destiny: like the Israelites in the Old Testament, Britain was an 'elect' nation in the eyes of God. Its superior religion, prosperity, empire and political system were testament to its special place in the world. This was consistent with a view of political liberty as an exclusive national tradition, handed down through the generations, rather than something that all peoples of the world could enjoy: the Englishman was 'freeborn' as the country of his birth conferred on him his inherited rights. As we saw in Chapter 1, the revered constitution was not a single document but was the culmination of centuries of settlements, precedents and institutional developments. The political rights of the citizen were therefore enshrined in the history of the nation itself.

Radicalism

The label 'radical' requires some justification. Rather than just meaning an extreme position, in British politics it refers to a particular political tradition and worldview. The radical movement developed in the last third of the eighteenth century, and was committed to the achievement of political, social and legal justice for the common people. Radicals at the time identified themselves as such but, strictly speaking, 'radicalism' is an anachronistic term. The '-ism' suggests a unified movement with a coherent ideology, which probably misrepresents the nature of radical politics, but 'radicalism' nevertheless remains a useful term of art. Sir Francis Burdett noted: 'A radical is a person who would apply an effectual remedy to an inveterate disease ... To *eradicate* means to root up.'[6] Most radicals in the eighteenth century subscribed to the view that the rights of Englishmen were enshrined in the ancient constitution, and that these had been lost through corruption and the abuse of power. Radical reform therefore entailed going back to the roots, to restore these ancient national rights, rather than necessarily moving forward.

Early radicalism was indebted to the 'Country patriot' tradition. In the 1760s, John Wilkes had taken 'patriotism' to a new level, becoming ever more virulent in his xenophobia and chauvinism, and applying its critique of the ruling class in a more radical way. Wilkes claimed to stand for 'the people' against a government that was not committed to the nation and its welfare, and won much support from the middling sorts in particular. For Wilkes, a love of liberty was inherent in the English national character: the Englishman 'will always be ready to stand forth for his king and country; and, according to the old *English* plan of liberty, will praise or censure any minister, or set of ministers, according to their behaviour'.[7]

In the 1770s, the American issue had profound implications for patriot radicalism. Wilkes sympathised with the plight of the rebels and made common cause with them: radicals generally saw the colonists as fellow Britons who were denied basic rights and were oppressed by the same corrupt government. Indeed, most Americans saw themselves as Britons too, and both sides in the dispute reasoned that they were protecting the British constitution. In this period, Britain and America shared a broadly common political culture. The American rebels were using ideas about government, liberty and resistance that were based upon English radical Whig thought, and they engaged in a transatlantic dialogue with British radicals. Some of the key texts of the American Revolution were produced by English radicals, such as Thomas Paine's *Common Sense* (1776) and John Cartwright's *Take Your Choice* (1776). This dialogue served further to radicalise English opposition thought and, as we have seen, inspired Wilkes to table the first motion for parliamentary reform in Britain. As the dispute developed, however, it became more difficult to articulate radicalism in a patriotic way. Once Britain went to war with the rebels, the radicals found themselves in the position of sympathising with the nation's military adversaries. This problem became more acute when France and Spain joined the war on the American side, given that these were the patriots' traditional enemies. British radicalism emerged battered from the experience of the American War and remained in the doldrums for much of the 1780s.

Radicalism revived at the end of the 1780s. The beginning of the French Revolution was generally greeted with optimism in Britain. Radicals rejoiced that France's absolutist regime had been deposed and were inspired by early revolutionary ideas. The Romantic movement captured the idealistic spirit of these early days of revolution: as the poet William Wordsworth recalled, 'Bliss it was in that dawn to be alive / But to be young was very heaven!'[8] This optimistic reaction to events in France was partly informed by the centenary of the Revolution of 1688–89. A year of celebrations emphasised that the Glorious Revolution had expelled absolutism and guaranteed the people's liberties: as Wilson notes, this 'elite' affair had by then taken on a 'popular' significance.[9] France appeared to be going through the same process that England had a century before: historical time was often thought about in cyclical terms in this period, so this recurrence of events (literally a 'revolution') appeared to make sense. Many Britons wished France well on this journey, but radicals were less inclined to be self-congratulatory about Britain's situation. On 4 November 1789, the Nonconformist minister Richard Price preached a sermon entitled 'A discourse on the love of our country'. Price's message was that the American and French Revolutions were also 'glorious', and they demonstrated that Britain should now finish the job that it started in 1688. For Price, the principles of the Glorious Revolution were:

> First; the right to liberty of conscience in religious matters.
> Secondly; the right to resist power when abused. And
> Thirdly; the right to chuse our own governors; to cashier them for misconduct; and to frame a government for ourselves.[10]

This would have been news to the Whigs of 1688 and demonstrates the extent to which the meaning of the Glorious Revolution had shifted in popular myth over the century. In the light of the American experience, Price argued that the revolution upheld the principles of popular sovereignty and government by consent.

Inspired by events in France, radicals in Britain mobilised. Moderate reformers such as the Whigs found themselves in an increasingly marginal position as the Revolution polarised British politics between radical and loyal extremes. The social composition of radicalism changed: whereas Wilkes had won support from the metropolitan middling sorts in the 1760s, the radicalism of the 1790s was much more working class. Marxist historians such as E. P. Thompson therefore portray the 1790s as the heroic age of British radicalism, when the oppressed and the marginalised achieved class-consciousness.[11] Indeed, the history of radicalism has traditionally been explained in terms of class, as a political 'reflection' of social circumstances. Rather than being a proto-socialist movement, however, radicalism drew upon older oppositional traditions and political critiques, and had a rich political culture that deserves to be studied in its own right. It mobilised the institutions of the public sphere in radical ways. Radicals across the country organised into Corresponding Societies, which corresponded with the French and with each other, sharing constitutional information. There was a proliferation of political print and radical newspapers increasingly went underground, evading both the censor and the stamp tax, keeping them affordable for working people and not contributing to the coffers of the hated government. Some radicals went further and planned to hold a 'convention', an alternative to parliament that would draw its legitimacy from the people and draft a new democratic constitution. Others armed and planned insurrection: the period is littered with failed plots and conspiracies.

The reaction of the government to all this was unequivocal. Pitt the Younger regarded radical activity as a threat to national security and countered it with the full force of the law. Radical organisations were infiltrated with spies, there were widespread arrests and parliament passed laws restricting freedom of expression and association. This in turn drove the movement further underground and reinforced the radicals' conviction that the government was suppressing popular liberty. Arguably the government overreacted, but we should not underestimate the extent to which contemporaries feared that revolution would spread across the channel, and that domestic radicals would facilitate this. In addition to the government response, popular opinion turned against the French. It soon became clear that their social and political experimentation went well beyond a rerun of the Glorious Revolution and, by 1793, news of violence and executions in France decisively turned British public opinion against them. The execution of the royal family horrified France's neighbours and drew Britain into war.

As with the American Revolution, the declaration of war placed British radicals in a difficult position. In particular, it was problematic to claim to be a 'patriot' in these circumstances. Many radicals like John Cartwright continued to argue in terms of patriotic constitutionalism. He appealed to the British nation, 'in whose service, as a sincere friend to its liberty and constitution, I have not been inactive'.[12] Cartwright sought to restore the ancient constitution, which he regarded as the source of the Briton's unique, historic liberties. One way he proposed to do this was through universal military service. Cartwright was an enthusiast for citizen soldiering – he was known as 'Major' Cartwright after his rank in the Nottinghamshire militia – and he invoked the classical argument that men should earn their citizenship by defending the nation. He advocated 'a substantial reform in the representation, and a restoration of the ancient system of arming' since, in his view, the two went hand in hand.[13] Unfortunately this meant going to war against the French Revolutionaries whom he so admired: it was not easy being a radical patriot in the 1790s.

Other radicals grappled with their patriotic legacy. Price argued that pursuing the interest of one's own country should not mean a disregard for other countries:

> We should love it ardently but not exclusively. We ought to seek its good, by all the means that our different circumstances and abilities will allow; but at the same time we ought to consider ourselves as citizens of the world, and take care to maintain a just regard to the right of other countries.[14]

We can see here a forerunner of the modern left's internationalism. Price's notion of 'citizens of the world' was powerful in the context of the Age of Revolution, when revolution knew no borders and promoted notions of universal rights. The radical who most completely turned his back on patriotism was Thomas Paine. His book *Rights of Man* (1791) became a sensation and was widely reprinted. Paine rejected the notion that political systems were national traditions that were handed down by previous generations, and which therefore could not be changed. The notion that future generations should be bound by our political institutions was 'governing beyond the grave'.[15] Instead, political sovereignty rested in the people, in the present day. Every individual possessed rights that they received directly from God and it was up to them how they constituted their political system. The ancient constitution and national political traditions were therefore irrelevant, since Paine was an internationalist who believed in universal human rights. He travelled to France to spread this message but, ironically, the revolutionary regime saw him as a threat and put him in jail. While in prison he wrote *The Age of Reason* (1794), which promoted free thought and critiqued organised religion, including Christianity. Meanwhile, back in Britain, Paine came to symbolise everything that the establishment and its supporters most feared.

Loyalism

Besides the government's repressive measures, there were numerous public initiatives to oppose the Revolution and its radical supporters. Groups were formed such as 'Church and King' societies and the Association for Promoting Liberty and Property Against Republicans and Levellers (known as Reeves Societies after their founder John Reeves). These associations were involved in activities such as disrupting radical meetings, organising prosecutions and burning Paine in effigy. In addition to this, there was an explosion of anti-Revolution publications, including newspapers, sermons and pamphlets. Some of these were specifically targeted at working people, with the aim of countering the spread of radical ideas.

The catch-all term for these diverse activities is 'loyalism'. Like 'radicalism', it has its problems as a label. It dates from the Victorian period, so we should be careful when applying it to the eighteenth century. It also tends to be used rather imprecisely by historians, to connote patriotism, conservatism, counter-revolution or reaction. If we are going to use the concept to think about the history of citizenship, we need to know to whom (or what) the loyalists were loyal, and what the nature of their loyalty was. It is clear that the loyalists of the 1790s were hostile to the French Revolution and its radical supporters, and that usually involved expressing loyalty to the monarchy, the church and the constitution. Their relationship with patriotism and even conservatism, however, was more complex and arguably shifted over the course of the decade.

It is vital to be precise about the nature of loyalism, since it has a big impact upon how we interpret this pivotal decade in British history. Loyalism was long ignored by historians, since it did not fit the Whig narrative about the onward march of liberty or the Marxist account of the radical working class. Its reactionary activities looked like the anti-communist witch-hunts of Senator McCarthy in the 1950s, and the social historians of the 1960s tended to regard it as having been orchestrated by the authorities. The 1980s, however, saw a re-evaluation of loyalism, since the electoral success of Margaret Thatcher encouraged historians to take popular conservatism seriously. Rather than a top down phenomenon, historians instead emphasised that loyalism had a genuinely popular basis. Frank O'Gorman, for example, demonstrated that the Paine burnings of 1792–93 were not just elite-sponsored, but drew participation from the middling and lower orders.[16] And Colley presented a more benign interpretation of British nationalism at the end of the long eighteenth century, suggesting that it was a source of social consensus and a way for ordinary Britons to express a sense of citizenship.[17] Loyalism can therefore help us to think about the relationship between the individual and the state.

One of the first hostile responses to the French Revolution was Edmund Burke's *Reflections on the Revolution in France* (1790). Burke had been a Whig, but broke with them over their view of the Revolution. He took issue with Price's sermon on the implications of 1688: 'Instead of a right to choose their own governors, they declared that the *succession* in that line (the protestant line drawn from James the First) was absolutely necessary.'[18] Burke argued that the strength of the British political system was its foundation in tradition, since it embodied the tried-and-tested wisdom of experience. People should therefore respect tradition and should seek to hand on the benefits of their political system to future generations. This is British conservatism in a nutshell and the *Reflections* is often regarded as its founding document. In contrast with his account of British solidity and contentment, Burke reacted with horror at what was going on in France. He argued that it was dangerous to take a leap in the dark based upon unproven abstract theories. Burke perceived that the French were embarking on a dangerous experiment that was doomed to failure, since their chosen path would lead to extremism, bloodshed and chaos.

The course of events in France seemed to prove Burke right. (He further argued that the resulting power vacuum would lead to the rise of a tyrant, so he is often credited with predicting Napoleon.) Conservative commentators that followed painted a similar picture, praising the virtues of stability, religion and obedience, and contrasting this with the chaos, atheism and subversion of the Revolution. They painted a picture of a cohesive, interdependent and God-ordained social order:

> We are all in a Chain. Providence has so ordered it that the Rich can't do without the Poor, nor can the Poor do without the Rich. As to being equal in Property ... it never was, and never can be.

The message to working people was that they benefit from the existence of the rich, who pay their taxes, purchase their goods and look after them in time of need.[19] They should therefore know their place and respect their betters, since they enjoy the benefits of 'real liberty'. This was opposed to the false liberty sought by the French, which would only destroy the social fabric that ultimately serves to protect them.

The most imaginative packaging of these ideas was the Cheap Repository Tracts. This was an initiative of a group of Evangelicals known as the Clapham Sect, which included the prolific writer Hannah More. The Cheap Repository's stated aim was 'to supplant the multitude of vicious Tracts circulated by hawkers, and to supply, instead of them, some useful reading, which may likely to prove entertaining also'.[20] Arguments in favour of religion, morality and obedience – and against atheism, immorality and revolution – were presented in short stories and ditties, using popular genres and accessible language. These were then sold cheaply or distributed gratis to working people, sometimes using the same distribution channels as the radical and bawdy literature that they sought to oppose. More and her colleagues were concerned both with moral reform and with counter-revolution, since in their view the two were inseparable. Evangelicals sought religious revival and a reformation of manners, since only a godly nation would prevail against the revolutionaries. Gender was central to this project: as we have seen, some historians credit the Evangelicals with popularising the notion of 'separate spheres' for men and women, whereby women's moral purity would be preserved within the domestic sphere. For the loyalists, therefore, politics began at home.

These domestic themes recur in the Cheap Repository Tracts, but some of them dwell explicitly on the dangers of Revolution. *Village Politics* (1792) concerns a dialogue between Tom, whose head has been turned by radical promises of equality, and his sensible friend Jack:

> *Jack.* [W]hen this levelling comes about, there will be no 'firmaries, no hospitals, no charity-schools, no Sunday-schools, where so many hundred thousand poor souls learn to read the word of God for nothing. For who is to pay for them? equality can't afford it: and those that may be willing won't be able.
>
> *Tom.* But we shall be as good as another, for all that.
>
> *Jack.* Aye, and bad will be the best ... My cottage is my castle; I sit down in it at night in peace and thankfulness, and 'no man maketh me afraid.' Instead of indulging discontent, because another is richer than I in this world, (for envy is at the bottom of how your equality works,) I read my bible, go to church, and think of a treasure in heaven.

Eventually, Tom is persuaded by Jack's reasoning ('I begin to think I'm not so very unhappy as I had got to fancy') but it is difficult to believe that all of More's readers would have been won over by her dour message of submission and religious observance.[21] Burke's basic argument from 1790 reached a wide audience, and would continue to be proffered by religious writers and moral reformers for decades to come, but it did not offer a particularly appealing model of national belonging. Early loyalists promoted passive subjecthood rather than active citizenship: they were conservative without being patriotic.

Military volunteering

The outbreak of war between Britain and France in February 1793 made the loyalist response to the French Revolution more urgent. The 'war of ideas' had now become a military war in which Britain's very existence was at stake, given its vulnerability to French invasion. The French state was committed to spreading Revolution by conquest, and to crushing its enemies. This involved a novel model of citizenship, since the huge war effort required the participation of whole population: David Bell therefore argues that the French Revolutionary and Napoleonic Wars were the 'first Total War'. On 23 August 1793, the National Convention famously declared the *Levée en Masse*:

> From this moment until such time as its enemies shall have been driven from the soil of the Republic, all Frenchmen are in permanent requisition for the services of the armies. The young men shall fight; the married men shall forge arms and transport provisions; the women shall make tents and clothes and shall serve in the hospitals; the children shall turn old lint into linen; the old men shall betake themselves to the public squares in order to arouse the courage of the warriors and preach hatred of kings and the unity of the Republic.[22]

If the people's Revolution was to survive, then the people had to be active in its defence. In particular, men were conscripted into the army on a massive scale. As in the American Revolution, the 'citizen soldier' was a vital figure in the French. A citizen soldier fights, not for pay or because he has been ordered to, but because he believes in what he is fighting for. In a century that placed a great deal of emphasis upon feeling, this supposedly made the citizen soldier invincible. What he may have lacked in professional training, he made up for with motivation, since he was fighting to defend his country, wife and children. It was therefore a highly gendered role and – given that it was commonly taken to be a key way that individuals earned their citizenship – an exclusively masculine one.

The British state therefore faced a military emergency and was under pressure to get large numbers of men under arms. This was both to meet the feared invasion and also to put down internal disturbances, at a time when taxes were high, the economy was dislocated and radicals were spreading discontent. Tellingly, it did not go down the route of conscription. The notion of conscription was so abhorrent to British notions of civil rights that it saw out the Napoleonic Wars and even half of the First World War without it. (This is not to say that forms of compulsory service were unknown in Britain, given the practice of naval impressment and the militia ballot.) In the Anglophone political tradition, citizenship trumped soldiering: the discourse around citizen soldiers concerned the individual's rights, in contrast to the French who emphasised his obligations to the state. The emphasis was instead upon voluntarism, either through willingly joining the regular services or through part-time, civilian soldiering. We should not assume, therefore, that the citizen soldier was solely a feature of the revolutionary regimes with which Britain was at war: Britain had its own brand of citizen soldiering and adopted it on a comparable scale.

Given the need to motivate British people to counter the Revolution, the loyalist rhetoric of the early 1790s was increasingly inadequate to the task. As such, the nature of loyalist argument began to change. Take this example of a handbill from the invasion scare of 1803:

> Hasten then to demonstrate to your DARDING INVADER, how high your National Spirit rises at the Insult, and that although his DISCOMFITURE

and RUIN be certain in the Attempt, let your strenuous and unceasing Efforts in General Armament manifest to the Foe, a firm Appearance of the same manly Vigour in Defence of every Thing dear to ENGLISHMEN, which were purchased with so much Blood, your envied LIBERTY and glorious CONSTITUION, and which can emanate only from the Spirit of BRITONS![23]

The tone of loyalist appeals was now completely different from those of the early 1790s. Instead of preaching passive obedience, loyalists increasingly urged Britons to action. Rather than telling people to accept their place in the world, appeals such as this encouraged them to take responsibility and show initiative: it encouraged manly independence rather than un-masculine dependence. Fundamentally, this was a highly patriotic appeal, revelling in 'National Spirit' and urging Britons to love their country. In many ways, it resembled earlier radical appeals from the likes of Wilkes or Cartwright: as radicals increasingly turned away from such language, the loyalists occupied the patriotic territory. Strikingly, however, patriotism in loyalist hands still retained some of its radical content: this handbill referred to Britain's constitution and its historic liberties, which had been won by the blood sacrifices of ancestors. The difference is that these were now imperilled by an external tyrant rather than an oppressive government: it was a straightforward manoeuvre to shift the focus from a culturally foreign domestic enemy to an actually foreign military one.

A key aim of such appeals was to encourage British men to offer their services in defence of the nation. In addition to the regular forces and the official militia, volunteer military associations were formed throughout the county. As well as providing a defence against invasion, these volunteer units were involved in police and riot control duties. Partly for this reason, J. R. Western argued that the volunteer movement was an anti-revolutionary movement, designed to bolster the forces of order and oppose the radicals.[24] More recent studies of the volunteers have emphasised their diverse social makeup and their non-conservative politics. Some volunteer regiments elected their officers and stipulated that 'the Voice of each Individual will be equal to that of another': 'the Virtues, Talents, & Valour of the Man who enters into this Corps ... are what they will respect and admire, more than his Gentility or Property (for what are they in Battle?)'.[25] Either way, men joined up in large numbers. The motives of individual volunteers are difficult to gauge and, certainly, there were reasons to join up other than patriotic enthusiasm or a desire to fight the French. Joining a volunteer unit got you out of the ballot for the militia, which was a much more onerous service: volunteer units were not subject to martial law and its harsh punishments, were only part-time and served close to home. Others may have been attracted by the fancy uniforms or the opportunities for networking and social climbing. Nevertheless, up to 400,000 men got involved in the volunteer movement.

The volunteers were a favourite topic for satirical prints. Some of these made predictable jokes about the amateur soldier's ineptitude but, in general, they celebrated volunteering and encouraged men to get involved. Charles Williams's

'The Consequence of Invasion or the Hero's Reward' (Figure 4.1) depicts a plump, John Bullish volunteer who has just routed the French army, apparently singlehandedly. He has impaled Napoleon's head on a spear (his diminutive features emphasised by his giant bicorne hat), which also bears the heads of several monstrous Frenchmen. Women crowd round in admiration, declaring 'Bless the Warrior who saved our Virgin charms' and taunting an effeminate 'poltroon' who failed to serve. Louise Carter has noted the phenomenon of 'scarlet fever' during the Napoleonic Wars, whereby women were attracted by the sight of a soldier's red coat.[26] The intended male viewer of the print is supposed to be drawn to the soldier's gallantry and the promise of sexual allure, but the print also casts active citizenship as a masculine station, side-lining women and un-masculine men.

This later loyalism was therefore very different to its predecessors. John Cookson argues that it should be called 'national defence patriotism' instead, but it remained loyalist in its attachment to the status quo and the establishment, and its hostility to radicalism and Revolution.[27] It was not necessarily conservative, however. Loyalist rhetoric from the invasion scares focused attention on homegrown freedoms and the defeat of tyranny. Moreover, this is the first time that the British state encouraged ordinary men to identify with a participatory and inclusive notion of citizenship. Fundamentally, they addressed their audience as 'citizens'.[28] Ordinary men were encouraged to see themselves as empowered, active agents with a vital role to play in the fate of the nation. Now that men had performed the duties of citizenship, it would be more difficult to deny them its rights in future.

Figure 4.1 Charles Williams, 'The Consequence of Invasion or the Hero's Reward' (1 August 1803). © Trustees of the British Museum.

Historians have emphasised that participation in the armed services during the French Wars served to enhance a sense of nationhood. Men who may otherwise have barely left their parish had opportunities to travel far and wide, and to feel involved in a national enterprise. The militia, for example, marched all over Britain and memoirists record the profound effect of this experience, as they encountered a diverse but unified country. The county militia regiments commonly encamped together at huge sites such as Coxheath in Kent, which had the feel of the nation in microcosm, with its many regional accents and traditions. In total, around one in four British men served in some capacity during the Revolutionary and Napoleonic Wars, a figure comparable to the 'total wars' of the twentieth century.[29] In addition to this, the Defence of the Realm Act of 1803 surveyed British men about their willingness to fight in the event of invasion, and a further half a million replied that they would. For Colley, this is evidence of the success of the British national project: men were so committed to their national community that they were willing to die for it.

The impetus of war also led to further integration of the four nations into a single unit. In the early years of the war, Scotland and Wales saw twice the volunteering rates as those in England.[30] The 1757 Militia Act had applied only to England and Wales, due to doubts about Scotland's loyalty in the wake of the Jacobite Rebellion, but Scotland got its own militia in 1797. The situation in Ireland was more complex. It too formed a militia in 1793, both to defend against invasion and in an attempt to keep order during a very turbulent decade. It was open to Catholics and Nonconformists, but the officers were drawn from Anglican gentry and its loyalty was to the Protestant establishment. Ireland also had a radical tradition of citizen soldering. In the 1770s and 1780s, the Patriots had been pushing for greater independence from Britain and an extension to the franchise, and they received support from the Irish Volunteer movement. They were moderate in their aims, however, and with the onset of revolution in France a more radical reform movement developed among the Catholic community. The Society of United Irishmen campaigned for parliamentary reform and Catholic emancipation, and became a mass underground movement committed to armed uprising against Britain. Kennedy has shown how leaders such as Wolfe Tone projected a masculine vision of citizenship, based both on civic humanist notions of the citizen soldier and on chivalric ideals, gallantly defending their womenfolk and the feminised Irish nation.[31] Tone travelled to France and sought military support for their revolution. A French landing failed and martial law was imposed, but by 1798 Ireland was in full rebellion, which was put down with bloody force. As with Scotland in 1707, the government ultimately came to the conclusion that an independent neighbour posed a military threat and a platform for French invasion, so Ireland was integrated into the British state. The Irish parliament was abolished and the Act of Union came into force on 1 January 1801, forming the United Kingdom of Great Britain and Ireland.

Radicalism revives

By the time of the invasion scare of the summer of 1803, patriotism was firmly on the side of the loyalist establishment and the radical movement was suffering from years of proscription. As the war dragged on, however, opportunities arose for radicals to recapture the patriotic initiative. In particular, political scandals revealing corruption and mismanagement in high places enabled radicals to make a case for reform. In 1809 it emerged that the Duke of York's former mistress had been selling army commissions. A radical MP Gwyllym Wardle brought the case to the attention of the House of Commons and forced the government to institute an investigation. Ultimately the case against the duke failed, but he attracted so much public opprobrium that he had to resign as commander in chief of the army, and the case galvanised the radical movement. Cases like these enabled radicals to make appeals on patriotic grounds, since political corruption was directly undermining the country's war effort. Patriotic citizens should be undaunted in exposing elite wrongdoing, and were encouraged to live up to the masculine values of independence, honesty and public spirit.[32]

Corruption was a key focus of the radical movement in the early nineteenth century. In this period, the term had its familiar political sense of dishonest or venal conduct, but it was also used to suggest decay or structural imbalance. The balanced constitution required a strict separation of powers, and it also required MPs to be independent and conscientious, and the same of the voters who selected them. Over time, however, the growth of places, pensions and bribery had enabled governments to control blocs of parliamentary votes, and members of the Lords interfered in the business of the Commons by manipulating the electoral system. This corrupted a delicate political mechanism so that it no longer functioned in the way that it should. Reform was therefore required to restore the system to its ancient perfection, whereby parliament would reflect the will of the people and would govern for the general good, rather than in the interests of a narrow elite. This class angle sharpened in the early nineteenth century, since the critique of 'Old Corruption' was particularly targeted at the aristocracy. Radical publications like *The Extraordinary Black Book* (1820–23) exhaustively listed the financial interests and political connections of the ruling classes, including the government, the royal family and the church. Cases like the Duke of York affair linked the elite's political conduct to their personal morality, focusing on their extra-marital affairs and their penchant for gambling and gluttony. The antics of the prince regent became ever-more offensive to a country struggling after two decades of war, high taxes and economic dislocation. Reformers contrasted this with their own preference for industry and domesticity, using the developing idiom of the 'middle class' to emphasise their superior virtue.

At the end of the Napoleonic Wars in 1815, British radicalism had a distinctive form. The rapid demobilisation of the armed forces threw thousands of men on the job market, leading to widespread unemployment and poverty. These economic conditions sharpened the impact on a working class that was already struggling with the effects of industrialisation. Some radicals were explicitly concerned with the effect of mechanisation on their livelihoods. The Luddite movement began around Nottingham in 1811, when textile workers protested that the new machinery was leading to unemployment and was rendering their skills redundant. Luddites protested by breaking the hated machinery and their rebellion spread across the region, tying down thousands of troops who would otherwise have been fighting the war against Napoleon. The last major Luddite act was a rising located in the Derbyshire village of Pentrich in 1817, which was infiltrated by a government spy and put down by constables and the military. Historians have debated the extent to which Luddism was sophisticated and organised, or whether they drew on far older traditions of agrarian protest.[33]

Post-war radicals also adopted the tactic of the mass meeting. One of the first of these took place at Spa Fields in November 1816, when 10,000 gathered to hear the radical Henry Hunt speak on the subject of a petition to the prince regent, calling for parliamentary reform and relief for distressed workers. Hunt was an example of the 'gentleman leader', a common radical tactic at the time. As Wilkes and Wyvill had done before, figures like Hunt and Burdett provided well-to-do figureheads for the movement. Their gentility licensed activities like the mass platform that might otherwise have seemed threatening, and their disinterestedness emphasised that they were incorruptible and aloof from party politics.[34] Such leaders addressed monster meetings, which both underlined the strength of the cause and the orderliness and respectability of working people who were trying to emphasise their worthiness for citizenship. Not all such meetings passed off peacefully, however. A second meeting at Spa Fields turned into a riot, as revolutionary Spenceans sought to spread disorder in order to seize the Tower of London and the Bank of England. The following month, the prince regent's coach was mobbed and its window broken, possibly by a bullet.

The government responded by suspending habeas corpus and reinstating the oppressive legislation of the 1790s, targeting political meetings and seditious print. This is the subject of George Cruikshank's print 'Liberty Suspended! with the Bulwark of the Constitution!' (Figure 4.2). The female figure of Liberty is literally suspended, hanging from a gibbet made from a printing press. On the gallows stand representatives of the church, the law and the government, and they are protected by the military and a 'band of gentleman pensioners'. In the background, John Bull weeps at a vigil, while the funeral cortege bears the legend 'For the funeral of British Liberty who died at St Stephens, March 1817', referring to the legislation passed by parliament. For commentators like Cruikshank, the loss of civil rights such as press freedom and freedom of association constituted the very death of liberty.

Radicals, however, persisted with the tactic of the 'mass platform'. The most famous mass meeting of this period ended in tragedy. On 16 August 1819, around 60,000 people gathered in St Peter's Field in Manchester to hear radical speakers including Hunt. Manchester had a population of 200,000 and was an industrial powerhouse, yet had no MP, so the meeting demanded parliamentary reform. The gathering was peaceful and there were women and children among

Figure 4.2 George Cruikshank, 'Liberty Suspended! with the Bulwark of the Constitution!' (March 1817). The Art Institute of Chicago, © Photo SCALA, Florence.

the crowd, but the local magistrates were concerned about the meeting so requested military assistance. In this period, there was no national police force and responsibility for keeping order was localised, voluntarist and ad hoc. Communities were lightly policed by constables, who in theory were volunteers from the community, since citizens were expected to take responsibility for policing. Before the New Police of the 1820s, proposals to professionalise the police foundered on concerns about continental absolutism and militarism. Ironically, this meant that the military were often called in to support the civil power, since the civilian authorities were unable to cope with crowd disorder. The Riot Act of 1714 required crowds to disperse within an hour of the Act being read by a magistrate, or the military were permitted to use lethal force against them, but crowds usually dispersed before violence was used.

At Manchester, the authorities had at their disposal regular infantry and cavalry, and also volunteer cavalry in the form of the Yeomanry. The Yeomanry had been created in 1794 as part of the drive to raise volunteer soldiers during the French Wars. They were therefore promoted by means of the same patriotic constitutional discourse used by the radicals, but the Yeomanry had a different character to other types of volunteer soldier. As mounted soldiers they drew heavily on the aristocracy and the gentry for their officers, and privates were often drawn from their tenants and farmers. They therefore tended to be regarded as interested parties in local disputes, and protesters regarded them with more hostility than regular troops.[35] They were often used against crowd disturbances, since mounted troops were mobile and being on horseback has its advantages for crowd control. The actions of the Manchester and Salford Yeomanry on that day, however, have gone down in infamy. The magistrates read the Riot Act and issued an arrest warrant for the speakers, so the Yeomanry ploughed into the crowd to get to the hustings. Civilians were trampled by the horses and when they got stuck due to the sheer weight of people, the Yeomanry hacked at the crowd with their sabres (instead of using the flat of their swords, which was usual practice for crowd control). Fifteen people died and hundreds were wounded. It became known as the Peterloo Massacre, in ironic reference to the military victory of Waterloo.

Peterloo had a profound effect on British radicalism. The government responded with a further clampdown on civil rights, passing the notorious Six Acts against meetings, military drilling and press freedom. This was effectively the end of the post-war 'mass platform', as key leaders were rounded up and large gatherings became too risky. The government's unwavering support for the authorities and lack of sympathy for the victims, however, further convinced radicals of the rectitude of their cause. They set up their own compensation scheme for the victims and a witness to the massacre, John Edward Taylor, founded *The Manchester Guardian*, which to this day is Britain's foremost centre left newspaper. Numerous prints and commemorative objects were produced, memorialising the victims and demonising the authorities. A medal was struck, bearing a depiction of the massacre on the front and a biblical quotation on the reverse: 'The wicked have drawn out their sword. They have cut down the poor and needy and such as be of upright conversation.' The practice of casting a medal referenced those awarded after a military victory such as Waterloo, of which one of the fatalities was a veteran. This medal was cast in pewter so it would be affordable even to the poor. Many examples feature a hole for string, suggesting that it was worn as a necklace, close to the heart; some appear to be well-worn.[36] Depictions of the event often emphasised the many female victims: although women composed around an eighth of the crowd, they were a third of the casualties, so they appear to have been singled out for especially brutal treatment. Emphasising female victimhood in representations like these had several effects. It underlined that the authorities were acting in an unmanly way, undermining their moral right to rule. It urged male onlookers to action in the cause of the radicals, playing on their chivalric expectations. And it emphasised that the common people were innocent victims of a corrupt and brutal establishment.

Conclusion

Radicalism therefore travelled a long way between Wilkes and Peterloo. Over the course of the half century surveyed in this chapter, its relationship with patriotism changed significantly, but by no means in a linear way. The experience of war and revolution abroad had enabled the establishment to occupy the patriotic ground, but even in their hands, the basic focus on home-grown, historic liberties persisted. Many radicals remained committed to patriotism as a critique, and incidents like the Duke of York affair showed that there were opportunities for patriot radicalism even in wartime. Key aspects of British radicalism, however, remained consistent throughout the period and beyond. Radicals fundamentally believed in representative politics. Their goal was the vote, since a parliament that was genuinely elected by the people would govern in their interests. Their vision of citizenship was therefore electoral above all. They were also committed to a range of other civil rights that we would today identify with citizenship – freedom of speech, of association, of conscience, against imprisonment, and so on – but none of these were secure while parliament remained unreformed. The theme of suffrage will therefore return in later chapters.

Notes

1 H. Cunningham, 'The language of patriotism, 1750–1914', *History Workshop*, 12, 1981, 8–33.
2 L. Colley, *Britons: Forging the Nation 1707–1837*, New Haven: Yale University Press, 1992.
3 K. Wilson, *The Island Race: Englishness, Empire and Gender in the Eighteenth Century*, Oxford: Routledge, 2002.
4 C. Kennedy, *Narratives of the Revolutionary and Napoleonic Wars*, Basingstoke: Palgrave, 2013, p. 85.
5 S. Johnson, *A Dictionary of the English Language*, 4th edn, London, 1777, vol. 2.
6 F. Burdett, *Reform of Parliament. To the Electors of Westminster*, London, 1820, p. 7.
7 *The North Briton*, 26–27 November 1762, emphasis in original.
8 W. Wordsworth, 'The Prelude' book X, lines 692–3, in *The Major Works*, ed. S. Gill, Oxford: Oxford University Press, 2000, p. 550.
9 K. Wilson, 'Inventing revolution: 1688 and eighteenth-century popular politics', *Journal of British Studies*, 28, 1989, 349–86 (p. 385).
10 R. Price, *A Discourse on the Love of Our Country*, London, 1789, p. 34.
11 E. P. Thompson, *The Making of the English Working Class*, London: Gollancz, 1963.
12 J. Cartwright, *A Letter to the Duke of Newcastle*, London, 1792, p. 41.
13 J. Cartwright, *An Appeal, Civil and Military, on the Subject of the English Constitution*, London, 1799, p. 126.
14 Price, *Discourse*, p. 10.
15 T. Paine, *Rights of Man*, 8th edn, London, 1791, p. 11.
16 F. O'Gorman, 'The Paine burnings of 1792–93', *Past and Present*, 193:1, 2006, 111–55.
17 Colley, *Britons*.
18 E. Burke, *Reflections on the Revolution in France*, 1790, ed. L. Mitchell, Oxford: Oxford University Press, 1993, p. 17, emphasis in original.
19 *Job Nott's Address to the Inhabitants of Birmingham*, Birmingham, 1792.
20 *Cheap Repository Shorter Tracts*, London, 1798, p. v.
21 [H. More,] *Village Politics: Addressed to all the Mechanics, Journeymen and Day Labourers in Great Britain. By Will Chip, A County Carpenter*, London, 1792, p. 17.
22 Quoted in D. Bell, *The First Total War: Napoleon's Europe and the Birth of Modern Warfare*, London: Bloomsbury, 2008, p. 148.
23 'Englishmen!' (handbill), 1803, from Frank K. and S. Hustvedt (eds.), *The Warning Drum: The British Home Front Faces Napoleon. Broadsides of 1803*, Berkeley and Los Angeles: University of California Press, 1944, p. 114.
24 J. R. Western, 'The volunteer movement as an anti-revolutionary force, 1793–1801', *English Historical Review*, 71, 1956, 603–14.

25 'To the Inhabitants of the Town and Neighbourhood of Aylesbury' (handbill), Aylesbury, 4 August 1803.
26 L. Carter, 'Scarlet fever: Women's enthusiasm for men in uniform 1780–1815', in K. Linch and M. McCormack (eds.), *Britain's Soldiers: Rethinking War and Society, 1715–1815*, Liverpool: Liverpool University Press, 2014.
27 J. Cookson, *The British Armed Nation*, Oxford: Oxford University Press, 1793–1815, pp. 211–13.
28 'Citizens of England' (handbill), 1803, from *Warning Drum*, p. 146.
29 S. Conway, *The British Isles and the War of American Independence*, Oxford: Oxford University Press, 2002, pp. 195, 28.
30 Colley, *Britons*, p. 293.
31 C. Kennedy, '"A gallant nation": Chivalric masculinity and Irish nationalism in the 1790s', in M. McCormack (ed.), *Public Men: Masculinity and Politics in Modern Britain*, Basingstoke: Palgrave, 2007, pp. 73–92.
32 P. Harling, 'The Duke of York Affair (1809) and the complexities of wartime patriotism', *The Historical Journal*, 39:4, 1996, 963–84 (pp. 982–3).
33 M. Roberts, 'Rural Luddism and the makeshift economy of the Nottinghamshire framework knitters', *Social History* 42:3, 2017, 365–98.
34 J. Belchem and J. Epstein, 'The nineteenth-century gentleman leader revisited', *Social History*, 22:2, 1997, 174–93.
35 G. Steppler, *Britons, To Arms! The Story of the British Volunteer Soldier*, Stroud: Sutton, 1992, p. 28.
36 Pewter medal commemorating the Peterloo Massacre, 1819: National Army Museum NAM. 1987-04-5-1.

Recommended reading

Colley, L., 'Manpower', in *Britons: Forging the Nation 1707–1837*, New Haven: Yale University Press, 1992.

Cunningham, H., 'The language of patriotism, 1750–1914', *History Workshop*, 12, 1981, 8–33.

Conway, S., *The British Isles and the War of American Independence*, Oxford: Oxford University Press, 2002.

Cookson, J. E., *The British Armed Nation 1793–1815*, Oxford: Oxford University Press, 1997.

Dinwiddy, J., *Radicalism and Reform in Britain, 1780–1850*, London: Bloomsbury, 1992.

Gee, A., *The British Volunteer Movement 1794–1814*, Oxford: Oxford University Press, 2003.

Kennedy, C., *Narratives of the Revolutionary and Napoleonic Wars*, Basingstoke: Palgrave, 2013.

Navickas, K., *Loyalism and Radicalism in Lancashire, 1798–1815*, Oxford: Oxford University Press, 2009.

Pedersen, S., 'Hannah More meets Simple Simon: Tracts, chapbooks and popular culture in late eighteenth-century England', *Journal of British Studies*, 25:1, 1985, 84–113.

Thompson, E. P., *The Making of the English Working Class*, London: Gollancz, 1963.

5 Women and political campaigning

This chapter focuses on the role of British women in the public sphere, from the late seventeenth to the mid-nineteenth century. We have encountered many examples of female political action already – and will do so yet more frequently in later chapters when we examine feminism, the women's movement and suffragism – but it is useful to pause our chronological survey and to analyse the broader themes that this raises. The usual story in British women's history in the eighteenth and nineteenth centuries is that the public sphere and the private sphere became more separate: women were increasingly identified with the home and family, whereas men monopolised the political world. Within this narrative, it is difficult to conceive of female political participation, but more recent work on women and gender has questioned the 'separate spheres' narrative. This chapter will survey this revisionist work, which has shown that there were indeed ways for women to participate in the public sphere. We will see that women frequently engaged in types of political campaigning and that – whereas the very presence of women in politics could be regarded as a radical statement – they often did so without challenging the gender norms of the time, nor indeed proffering a 'radical' political message. Reinstating women to the political picture does, however, require us to think differently about the nature of that world and how historians should go about studying it.

Separate spheres?

Women rarely feature in histories of British political life, and this is particularly the case when considering periods before the mid-nineteenth century. Political history in general often has a masculine bias, focusing on male actors without seeking to question why men dominated this sphere. This partly reflects the way that political history has traditionally been done, since it tends to focus on the official structures of politics – the institutions of government and the electoral system – where men predominated. Political histories of Britain in the eighteenth and nineteenth centuries were largely content to describe these institutions' male personnel, without questioning why women were excluded from them.

Political history was therefore a prime example of women's 'invisibility' in history, which the new women's history of the 1970s sought to challenge. It is only more recently, however, that historians of women and gender have systematically studied the role of women in politics. This is partly because of the explanatory scheme that came to dominate British women's history, the emergence of 'separate spheres'. This theory posits that, from the later eighteenth century, Britain underwent a reorganisation of social life along gendered lines. Men came to dominate the 'public' worlds of economics, the law and politics: this male world has latterly been mapped onto Habermas's conception of the 'bourgeois public sphere' that we explored in Chapter 1. Women, on the other hand, were increasingly identified with the domestic sphere, and roles within it such as motherhood and homemaking. This was accompanied by a redefinition of sexual difference, whereby men and women were held to possess natures that were appropriate to their allotted sphere: men were identified with physical strength, rationality and independence, whereas women were seen to be physically and mentally weaker, but instead possessed nurturant and sympathetic qualities. They therefore required protection in the private sphere, because the rough public world would corrupt their delicate virtues. These ideas were particularly identified with the new middle class, who subscribed to the cult of the male breadwinner and citizen, and who placed great emphasis on domestic privacy and the separation of the family unit from the community. The emergence of separate spheres therefore shared its chronology with the emergence of the class society, which dominated Marxist social history. Women's history partly came out of social history and shared its ethos of studying history from below from a radical left perspective, rescuing historically marginal groups from scholarly invisibility.

Perhaps because of these origins in social history, and because political history typified the 'traditional' history that it defined itself against, relatively little early women's history focused on politics. We will see that many of the women who were politically active in the eighteenth and nineteenth centuries came from the social elite, who provided unpromising material for Marxist-feminist historians. Since the 1990s, however, there has been a concerted drive to write a history of women in politics. A key context for this has been the rise of gender history and its critical approach to the methods of women's history. The 'separate spheres' narrative has now been thoroughly critiqued.[1] A key way of doing this was in demonstrating that actual practice did not fit the model, and work on women in politics (as well as male domesticity, which provided a focus for early work on masculinity in British studies[2]) was central to this. As well as empirically demonstrating that the model did not work in practice, the debate also focused critical attention on aspects of the theory – such as language, space and social class – providing a more nuanced understanding of what gender difference is and how it relates to society.[3]

Work on women and politics therefore changed our approach to gender history, but it had equally important implications for political studies. In order to study women's contribution to politics in this period, it is necessary to look beyond the MPs, the Lords, the civil servants and the voters, and instead to think about informal and unofficial roles. These roles are often less visible, so can require a different approach to our source material. To reveal these kinds of interactions it is often necessary to use more personal sources, or not to take 'public' sources at face value. For example, Kathryn Gleadle notes that women may not be listed among the attendees at election dinners, but attended after the food for the speeches.[4] It also involves exploring the hidden worlds of family and personal connection. Studying women and politics requires a more social approach to the political world, which in turn reveals that politics was not a discrete activity, but one that seeped into the minutiae of everyday life. Gender history has therefore helped to foster a broader conception of 'politics', which we need if we are going to understand the history of citizenship, since it requires a holistic understanding of the place of the individual within the political community.

Before we explore the practical ways in which women from all classes engaged in politics, it is worth examining some commentaries from the time, to see how they conceived of female political action. It is striking how even ostensibly conservative commentators were prepared to acknowledge a political role for women, suggesting that they conceived of 'separate spheres' rather more flexibly than some twentieth-century historians. For example, the evangelical Sarah Lewis's *Woman's Mission* (1839) was a bestselling celebration of domestic womanhood.[5] In common with many Victorian commentators, she argued that men and women had fundamentally different natures that befitted different roles. Men were suited to public political contests, whereas women possessed an 'unselfish and unworldly spirit' that was instead suited to familial nurturing and religious devotions. Her conclusions about politics, however, might seem surprising to modern readers:

> It is by no means my intention to assert, that women should be passive and indifferent spectators of the great political questions, which affect the well-being of the community, neither can I repeat the old adage, that 'women have nothing to do with politics'; they have, and ought to have, much to do with politics. But in what way?

Lewis concurred with her contemporaries who felt that it was undesirable for women to participate in 'scenes of popular emotion', since this would 'warp' the qualities that made women special and would be 'fatal to the best interests of society'. Instead, she argued that women should approach politics in a manner that made the most of their distinctive nature and station:

> As moral agents; as representatives of the moral principle; as champions of the right in preference to the expedient; by their endeavours to instil into their relatives of the other sex the uncompromising sense of duty and self-devotion, which ought to be their ruling principles! The immense influence which women possess will be most beneficial, if allowed to flow in its

natural channels, viz., domestic ones, because it is of the utmost importance to the existence of influence, that purity of motive be unquestioned.[6]

Lewis therefore proposed an indirect way into politics, emphasising women's beneficial influence over their menfolk. The emphasis on morality was key: overt participation in public life could bring their moral character into question, which would imperil the key perspective that women were able to offer, and would prevent them from exercising this influence.

Another widely read work from this period that reflected on gender difference is *Sesame and Lilies* (1865) by the critic and social commentator John Ruskin. Many modern critics hold it up as the epitome of the 'normative beliefs of the Victorian middle class'.[7] Ruskin did indeed believe that men and women had 'separate' characters, and that these were complementary:

> The man's power is active, progressive, defensive. He is eminently the doer, the creator, the defender. His intellect is for speculation and invention; his energy for adventure, for war, and for conquest wherever war is just, wherever conquest is necessary. But the woman's power is for rule, not for battle, – and her intellect is not for invention or creation, but for sweet ordering, arrangement and decision. She sees the qualities of things, their claims, and their places.

Whereas his list of male qualities was predictable, his list of female ones was not, and this led to some nuanced reflections on the role of women in politics. 'Generally, we are under an impression that a man's duties are public, and a woman's private. But this is not altogether so.' Ruskin conceived of women as rulers, who were able to discern the bigger picture and make considered decisions in a way that men were not. (It is interesting to speculate which specific women he had in mind when writing this passage: possibly Queen Victoria, or indeed his own mother, a formidable character with whom he had a complex relationship.) Although he saw the home as women's domain, he argued that 'this home is always around her' wherever she may be, and that this allowed her to exercise her beneficent moral leadership in other spheres. He urges his contemporaries to 'expand' the duties of women, so they could 'assist in the ordering, in the comforting, and in the beautiful adornment of the state'.[8]

In Lewis and Ruskin, we can see how even explicit statements of separate spheres and separate natures could nevertheless include opportunities for female political action. We will now explore how this played out in practice, by thinking about the full range of female political activity and how this manifested itself in different social classes. Themes from these two commentators will be apparent – such as the role of female influence, their role in moral causes, and the expansion of the domestic role – and we will see how there were accepted ways that women could participate in politics without challenging contemporary notions of sexual propriety. On the other hand, we will also see how women were able to push at the boundaries of social acceptability, and how experience gained in mainstream activities could later be put to use in establishing an autonomous female politics.

Women of the upper classes

Women born into the British upper classes could expect politics to be a significant part of their lives. Politics in the eighteenth and nineteenth centuries was dominated by aristocratic families, for whom politics was the family vocation. Wives and daughters would be expected to take an interest in the political careers of their menfolk, and often to provide support in practical ways. Women often acted as intermediaries in a high-political community that was held together by ties of marriage and personal connection. Political meetings would often take place in private houses, or at dinners for which women were the hostesses. Daughters would act as assistants to their politician fathers, providing administrative support. (The practice is still widespread and is now a paid role: around a fifth of British MPs employed family members as assistants or secretaries in 2017, when new rules came into force to discontinue the practice.[9]) Female relatives could even contribute to the writing of speeches or political works that bore the authorial signature of a male relative, but which were in reality collaborative efforts.[10]

We saw in Chapter 3 how elections in particular were a family effort. Elections required considerable input from women of this class, who acted as canvassers, organisers, hostesses and even controllers of voting blocs. The most prominent such woman in the eighteenth century was Georgiana the Duchess of Devonshire, who endured fierce criticism for her role in the 1784 Westminster election: not because she was a woman per se, but because she was acting on behalf of a non-relative, and also because of her wider reputation for scandal. In the light of this experience, she withdrew from public politics. Acting from behind the scenes, however, she arguably exercised more real power than she ever did in the public arena. She remained a leading figure in the Whig party. Georgiana contributed to their informal milieu, running a *salon*. This was a mixed social gathering on the French model that was adopted by the Francophile Whig *beau monde*. As hostess, she had an opportunity to facilitate political discussion, make new connections and introduce new talent. She also acted as a political fixer, playing a key role in coordinating a political grouping that was characterised by its close personal and familial connections. The Whig party endured a difficult 1790s, but at the turn of the century Georgiana succeeded in reconciling its factions and maintaining its links with the Prince of Wales, which was vital for a government in waiting. Her role was instrumental in the formation of the coalition government of 1806, which was the only time the Whig party got into power in half a century.[11] Georgiana therefore epitomised the difficulties that women faced when entering the political world, but she also demonstrated how an effective political role could be achieved behind the scenes, or when working *within* contemporary expectations of femininity.

There were ways in which well-to-do women could access the hallowed masculine space of parliament itself. Peeresses attended the opening of parliament in all their finery and elite women viewed debates in the Lords from the gallery. Although in theory women were excluded from the galleries after the 1778 ruling on 'Strangers' attending debates, they continue to be admitted to the Lords' galleries, and they could view the Commons by sitting in the 'ventilator' above the chamber. Sarah Richardson argues that this compromise meant that women 'could listen to debates but were not officially part of the House'.[12] This room was cramped, humid and untidy, but there was much demand for the 25 ticketed seats and a lively female political community developed within it. After the building was destroyed by fire in the 1830s, women were allotted a dedicated gallery in the new Palace of Westminster, but they were separated from the Commons chamber by a metal grille. Parliament was therefore defined as a male space, from which they were physically excluded, and later suffrage campaigners regarded the 'cage' as being symbolic of their plight.[13] Female spectators were, however, able to make their presence felt audibly by voicing their protests during debates.

Finally, there were opportunities for women of the upper and middle classes to vote and stand for public office. Women were, of course, excluded from voting or standing in parliamentary elections, and the Municipal Corporations Act of 1835 also excluded them from voting in local elections and for Poor Law boards. But women were able to vote and stand for parish offices. Gleadle shows how later legislation such as the Public Health Act of 1848 and the Towns Improvement Act of 1854 did not exclude female voters, but that it was haphazard and much debated whether they were allowed to vote in practice. This both provided contemporaries with examples of female voting and 'simultaneously reaffirmed women as secondary, borderline citizens'.[14]

Women of the middle classes

If well-connected women could engage with 'official' politics, there were opportunities for women from other classes to be politically active in other ways. We saw in Chapter 1 how women were involved right across the public sphere, suggesting that it was far from being an exclusively male domain in practice. Women were readers and writers of political texts, and consumed news just as much as their menfolk: the reading of the newspapers was a daily ritual among many families. Women of the middle classes joined lending libraries and debating societies, were canvassed at election time, and were spectators to public electoral and civic rituals.

Probably the most significant opportunity for middle class women to get involved in politics was presented by philanthropy. Lewis argued that women possessed a 'missionary spirit', which combined a natural inclination to morality and religion with an unselfish desire to help those less fortunate.[15] Evangelical and Nonconformist Christianity, which were so significant among the British middle classes from the later eighteenth century, emphasised a practical brand of Christianity that involved doing 'good works' in society. This often involved charity work, but political campaigns that had a moral or religious edge were also legitimate avenues for female activity. So although this could be a conservative vision of womanhood, which upheld notions of sexual difference, it nevertheless provided many opportunities in the public sphere.

These campaigns could take many forms. Some were concerned with social conditions, particularly where women and children were concerned, such as in factories or workhouses. The Quaker Elizabeth Fry was involved in a range of humanitarian campaigns, and the most celebrated of these concerned prison conditions. She visited Newgate Prison in 1813 and was appalled by the conditions endured by the women and children. After providing direct help in the form of food and clothes, she established a prison school and continued to campaign for the rights of female prisoners and transported convicts. She established the British Ladies Society for Promoting the Reformation of Female Prisoners in 1821, which is widely regarded as the first nationwide women's organisation in Britain. Other more mainstream political causes could draw female participation if they had a moral aspect. The Anti-Corn Law League, for example, sought to remove the duties on imported corn, which were designed to protect the landed interest but which kept the price of food high. This cause was beloved of the Liberal party, since it sought to end the privileges enjoyed by Tory landowners and to usher in an economic policy based on free trade. For Liberals, this was a moral issue in itself, but the fact that it affected the ability of working people to afford bread brought it within the ambit of female philanthropy, and many Liberal women got involved in the League.

The most significant female political campaign of the eighteenth and nineteenth centuries was the abolition of slavery. Women were involved in the campaign against the Atlantic slave trade from its beginnings in the 1780s. The first anti-slavery societies were established by Quakers and Evangelical Anglicans, so it was from the outset a religious cause. The Evangelical Hannah More published a poem entitled *Slavery* in 1788, and other prominent women in the movement included the Methodist Elizabeth Heyrick and the Quaker Anne Knight. The first women's abolitionist society was the Birmingham Ladies' Society for the Relief of Negro Slaves, formed in 1825, and by the mid-nineteenth century the majority of anti-slavery societies were run by women. Anti-slavery was seen as a peculiarly female political cause: as one commentator put it, 'pity for suffering and a desire to relieve misery are the natural and allowed feelings of Women'.[16] Anti-slavery campaigning literature tended to emphasise the plight of slave women and children in particular, in an attempt to horrify male opinion, and this cast British women as their natural defenders. Isaac Cruikshank's cartoon 'The Abolition of the Slave Trade' (Figure 5.1) portrays female slaves as victims of male abuse and lust, with the ship's captain as a melodramatic villain: the viewer is invited to identify with the decent common sailors who voice their disgust at his unmanly behaviour.

Female abolitionists used various distinctive campaigning methods. They were prominent in petitioning parliament and the queen, and in writing tracts

Figure 5.1 Isaac Cruikshank, 'The Abolition of the Slave Trade' (1792). Courtesy of the Lewis Walpole Library, Yale University.

and poems. One example of which is *Poem on the African Slave Trade* (1792) by the Irish Quaker Mary Birkett. Birkett addressed her poem 'to Her Own Sex', urging her countrywomen to follow the example of their English sisters. The poem is in a sentimental idiom, and emphasises how the cause is suited to a woman's natural sense of charity and sympathy:

> To you the Muse would raise her daring song,
> For Mercy's softest beams to you belong;
> To you the sympathetic sigh is known,
> And Charity's sweet lustre – all your own;
> To you gall'd Mis'ry seldom pleads in vain,
> Oh, let us rise and burst the Negro's chain!
> Yes, sisters, yes, to us the task belongs,
> 'Tis we increase or mitigate their wrongs.
> If we the produce of their toils refuse,
> If we no more the blood-stain'd lux'ry choose...

As Birkett relates, a key way that women could exercise power was by boycotting consumer goods. Women controlled household budgets and made consumer decisions, so women organised boycotts of slave-produced items such as cotton and sugar. (There is an analogy today in the Fairtrade movement, where consumers are encouraged to make ethical choices in order to provide a better deal for producers in developing countries.) Birkett also urged women to use their influence on their husbands, brothers and friends: 'Will these reject your small, your just request, / When urg'd with meekness, yet with warmth exprest?'[17]

Women's support for anti-slavery was instrumental in the abolition of slavery in the British empire in 1833. As women tended to take the moral side in the argument, they were key to the achievement of full abolition, rather than the compromises proposed by some pragmatic male politicians. There were also comparable campaigns that concerned the welfare of women in the empire. For example, in the 1810s and 1820s there was a campaign to abolish the practice of Sati, a Hindu ritual whereby the widow was burned alive on her deceased husband's funeral pyre. This was seen as a women's cause, both because it concerned women's welfare but also as it had a religious edge.[18] This was a missionary campaign in which many Evangelical women took a leading role, since it concerned ending 'heathen' practices and Christianising the empire. Our evaluation of this movement therefore needs to balance its concern for women's rights with its role in providing a moral justification for British rule in India. Slave abolition, too, combined obviously laudable objects with a self-congratulatory notion of Britain as a moral leader on the world stage, whereas its empire had played a key role in creating the Atlantic trade in the first place.

However we evaluate these moral campaigns themselves, participation in them was a crucial experience for British women. They gained vital experience of political tactics, of political methods such as petitioning, letter writing and lobbying, and of political organisation, including large societies that could even be nationwide in scope. We will see in Chapter 7 how the anti-slavery campaigns in particular gave women a vocabulary and a range of concepts that helped them to argue against their own subordination. Historians of women in politics therefore argue that these campaigns 'heightened the consciousness of women', and that this would be brought to bear in the feminist and suffragist campaigns that followed.[19]

Women of the working classes

Women of the working classes also had opportunities for political expression. The electoral street theatre was socially inclusive, and we saw in Chapter 3 how women from this class needed to be knowledgeable about political affairs since they engaged with canvassing parties, and could well be financially implicated as landladies of pubs or lodging houses. The minutes of the poll at Northampton's 1768 election show how women acted as witnesses when voters came to the poll to claim their vote. A recurring figure in this source is the formidable Mrs Cross, who contributed evidence for and against on nine occasions, establishing whether claims to a vote on the basis of residency were legitimate. Given how these voters then cast their vote, it is clear that she was working for one of the candidates and presumably was rewarded handsomely for her services. Zoe Dyndor has demonstrated the extent of plebeian women's involvement in elections as householders and witnesses.[20] The latter role ceased with the introduction of prior electoral registration in 1832: another example of how the Great Reform Act was exclusionary for women.

A key form of political expression for working women was crowd protest. Robert Shoemaker argues that women tended to riot in response to a narrower range of grievances than men, 'where they were seen to have had a particular authority'.[21] As moral guardians of the community, women could protest where those moral standards had been offended, such as the tradition of 'rough music' whereby women would noisily shame a wife-beater or a cuckold.[22] As managers of household budgets and provisioning, women were prominent in protests concerning the price of foodstuffs (the 'just price' of which was conceived of in moral terms) or the loss of traditional rights to common lands or gleaning. Women protested about the prospect of their menfolk being balloted for the militia, such as in Scotland in 1797.[23] Women tended not to be involved in employment disputes as worker's organisations were men-only, but there were exceptions. Women participated in machine-breaking in the late eighteenth and early nineteenth centuries, and they took a supporting role in the Luddite and Captain Swing disturbances. In general, women were less likely to be involved in violent crowd protests than men, instead using defamatory or seditious language as individuals. Although all such actions are 'political', women were rarely involved in political riots in its narrow, parliamentary definition: the highest recorded participation of the eighteenth century was during the Gordon Riots of 1780, where 20 out of the 110 prosecuted rioters were women.[24]

Finally, women were involved in radical politics. Working-class radicalism in the 1790s tended to have a strongly masculine emphasis. Thomas Paine's egalitarian theories of rights could have led to an interest in sexual equality, but although feminists such as Mary Wollstonecraft used his ideas in this way, most plebeian radicals were committed to the rights of men. Radicals claimed rights for males on the basis of their independence and their position as the heads of households, and their campaign for the vote consistently focused on manhood suffrage. The post-war radical movement did, however, have wider female involvement. The impetus swung to the industrial north, where women were often in employment and enjoyed a higher status. In northwest England, women attended reform meetings and set up their own reform societies. The Female Reform Society of Blackburn achieved notoriety after its activities were widely reported. Alice Kitchen presented a cap of liberty to a reform meeting and delivered a short speech, expressing support for 'those brave men who are nobly struggling for liberty and life'. Their written address expressed support for the men's campaign for the vote, since a reformed parliament was necessary to end the tyrannical system whereby the people's taxes supported the rich, while their 'innocent wretched children' starved. They therefore positioned themselves in a feminine auxiliary role and expressed themselves in sentimental, familial terms. But the conservative paper *The Courier* expressed its horror that these '*degraded females*' should have 'abandoned ... the *domestic character of women*':

We consider, therefore, the fact of these women, thus *deserting their station*, as a painful evidence that their male kindred, in the pursuit of their guilty objects, have disunited themselves from all those social ties and endearments which are the best pledges of their *fidelity to their God, their country and their King.*[25]

The cartoonist George Cruikshank produced a satirical print about the meeting, 'The Belle Alliance, or the Female Reformers of Blackburn!!!' (Figure 5.2). He portrays the plebeian radicals in grotesque and dishevelled terms, making visual references to the horrors of the French Revolution. The female reformers are depicted in a decidedly unfeminine way, their skirts tucked into their underclothes as they suggestively place the cap of liberty on a phallically erect staff. Cruikshank here aims to undermine the radicals' claim that men deserved the vote on the basis of their manly independence and domestic respectability. Women continued to be a presence during mass radical meetings, however: a third of the wounded protesters at Peterloo in 1819 were women.

The Queen Caroline affair

The next key event in the history of British radicalism was its support for Caroline of Brunswick, the wife of the prince regent. The 'Queen Caroline affair', as it has come to be known, provides a useful case study with which to conclude this chapter. It is a key example of how a mainstream political issue drew wide

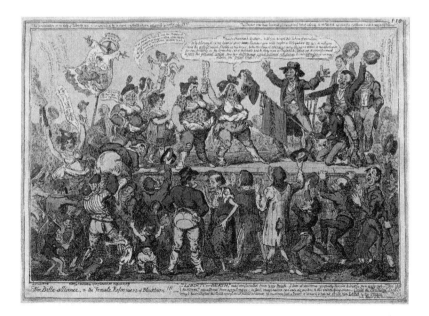

Figure 5.2 George Cruikshank, 'The Belle Alliance or the Female Reformers of Blackburn!!!' (1819). The Art Institute of Chicago, © Photo SCALA, Florence.

female interest and participation from all classes. It also focused on issues that explicitly related to women's position in society, and shows how questions of gender and sexuality were fundamentally about political power.

The Queen Caroline affair concerned the marital status of George, the Prince of Wales and heir to the throne. George had secretly married Maria Fitzherbert in 1785, but the marriage was not legal as she was Catholic and therefore excluded from the succession, and nor did he have his father's permission. In return for increasing his allowance, he agreed to marry Caroline, a princess from Brunswick, in 1795. They had never met before and disliked one another, so quickly lived apart. Caroline was ostracised from the court and kept away from their daughter, Charlotte. She was accused of having affairs, something that George was by no means innocent of himself. Unhappy with her treatment, in 1814 she got a deal from the government whereby she would live abroad in return for an allowance. George, meanwhile, became prince regent in 1811, exercising the powers of king while George III was incapacitated with mental illness. The prince regent was not a popular ruler like his father, however. He spent lavishly and ran up huge debts, so was commonly a focus for radical critics of the civil list and its 'tax eaters'. His opulent lifestyle became increasingly offensive as Britain endured two decades of war, high taxation and unemployment: cartoonists like James Gillray famously played on his obesity to emphasise his greed.

Caroline's status became a political issue in 1820 when George III died. The prince regent became George IV, but he had no intention of Caroline becoming his queen. The government attempted to buy her off, but Caroline refused and returned to Britain to press her claim. On her arrival, riots broke out in support of Caroline and against the unpopular king. George was still determined to divorce her, so instructed the government to pursue this. A Bill of Pains and Penalties was brought in, with a view to divorcing her and stripping her of the title of queen. This involved revealing lurid details of her private life and alleged affairs, information that had been extensively gathered by the government, with a view to providing grounds for divorce. The Tory government, however, was weak and unpopular and Caroline's cause was taken up by the Whig opposition and the radicals. There was no doubt some pragmatism in this, given her popularity and the opportunity to embarrass the government. But radical commentators made explicit links between the treatment of Caroline and the wider political system. They alleged that parliament was acting contrary to the will of the people, which demonstrated how unrepresentative it was, and how amenable it was to corruption by the Crown. A representative parliament would never act in this dishonourable way and persecute an innocent woman: it therefore demonstrated the urgency of parliamentary reform.

Caroline enjoyed wide support in British society. Her cause was widely seen as a women's cause, as women were encouraged to identify with her plight:

> Attend ye virtuous British wives
> Support your injured Queen,
> Assert her rights; they are your own,
> As plainly may be seen.[26]

Women and political campaigning 99

Women of the working and middle classes took up the cause, and thousands of women throughout the country signed addresses in support of the queen.[27] Women also participated in processions, attended meetings and followed the details of the trail in the press. Although the status of a queen might seem distant from ordinary women's everyday concerns, her case nevertheless highlighted women's unequal status to men with respect to issues such as marriage, divorce and child custody. This was therefore a legitimate political cause for women, since it had a moral basis and concerned women's issues: in supporting Caroline as a wife and mother, the campaign arguably took a conservative view of gender relations rather than offering a critique of them. The phenomenon of female support for Caroline was depicted in one of the many satirical prints produced about the affair, 'The Blanket Hornpipe' (Figure 5.3). George is being tossed in a blanket by five women, a traditional community punishment for wife-beaters. 'Blanket hornpipe' was also a euphemism for sex, giving a flavour of the bawdy nature of many of the cartoons. The women are gaudily and revealingly dressed, suggesting that they are prostitutes: this signals their lowly social status, but perhaps also what the artist thinks about the campaign's propriety. The two sentries egg them on ('Well done lasses – go to it') while a sign proclaims that the palace in the background is protected by 'steel traps and spring guns': this was therefore a campaign of the people against a remote and hostile establishment.

As well as being important for British women, the campaign also tells us a lot about the role of masculinity in Georgian politics. Criticisms of George focused

Figure 5.3 'The Blanket Hornpipe, by Signor Non Ricordo' (1820). Heritage Image Partnership Ltd/Alamy Stock Photo.

on his failings as a man, and his ministerial supporters were characterised as being immoral, corrupt and unchivalrous in their oppression of a helpless woman. The king's supporters, by contrast, argued that 'the true British man should be characterised by his private virtue, his respect for women, his obedience to God, and his active patriotic citizenship'.[28] Socially speaking, this was potentially an inclusive identity: emphasising virtuous masculinity as a basis for citizenship – as opposed to station or wealth – therefore suited radical arguments in favour of rights for men. Despite encouraging female political participation, therefore, the Queen Caroline affair arguably reinforced radical arguments about citizenship that were exclusive to women. The campaign offered radical men an opportunity to reassert their standing as men, following as it did the crushing experience of Peterloo, where men and women alike were portrayed as passive victims of an oppressive state.

Such was the scale of the public campaign that the government abandoned its Bill of Pains and Penalties, but with the end of the trial the campaign fizzled out. Caroline was excluded from the coronation the following year, despite turning up and trying to force her way in. She died shortly afterwards, amid rumours that she was being poisoned. The Queen Caroline affair was therefore a typical Georgian scandal, which intensely focused attention on the issues of the day for a short period before disappearing without trace. It was also the last of its kind, since the bawdy, saturnalian tone of its cartoons, processions and print commentaries would be inimical to the Victorians. Perhaps because of this tone, it was long dismissed by historians as an 'affair', whose melodrama and sexual scandal were a distraction from proper politics.[29] Gender historians, however, have demonstrated that it is precisely these elements that require us to take it seriously as a political event. Anna Clark argues that melodrama was an ideal medium for working-class radicals, since its plots were accessible and concerned sex and power.[30] The villain of melodrama was an aristocratic libertine, who was trying to oppress the helpless heroine: it was straightforward to cast George and Caroline in those respective roles. The hero was a virtuous plebeian man who defended the heroine against the villain: by casting themselves in this emotive role, radicals personalised the fight of working people against 'Old Corruption'. In helping contemporaries to conceive of their place within the national drama, these gendered political idioms therefore contributed to a sense of citizenship.

Conclusion

After surveying the full range of female political activity up to the mid-nineteenth century, how then should we evaluate the 'separate spheres' interpretation? It should be clear that politics does not correspond to the 'male' and 'public' side of a two-way divide. Politics has its public and private aspects, and the line between them is blurred. We have seen how women were able to engage in a wide range of activities in the public world, partly by expanding the notion of what the private sphere consisted of. If mainstream political studies tends to miss a lot of this activity, it is because it is too male-centric and too committed to a narrow definition of 'politics'. If we look beyond the official structures of politics and take on board its more informal and personal manifestations, then a wide range of additional activities and participants come to light. Citizenship is therefore a useful concept as it captures the full range of ways that an individual engages with the political world. Kathleen Canning and Sonya Rose argue that it is important to 'link collective or public prescriptions and invocations of citizenship, to the interior individualised meanings of citizenship', rather than to establish a firm boundary between public and private.[31]

This chapter has explored how women of all classes engaged in mainstream politics. To a certain extent, class was the factor that determined the nature of their participation, but there were nevertheless important commonalities between the classes. We have seen how women were able to carve out a political role as matriarchs, as hostesses, as consumers and as moral leaders. Rather than being restricted to the private sphere as such, women's action was informed by expectations of feminine behaviour that were considered appropriate to their class. As we have seen, many women worked within these 'private' roles and exercised very real political power in the 'public' world as a result. In later chapters we will explore the women's movement and the suffrage campaigns, but it is important to recognise that the political history of British women predated these. Indeed, the experiences gained in mainstream political activities in the preceding century were to provide vital foundations for the campaigns for full female citizenship.

Notes

1 For example: A. Vickery, 'Golden age to separate spheres? A review of the categories and chronology of English women's history', *The Historical Journal*, 36:2, 1993, 383–414.
2 Notably the work of John Tosh: *A Man's Place: Masculinity and the Middle-Class Home in Victorian Britain*, New Haven: Yale University Press, 1999; *Manliness and Masculinities in Nineteenth-Century Britain*, Harlow: Longman, 2005.
3 For a survey of this debate, see M. McCormack, 'Men, "the public" and political history' in his *Public Men: Masculinity and Politics in Modern Britain*, Basingstoke: Palgrave, 2007, pp. 13–32.
4 K. Gleadle, *Borderline Citizens: Women, Gender and Political Culture in Britain, 1815–1867*, Oxford: Oxford University Press, 2009, p. 63.
5 C. Midgley, *Feminism and Empire: Women Activists in Imperial Britain, 1790–1865*, London: Routledge, 2007, p. 109.
6 S. Lewis, *Woman's Mission*, London, 1839, pp. 50–1.
7 K. Millett, *Sexual Politics*, New York: Columbia University Press, 2016, p. 89.
8 J. Ruskin, *Sesame and Lilies: Two Lectures Delivered in Manchester in 1864*, New York, 1865, pp. 90, 109.
9 R. Sayal, 'MPs to be banned from using public money to hire relatives', *The Guardian*, 15 March 2017.
10 Gleadle, *Borderline Citizens*, pp. 225, 233.
11 A. Foreman, *Georgiana: Duchess of Devonshire*, London: HarperCollins, 1998, p. 402
12 S. Richardson, *The Political Worlds of Women: Gender and Politics in Nineteenth-Century Britain*, Oxford: Routledge, 2015, p. 130.
13 C. Eustance, 'Protests from behind the grille: Gender and the transformation of parliament, 1867–1918', *Parliamentary History*, 16:1, 2008, 107–26.

14 Gleadle, *Borderline Citizens*, p. 41.
15 Lewis, *Woman's Mission*, p. 128.
16 *The Missionary Register*, London, 1830, p. 344.
17 M. Birkett, *A Poem on the African Slave Trade: Addressed to Her Own Sex*, Dublin, 1792, part I, p. 13; part II, pp. 21–2.
18 C. Midgley, 'From supporting missions to petitioning parliament: British women and the evangelical campaign against *Sati* in India, 1813–30', in K. Gleadle and S. Richardson (eds.), *Women in British Politics, 1760–1860: The Power of the Petticoat*, Basingstoke: Palgrave, 2000, pp. 75–92.
19 L. Billington and R. Billington, '"A burning zeal for righteousness": Women in the British anti-slavery movement, 1820–1860', in J. Rendall (ed.), *Equal or Different? Women's Politics, 1800–1914*, Oxford: Blackwell, 1987, pp. 82–111 (p. 82).
20 Z. Dyndor, 'Widows, wives and witnesses: Women and their involvement in the 1768 Northampton borough parliamentary election', *Parliamentary History*, 30:3, 2011, 309–23.
21 R. Shoemaker, *Gender in English Society 1650–1850: The Emergence of Separate Spheres?*, Harlow: Longman, 1998, p. 237.
22 E. P. Thompson, *Customs in Common*, London: Penguin, 1993, chapter 8.
23 A. Clark, *The Struggle for the Breeches: Gender and the Making of the British Working Class*, University of California Press: Berkeley and Los Angeles, 1995, p. 151.
24 Shoemaker, *Gender in English Society*, p. 233.
25 Quoted in *Cobbett's Weekly Political Register*, 23 October 1819, pp. 258, 264, emphasis in original.
26 Quoted in L. Davidoff and C. Hall, *Family Fortunes: Men and Women of the English Middle Class 1780–1850*, London: Hutchinson, 1987, p. 152.
27 L. Colley, *Britons: Forging the Nation 1707–1837*, New Haven: Yale University Press, 1992, p. 265.
28 L. Carter, 'British masculinities on trial in the Queen Caroline affair of 1820', *Gender & History*, 20:2, 2008, 248–69 (pp. 260–1).
29 T. Laqueur, 'The Queen Caroline affair: Politics as art in the reign of George IV', *Journal of Modern History*, 54, 1982, 417–66.
30 A. Clark, *Scandal: The Sexual Politics of the British Constitution*, Princeton: Princeton University Press, 2004, p. 219.
31 K. Canning and S. Rose, 'Gender, citizenship and subjectivity: Some historical and theoretical considerations', *Gender & History*, 13:3, 2001, 427–43 (p. 436).

Recommended reading

Billington, L. and Billington, R., '"A burning zeal for righteousness": Women in the British anti-slavery Movement, 1820–1860', in J. Rendall (ed.), *Equal or Different? Women's Politics, 1800–1914*, Oxford: Blackwell, 1987, pp. 82–111.
Carter, L., 'British masculinities on trial in the Queen Caroline affair of 1820', *Gender & History*, 20:2, 2008, 248–69.
Chalus, E., *Elite Women in English Political Life, c. 1754–1790*, Oxford: Oxford University Press, 2005.
Clark, A., *Scandal: The Sexual Politics of the British Constitution*, Princeton: Princeton University Press, 2004.
Gleadle, K., *Borderline Citizens: Women, Gender and Political Culture in Britain, 1815–1867*, Oxford: Oxford University Press, 2009.
Gleadle, K. and Richardson, S. (eds.), *Women in British Politics, 1760–1860: The Power of the Petticoat*, Basingstoke: Palgrave, 2000.

Klein, L., 'Gender and the public/private distinction in the eighteenth century: Some questions about evidence and analytical procedure', *Eighteenth-Century Studies*, 29:1, 1995, 97–105.

Midgley, C., *Women Against Slavery: The British Campaigns, 1780–1870*, Oxford: Routledge, 1995.

Shoemaker, R., *Gender in English Society, 1650–1850: The Emergence of Separate Spheres?*, Harlow: Longman, 1998.

Vickery, A., 'Golden age to separate spheres? A review of the categories and chronology of English women's history', *The Historical Journal*, 36:2, 1993, 383–414.

6 Reform, domesticity and citizenship, 1820–48

This chapter resumes our chronological survey, and focuses on a pivotal event in British political history, the First Reform Act of 1832. The 'Great' Reform Act was the first wholesale change to the electoral system in England and Wales, and there were parallel Acts for Scotland and Ireland that had an even greater impact. It was one of the most contentious issues of the century, which involved a huge campaign that its opponents feared would bring Britain to the brink of revolution. Where you stand on 1832 therefore defines what sort of historian you are. The Act always had a huge status in Whig history, not least because it was the Whigs who passed it. Whig history portrays the Act as a triumph for peaceful, gradualist democratisation, which averted revolution and ushered in Victorian prosperity and consensus. Tory historians are sceptical about this narrative, but agree that it was dramatic: J. C. D. Clark portrays it as a capitulation by the ruling classes and the end of the *ancien régime*.[1] Other revisionists have downplayed the extent to which it was a great watershed, suggesting that it was characterised more by continuity and a desire to preserve the best aspects of the old system.[2]

More recently, a fourth interpretation has been proposed, which has been informed by cultural history and gender history. In the opinion of the 'new political history', the First Reform Act was indeed dramatic, but not in a positive way. Rather, it was a concerted attempt to narrow opportunities for popular political expression and participation.[3] A key aspect of this was the drive to define the citizen for the first time in legislative terms, and to do so in an exclusive way. The reform debates of 1830–32 returned again and again to the question of what sorts of people were fit to exercise the franchise, defining this in terms of class and gender. As we will see in this chapter, the idea of the middle-class householder was central to the Reform Act, and would be an enduring political principle for decades to come. We therefore need to think about domestic masculinity and how this relates to political citizenship, linking histories of the private sphere to those of the public. The chapter concludes by focusing on the Chartist movement, which continued the campaign for the vote after the working classes were let down by the Reform Act. They too, however, demanded the vote for men only in terms of their manly independence and domestic respectability. The histories of political reform and radicalism, therefore, look a lot less like stories of progress when gender is taken into consideration.

Whig reform

The Reform Act of 1832 was passed by a coalition led by the Whig party. It is therefore worth focusing on the political ideas of the Whigs, to get a sense of what they were trying to achieve. We saw in Chapter 1 how the Whig party originated in the late seventeenth-century struggles around religion and the succession: the 'Whigs' were those who sought to exclude James II, due to his Catholicism and abuse of royal prerogative, and who engineered the revolution of 1688. They therefore stood up for the rights of 'the people' against executive power, but they were no democrats and their critique was an elitist one. They were themselves very aristocratic – much more so than the Tories – and they saw their role as custodians of the people's rights. When they dominated government in the first half of the eighteenth century, therefore, they were avowedly governing on the people's behalf and working with monarchs who accepted the limitations on their power.

The arrival of George III changed the situation, as he sought a more active role in government and favoured the Tories. The Whigs therefore took a more popular course, both to attack their rivals and because they needed alternative sources of support. They got their fingers burnt with Wilkes, but subsequent Whigs took a populist and reformist stance themselves. Their leader Charles James Fox styled himself as a 'man of the people' and championed popular rights and parliamentary reform. The Whigs had always styled themselves as defenders of popular liberties, but after they were excluded from power from 1784 they also had a motive to reform a system that was not working for them. We therefore have the paradox that the most aristocratic political party in the eighteenth and early nineteenth centuries was also the most liberal.

The Whigs took this pro-reform attitude into the era of the French Revolution. They sought to steer a middle course between the conservatives and the radicals, proposing a modest change to the system in order to head off the revolutionaries and to restore confidence in the system. As before, they took a paternalistic attitude towards plebeian radicals, presenting themselves as leaders and patrons. Their pro-reform organisation was dubbed 'The Friends of the People' and had a steep membership fee that restricted its membership to aristocrats and substantial gentlemen. Charles Grey proposed various motions for parliamentary reform in this period, the motion of 1797 in particular prompting a substantial debate in the Commons. It was voted down and the Whigs found themselves out in the political cold for much of the next three decades. In a sense, it was always doomed to failure: in the polarised politics of the 1790s it was difficult to generate support for moderate reform, and 1797 also witnessed one of the most serious invasion scares of the war. It is worth taking this debate seriously, however, as the Whigs used much the same arguments as they would in 1830–32, so it gives us an insight into what they were trying to achieve.

The Whigs were clear that they did not propose universal suffrage. They argued this would give the vote to people who would be susceptible to influence, which would only give more power to those who sought to influence them.

Instead, Fox argued that 'the best plan of representation is that which shall bring into activity the greatest number of independent voters'. This independence was partly measured in terms of property, although they were vague about exactly at what point the qualification should be set. Instead, the required 'independence' was primarily measured in terms of gender: the voter should be a male householder. Grey noted that, 'a man, arrived at the respectable situation of being a father, and consequently master of a family ... was not unworthy of a share in the legislation of the country'. By supporting a household he had demonstrated his responsibility, and by having people who depended upon him he had demonstrated his public spirit and capacity for governance. Furthermore, his dependants were a guarantee of his reliability. Thomas Erskine evoked a sentimental vision of the bourgeois family:

> Will you say that the masters of families, householders, every one of whom has some relation, some tie, some members of a little circle round his fireside, to whom he is attached, have no stake in the public fate, and are unworthy to enjoy political rights?[4]

He assumed that the paternal affection of the father and husband was a guarantee that he would act in the best interests of those who he virtually represented. The imagined male citizen of Whig reform was therefore defined in terms of his domestic station and attachments.

The 1832 Reform Act

Given that the campaign for parliamentary reform had existed for over 60 years, it would be tempting to portray the 1832 Reform Act as a product of long-term pressure. In reality, however, it was the result of a brief and intense political crisis. After the colourful conflicts of 1820, the rest of the decade was fairly quiet politically. Lord Liverpool was at the helm of a secure Tory administration. The Whigs were the official opposition but were disorganised and reform was off the agenda. Reform was precipitated by the end of this stable Tory leadership. In 1827, Lord Liverpool resigned and the government went through two unstable ministries, before settling on the Duke of Wellington as prime minister. Wellington had a huge reputation as a military hero and was certainly a clear leader, but he was also inflexible and undiplomatic, and a fierce opponent of any reform in church or state. These attributes meant that he was not best-placed to deal with the constitutional conflicts that occurred on his watch.

These conflicts began with the issue of religion. Up to this point, Catholics and Protestant Nonconformists had been second-class citizens and, partly for this reason, Nonconformists in particular were often drawn to radicalism and reform. The Corporation Act of 1661 barred anyone who did not take the Anglican Communion from taking up office in government or a corporation, and the Test Acts of 1692 additionally required candidates for office to acknowledge the monarch as the head of the Church of England and to reject the Catholic belief of transubstantiation. These Acts had long been unpopular and in 1828 the Lords and the king finally bowed to public pressure and allowed them to be repealed. The question of Catholic disabilities was, however, more thorny since it concerned the status of Ireland within the Union. Disaffection was growing in Ireland. The radical Daniel O'Connell set up the Catholic Association and won an election in County Clare in 1828. This tested the government's resolve since, as a Catholic, he was unable to take up his seat in Westminster. Wellington and Robert Peel could either uphold his exclusion and inflame Ireland, or risk the ire of their own party by addressing the political status of Catholics.

With great reluctance, they took the latter course, and this had several important effects. First, it dispelled the myth that the constitution could not be reformed. By passing the Roman Catholic Relief Act of 1829, the government was making sweeping changes to civil rights and altering the status of the Anglican Church within the constitution. Second, it also started the process of reforming the electoral system. The government were concerned about the prospect of large, working-class Irish electorates, so raised the property qualification in an attempt to restrict the franchise to the middle class. Once the process of parliamentary reform had begun it would be impossible to stop: indeed, the approach to the Irish electorate would be replicated for the rest of the UK in 1832. Third, Catholic emancipation caused the Tory party to self-implode, giving an opportunity to the Whigs. Defence of the state church was a key tenet of Toryism, so Wellington and Peel lost the confidence of their party for 'ratting' in this way. Some 'Ultra' elements in the party even converted to parliamentary reform, since they were convinced that a party that represented the will of the people would never have emancipated the Catholics.

George IV had always opposed reform, so his death in 1830 removed a key obstacle in its way and also necessitated a general election. This election revealed much support in the country for reform, and the Tories endured defeats in key constituencies. Wellington struggled on, but when he declared that 'the system of representation possessed the full and entire confidence of the country', few believed him.[5] Peel's supporters in the Commons ebbed away until William IV was forced to call upon the Whigs. Charles Grey agreed to form a government on the condition that they could bring in a Reform Bill. The Whigs had a clear vision of what the electorate should look like. A committee of four leading Whigs was tasked with working out the details, and their report argued that they should create 'a constituent body including all the intelligence and respectability of the independent classes of society'. In order to do this, they should exclude from the vote 'those whose want of education and state of dependence render them quite unfitted for its exercise'. The question of who should receive the vote therefore entailed talking about society, working out which social groups possessed the requisite personal attributes, and which did not. Dror Wahrman argues that the debates on reform led to the creation of a 'middle-class idiom', which lauded the responsibility and respectability of the social middle. Rather than reflecting the existence of a 'class' society, it was the political debate on reform that created the notion of three social tiers in public discourse, since the dividing line between citizens and non-citizens was drawn between the middle and the working class.[6] Indeed, the committee's notion of 'the independent classes' was not really a sociological understanding of class at all, rather it was a political one: those who were of sufficient virtue and station to make political decisions for themselves.

The image of the male, independent, middle-class, householder citizen pervaded the debates of 1830–32. This often entailed using explicitly domestic language. Earl Grey declared that the Act gave the vote to 'married men and the fathers of families', since their familial and domestic situations underwrote their respectability, responsibility and capacity for government. He asked if anyone 'would venture to say we cannot intrust men such as these with the Constitutional Privilege of choosing their own Representative in Parliament?'[7] He meant 'men' quite deliberately, since the Act legislatively excluded women from voting for the first time. Kathryn Gleadle downplays the importance of this, since women could not vote in practice anyway; the same parliament allowed female participation in the Vestries Act; and the Scottish Reform Act contained no such proscription.[8] Historians who argue that the Reform Act played a key role in defining the Victorian citizen, however, make much more of it. In formally excluding women from parliamentary politics, it established a principle that would not be overturned until 1918.[9]

The Act was the outcome of two years of debate inside and outside of parliament. There were three general elections in quick succession, and a huge popular campaign got behind the Bill. It would therefore have been a politicising experience, even if the Bill had not passed. Riots broke out throughout the country and the militia was embodied for the first time since the Napoleonic Wars to deal with the disturbances. Requiring military service from the disenfranchised, however, only drew attention to the reciprocal nature of citizenship: why should men who did not enjoy the rewards of citizenship perform its duties? The National Union of the Working Classes declared 'No Vote, No Musket', and some radicals noted that the lists of men liable for militia service provided an electoral roll.[10] Similarly, some campaigners advocated non-payment of taxes, both to put pressure on Wellington and to highlight a key duty of citizenship. Women too participated in the reform campaign, although Catherine Hall judges that they were 'spectators and supporters, rather than being active in their own right and on their own behalf'.[11]

The case against reform was equally powerful. The spectre of the French Revolution was never far away, and events in France in 1830 as well as the threat of violence at home contributed to a sense that Britain was on the verge of revolution. Conservatives feared that reform was a dangerous experiment that could bring the whole social and political order crashing down: there was much more at stake than merely the shape of the electoral system. Miles Taylor has pointed out that there was also an international dimension to the debate, since imperial interests and territories argued that they relied on the threatened pocket boroughs to get their men into parliament. Switching to a system that directly represented parts of the UK, rather than virtually representing the whole empire, would therefore disenfranchise them.[12] Although the coalition of Whigs, radicals, Catholics and former Tories had a majority in the Commons, the Lords was more conservatively inclined and repeatedly rejected the Bill. In the end, the government prevailed on the king to create large numbers of new lords, so the Whigs could command a majority there. This was a less drastic course of action than overruling the will of that house, but it permanently altered the balance of power between Lords and Commons. Whereas the former was diluted, the status of the latter was enhanced, and it was clear that the elected house would take precedence thereafter.

The Act had two main provisions: a change to the franchise and a redistribution of constituencies. The 40 shilling freeholder franchise in the counties remained in England and Wales, but there was a big change to the borough franchise. All the old local franchises were swept away and they were replaced by a uniform, national franchise for the first time. Voters now had to meet a substantial property qualification, so their house had to be worth £10 per year to qualify. The Scottish and Irish Reform Acts stipulated similar borough qualifications. Voters who had qualified under the old rules could retain the vote in their lifetime, but the rhetoric around the Act emphasised that this measure was intended to give the vote to the middle class. Voters also had to register in advance, therefore ending the lengthy process of applying for a vote at the poll itself, and other practical innovations ensured that elections could be conducted much more quickly – if not, as we will see, more inclusively.

The redistribution of constituencies was equally bold. The Act for England and Wales swept away 144 seats, removing the 'rotten' and 'pocket' boroughs, and reducing the representation of small towns from two members to one. Sixty-five of these seats were given to new constituencies or were used to bolster the county representation. More seats were then given to Scotland and Ireland, whose total number of MPs increased from 45 to 53 and from 100 to 105 respectively. The three 1832 Reform Acts therefore removed the most glaring abuses from the system, gave the vote to industrial centres like Manchester and Leeds for the first time, and went some way to addressing the imbalance of power within the Union. Although there was some movement in favour of representing where people actually lived, there was no attempt to reflect population in a mathematical way, despite the availability of the census (the most recent being 1831). Geographically defined constituencies containing roughly equal numbers of people would have to wait until 1885: such an excursion in utilitarian political arithmetic was too radical and French-looking for 1832. The basic shape of the borough and county representation was therefore retained.

To what extent, therefore, did the Reform Act really change British politics? Some historians are sceptical about this. John Cannon notes that the Act may have appeared bold, but was in reality more about preservation and continuity; and Frank O'Gorman judges that 'the electoral system gave way ... to one remarkably like itself'.[13] In England and Wales the electorate increased by around 50 per cent, but that only represented a rise from 14 to 18 per cent of adult males. There were more dramatic increases in Ireland, where the proportion doubled, and especially in Scotland, where it increased 16-fold. Arguably more important than the numbers of voters was the question of what *sorts* of voters. Men of the middle classes could now generally vote, whereas many of them had been excluded by the old qualifications that required the completion of an apprenticeship or residency in a particular area. Working-class voters who had qualified under the old rules were allowed to retain their voting rights in their lifetime, but as these died off the proportion of adult males able to vote actually decreased in some constituencies. James Vernon therefore argues that the Act was 'a restrictive step backwards, an attempt to limit popular representation by establishing uniformly exclusive electoral qualifications'.[14]

If the social composition of the electorate was changing, this did not result in a change to the composition of parliament. There was no influx of middle-class MPs and the vast majority of MPs after 1832 continued to come from landed backgrounds. MPs still had to pass a property qualification and received no salary, so it remained a vocation for leisured gentlemen. In terms of party politics, however, the effect was profound. The reform crisis redrew the political battle-lines and gave us our modern party nomenclature. The Liberal Party emerged over the 1830s and 1840s from the coalition who had supported reform, and the first recorded use of the label 'Conservative Party' was in the *Quarterly Review* in January 1830, to refer to those who sought to conserve the constitution. Party politics also became much more of an issue nationally, as politics in the constituencies became much more closely linked to that of Westminster. Candidates would now avow their party membership, instead of downplaying it as something suspect and a threat to their independence. If only around a third of voters voted consistently along party lines before the Act, around three-quarters did so afterwards. Parties became much more of a presence in the constituencies, as they began to establish the nationwide electoral machinery that we know today.

This was because electoral politics after the Act gave parties a lot more to do. Elections were a lot less predictable than before. Now that the tiny boroughs had been swept away and borough electorates were bigger, contested elections were the norm rather than being in a minority. The effect of this was even more profound outside of England: no Scottish voter had voted in 1826, and no Welsh voter in 1830, due to a lack of contests. Instead, parties could now expect contests to happen on a regular basis in all constituencies, and so had to work continuously to build their support, rather than relying on the efforts of individual candidates in the event of a contest. They also had to ensure that their voters were on the new electoral roll. Inclusion on the electoral roll was not automatic, since voters had to apply and reapply, and the process was expensive and complicated. Parties therefore established registration societies, providing potential supporters with financial and legal help to ensure that they could vote. This therefore created more work for parties in the constituencies, but also served to render the system more exclusive and more controllable. For many voters, the system was a lot less accessible than the old method of arguing your case at the poll. Furthermore, open voting continued, so party agents had poll-book data about the whereabouts and voting histories of the voters in a constituency, making it easier to target and put pressure on potential supporters. The secret ballot had been discussed during the reform debates, and radicals such as O'Connell had argued that it was the only way 'of making every man, however poor, independent'.[15] The consensus in parliament, however, was that secret voting was suspect and un-English, and would remove the 'beneficial' forms of influence that the Whigs sought to promote. This suggests that voting was still regarded as a public trust rather than a private right.

Other changes to electoral procedure also had a big impact on the nature of political participation. Instead of taking weeks, polls now took place over two days, shortened to a day in boroughs from 1835.[16] The hours of the poll were also restricted, to times when many working men were at work. Instead of a single poll, which provided a focus for the election crowd, constituencies now had multiple polling places. As with the electoral roll, measures that on the face of it appeared to favour efficiency could have served to reduce popular access. We saw in Chapter 3 how the unreformed electoral system was as much about the process as the result, and that non-voters had many opportunities to participate in the street theatre and the communal events. The Reform Act sought to narrow these opportunities and to make elections solely about the electors. Women were now not only excluded from voting in theory, but their former opportunities as non-voters were now eroded in practice, including their agency as witnesses at the poll. The poor also found it much more difficult to participate, and recipients of poor relief were formally excluded from voting. The same government passed the Poor Law Amendment Act in 1835, which abolished 'outdoor' relief and established the workhouse system: in encouraging male workers to be 'independent' and demonising the 'dependent', it arguably embodied the same rationale of citizenship as the Reform Act.[17]

The reputation of the Reform Act in the current historiography is therefore mixed and continues to be debated. There is one further argument in favour of the 'continuity' thesis, however. When the new constituencies had their first elections in 1832, they adopted the old electoral culture wholesale. New towns like Manchester – bastions of industrial progress and rational liberalism – held chairing ceremonies. However much the Whigs of 1832 and subsequent Victorian reformers tried to reform away the electoral culture of the eighteenth century, it proved to be very enduring. Indeed, in preserving the basic shape of the old system, the Reform Act ensured that many aspects of the Georgian system remain with us to this day.

Chartism

The Whigs presented their Reform Act as a final, once-and-for-all solution to the question of the electoral system. This was no doubt in part to assuage anti-reformers that it did not open the floodgates to further democratic reforms, but it is likely that the Whigs believed their own rhetoric. They presented a very clear idea about to whom the vote could safely be given and, if the Act excluded the vast majority of men for the time being, it also presented a standard to which all men could aspire. Many of the men who had campaigned for the vote and found themselves excluded by the Act did not accept this, however. The campaign continued and conservatives turned out to be correct in predicting that 1832 was only the first in a series of Reform Acts.

British radicalism diverged in class terms after the Reform Act. The middle classes now had the vote, so middle-class radicals were drawn towards campaigns such as free trade and ultimately the Victorian Liberal party. Working-class radicals, however, continued to campaign, both for political reform and also for social causes, protesting about poverty, working conditions and the imposition of the New Poor Law. In the later 1830s these campaigns cohered around the Chartist movement. Chartism was named after their demand for a People's Charter, formulated by its founding committee in 1838, which included the following six points:

1. A vote for every man twenty one years of age, of sound mind, and not undergoing punishment for crime.
2. THE BALLOT. – To protect the elector in the exercise of his vote.
3. NO PROPERTY QUALIFICATION for members of Parliament – thus enabling the constituencies to return the man of their choice, be he rich or poor.
4. PAYMENT OF MEMBERS, thus enabling an honest tradesman, working man, or other person, to serve a constituency, when taken from his business to attend to the interests of his country.
5. EQUAL CONSTITUENCIES, securing the same amount of representation for the same number of electors, – instead of allowing small constituencies to swamp the votes of larger ones.
6. ANNUAL PARLIAMENTS, thus presenting the most effectual check to bribery and intimidation...[18]

Chartism is hugely significant in the history of the British working class. It was the first nationwide working-class political movement and it drew mass participation. Hundreds of thousands attended Chartist rallies all over the country, culminating in a monster meeting at Kennington Common in 1848. They had several newspapers, the most famous of which was Leeds's *Northern Star*, which had the highest circulation for a provincial newspaper. Chartists collected millions of signatures in support of their charter, and presented successive petitions to parliament. In 1839 they established a National Convention, on the model of that of revolutionary France. This was ostensibly to facilitate the presentation of their petition, but it also had the character of an anti-parliament, which claimed more popular legitimacy than the current one and therefore sought to replace it. In the meantime, Chartists stood for election, and their leader Feargus O'Connor succeeded in becoming MP for Nottingham; others won great support at the show of hands, but did not proceed to the poll in protest at the unfairness of the system. Over the course of the movement, a division emerged between the 'moral force' Chartists who persevered with these political tactics, and those who advocated 'physical force'. The 1839 Newport Rising was conceived of as the start of a national uprising, and the 1840s witnessed several plots and outbreaks of violence, which were brutally put down by the military and the newly professionalised police force. These outbreaks of violence often coincided with strikes, linking the Chartist demands with those of industrial workers.

Given its 'class' character, its size and these examples of insurrection, Chartism was long regarded as the political expression of the working class. Within the Marxist interpretation, the key determinants of historical change are economic, as social classes perceive that their interests are in conflict with those of other classes. The arrival of Chartism could therefore be seen as a reflection of the existence of a mature, conscious working class. Reading politics as a reflection of class, however, makes the People's Charter difficult to explain, since we can see that its six points focus on narrowly political demands. For Asa Briggs, the Charter was merely a 'symbol of unity' and other historians agreed that the movement's demands were really social and economic ones.[19] Since the 1980s, however, historians have questioned this interpretation. Gareth Stedman Jones argued that it is not methodologically appropriate to regard political language as a reflection of class, and instead that historians should attend to what the Chartists themselves actually said. His groundbreaking essay 'Rethinking Chartism' presented a very different picture of the movement and his conclusions have been hotly debated by historians of radical politics ever since.[20]

Applying this approach to the six demands of the People's Charter can tell us a great deal about the nature and origins of Chartist political thought. All six demands concerned changes to the representative system. The headline demand was the suffrage, but even this was not universal: there was no demand for women's suffrage, and certain males were excluded such as minors, criminals and the insane. The second demand was the ballot, which was of particular concern to working-class voters since they were vulnerable to intimidation. The third and fourth demands concerned the exclusive nature of becoming an MP, since working men could not meet the property qualification or serve without payment. The fifth demand for equal constituencies suggested that the redistribution of 1832 did not go far enough, and that the people would only truly be represented by proportionate constituencies. This would not happen until the Third Reform Act of 1884–85: indeed, none of these demands would be achieved during the lifetime of the movement, but the first five were all achieved by 1918.

The demand that was never achieved, and which seems most alien to modern readers, was the sixth for annual parliaments. The Chartists claimed that it would put a stop to corruption, since nobody could afford to buy off a constituency that frequently, and it would also make MPs more regularly accountable. Such regular elections would make politics impracticable, however, putting parties in a continual state of campaigning and giving governments too short a period to get meaningful business through. The demand is instead significant for what it tells us about where the Chartists got their ideas from. Annual parliaments had been a demand of the 'Country party' since the seventeenth century – when the length of parliaments was a serious constitutional issue – and was consistently a plank of the radical programme through the eighteenth. All six of the Chartist demands put them squarely within the tradition of British radicalism, which prioritised political reform. The vote was hugely significant in its own right – as badge of citizenship and full manhood – but also in terms of what it could achieve. Radicals believed that the political system was at the root of the ruling classes' privileged position in society, and that the vote was the key to breaking this monopoly. Obtaining the vote would lead to the return of good MPs in parliament, who would govern in the interests of all. The Chartists therefore did seek to achieve social and economic change, but indirectly via political methods. For Stedman Jones, this helps to explain why Chartism declined in the late 1840s. Peel's second administration ushered in a period of prosperity, abolished the Corn Laws and passed acts regulating factories and mines: if an unreformed system could deliver such measures, then Chartism's critique that it was incapable of doing so was fatally undermined.[21]

As well as being important for historians of politics and labour, Chartism has attracted the interest of gender historians as it witnessed large-scale female participation. Women served in a number of capacities. Much of their support was 'auxiliary', providing support for a predominantly male movement that sought male political rights. Women campaigned for the People's Charter, made banners, organised consumer boycotts and even supported the uprisings. Other women were more direct in their activity. Anne Knight sought to change the People's Charter to include a demand for women's suffrage and William Lovett, one of the Chartist leaders, was sympathetic to the idea: he had included it in an early draft of the original Charter but removed it for pragmatic reasons. At a large meeting to establish a Female Chartist Association in October 1842, Mary Anne Walker spoke powerfully about the common plight faced by working men and women:

> The events which were at that moment taking place in the north, where their sisters and brothers were being cruelly and unjustly transported, or else plunged into a dismal and pestiferous dungeons, for no other cause than standing up for their own rights and demanding bread to appease their hunger and save themselves from dying of starvation in their native land, were unfortunately of a nature to drag woman from her retirement, and call upon her to lift up her voice against such deeds.

Her speech was greeted by 'Cheers from the men, and hear, hear, accompanied by waving of handkerchiefs, by the ladies'.[22] The reference to 'pestiferous dungeons' in that speech highlights the strong strain of melodrama in Chartist rhetoric: they tended to be 'plunged' into 'dungeons' rather than put in prison. Chartists often appealed to an idealised vision of working-class life, which had been disrupted by aristocratic villainy, but which could be restored by the simple heroism of working people.

Chartist rhetoric also appealed to domesticity. Anna Clark argues that Chartists sought to reform the rough masculine world of the working class, aiming instead for domestic respectability. This both served to contest the arguments of their critics, who argued that working men were not moral or responsible enough to be entrusted with the vote, and also offered an appealing vision to their supporters. For Chartist women, it suggested that their menfolk could be good husbands, who were temperate and brought home a good wage. Chartist men were in turn attracted by the prospect of becoming substantial householders, rather than competing with women for deskilled, low-wage work. Domestic respectability was therefore part of the Chartist claim for manhood suffrage. In much the same way that the citizen of 1832 was defined in terms of his masculine position as a father, husband and householder, the Chartists claimed that humble men too deserved the vote on that basis. Replacing property with skill lowered the bar for the 'independence' required for citizenship, but this remained independence of an exclusively masculine type. Ultimately, this meant that Chartist men 'denigrated the very females they sought to protect, in the process bolstering their own status as male citizens, skilled workers and breadwinners'.[23]

Respectability was an important part of the Chartist claim. The Kennington Common demonstration of April 1848 provoked fears of revolutionary violence, and the government ordered thousands of troops into the capital in the event of trouble. In the end, it passed off remarkably peacefully: like many radicals before them, the Chartists used mass peaceful demonstrations both to demonstrate their strength and also their suitability for citizenship, through responsible and respectable behaviour. Following Kennington Common, however, there was a revival of physical force tactics. That summer, some Chartists engaged in military-style drilling and plotted insurrection. This is the subject of John Leech's *Punch* cartoon, 'A Physical Force Chartist Arming for the Fight' (Figure 6.1). The cartoon depicts the black Chartist William Cuffay, one of the plotters who was transported to Australia. Tellingly, the scene is a domestic one, as a wifely figure helps him to prepare for battle. This is the auxiliary role that typified female Chartist participation, but at the expense of keeping house to middle-class standards. The house is disorderly, with objects scattered over the floor and an upturned table: the artist is therefore undermining the Chartists' claim on the basis of domestic respectability. The Chartist himself is comically attired, improvising a suit of armour from household implements; his drooping sword is between his legs, which would cause him to trip. He is also physically slight and looks terrified, so does not represent vigorous British masculinity nor appear to be much of a threat. Leech plays on the male Chartist's gender, race and class to suggest that he is not worthy of citizenship.

Conclusion

Explaining the failure of Chartism therefore requires us to look beyond political factors and the repressive actions of the state. Clark suggests that the Chartists failed to address the tensions in working-class family life: 'the movement could not reconcile its egalitarian ideals with its commitment to working-class patriarchy'.[24] This would continue to be an issue for the British left, as it remained committed to a masculine notion of political entitlement, based on the claim of the skilled male breadwinner. This was in part a consequence of working-class culture itself, but these were also the gendered terms within which political citizenship had long been negotiated. The Whig reformers of 1832 had presented a

116 *Reform, domesticity and citizenship*

Figure 6.1 John Leech, 'A Physical Force Chartist Arming for the Fight', *Punch*, 26 August 1848. Chronicle/Alamy Stock Photo.

vision of political belonging based upon the independent male householder, who owned property and was the head of a nuclear family. In R. W. Connell's scheme of masculinities, the Chartists promoted a 'complicit' form of masculinity in trying to make a case for political inclusion along these lines.[25] This was not just a pragmatic manoeuvre, however. The ideal of the masculine householder citizen was deeply embedded in British political culture: it was central to the Chartists' radical heritage and would inform reformist politics for decades to come.

Notes

1 J. C. D. Clark, *English Society, 1688–1832*, Cambridge: Cambridge University Press, 1985.
2 For example: F. O'Gorman, *Voters, Patrons and Parties: The Unreformed Electorate of Hanoverian England*, Oxford: Oxford University Press, 1989, p. 392.
3 For example: J. Vernon, *Politics and the People: Politics and the People: A Study in English Political Culture, 1815–1867*, Cambridge: Cambridge University Press, 1993.

4 W. Cobbett (ed.), *The Parliamentary History of England*, 36 vols, London, 1806–20, vol. 33, pp. 726, 660, 650. On this debate, see M. McCormack, *The Independent Man: Citizenship and Gender Politics in Georgian England*, Manchester: Manchester University Press, 2005, pp. 120–5.
5 *Hansard's Parliamentary Debates*, Third Series, London, 1831, vol. 1, col. 53.
6 D. Wahrman, *Imagining the Middle Class: The Political Representation of Class in Britain 1780–1840*, Cambridge: Cambridge University Press, 1993, chapter 9.
7 *Hansard's Parliamentary Debates*, Third Series, vol. 12, col. 19.
8 K. Gleadle, *Borderline Citizens: Women, Gender and Political Culture in Britain, 1815–1867*, Oxford: Oxford University Press, 2009, p. 159.
9 A. Clark, 'Gender, class and the constitution: Franchise reform in England, 1832–1928', in J. Vernon (ed.), *Re-Reading the Constitution: New Narratives in the Political History of England's Long Eighteenth Century*, Cambridge: Cambridge University Press, 1996, pp. 239–53.
10 M. McCormack, *Embodying the Militia in Georgian England*, Oxford: Oxford University Press, 2015, p. 195.
11 C. Hall, *White, Male and Middle Class: Explorations in Feminism and History*, Cambridge: Polity, 1992, p. 161.
12 M. Taylor, 'Empire and parliamentary reform: The 1832 Reform Act revisited', in J. Innes and A. Burns (eds), *Rethinking the Age of Reform: Britain 1780–1850*, Cambridge: Cambridge University Press, 2003, pp. 295–311.
13 J. Cannon, *Parliamentary Reform 1640–1832*, Cambridge: Cambridge University Press, 1972, pp. 252–4; O'Gorman, *Voters, Patrons and Parties*, p. 392.
14 Vernon, *Politics and the People*, p. 39.
15 *Hansard's Parliamentary Debates*, Second Series, vol. 34, col. 1214.
16 P. Salmon, *Electoral Reform at Work: Local Politics and National Parties, 1832–1841*, Oxford: Boydell and Brewer, 2002, p. 244
17 McCormack, *Independent Man*, p. 192.
18 'The Six Points of the People's Charter' (handbill, 1837) quoted in G. D. H. Cole and A. W. Filson (eds.), *British Working Class Movements: Select Documents 1789–1875*, London: Palgrave Macmillan, 1965, p. 352.
19 A. Briggs, *Chartist Studies*, London: Macmillan, 1959, p. 26.
20 G. Stedman Jones, 'Rethinking Chartism', in *Languages of Class: Studies in English Working-Class History 1832–1982*, Cambridge: Cambridge University Press, 1993, pp. 90–178.
21 Stedman Jones, 'Rethinking Chartism', p. 178.
22 *Caledonian Mercury*, 24 October 1842.
23 A. Clark, *The Struggle for the Breeches: Gender and the Making of the British Working Class*, Berkeley and Los Angeles: University of California Press, 1995, p. 237.
24 Clark, *Struggle for the Breeches*, p. 246.
25 R. W. Connell, *Masculinities*, Cambridge: Polity Press, 1995.

Recommended reading

Burns, A. and Innes, J. (eds.), *Rethinking the Age of Reform: Britain 1780–1850*, Cambridge: Cambridge University Press, 2003.
Chase, M., *Chartism: A New History*, Manchester: Manchester University Press, 2007.
Clark, A., 'Gender, class and the constitution: Franchise reform in England, 1832–1928', in J. Vernon (ed.), *Re-Reading the Constitution: New Narratives in the Political History of England's Long Eighteenth Century*, Cambridge: Cambridge University Press, 1996, pp. 239–53.

Clark, A., *The Struggle for the Breeches: Gender and the Making of the British Working Class*, Berkeley and Los Angeles: University of California Press, 1995.

McCormack, M., *The Independent Man: Citizenship and Gender Politics in Georgian England*, Manchester: Manchester University Press, 2005.

Roberts, M., *Political Movements in Urban England 1832–1914*, Basingstoke: Palgrave, 2009.

Smith, H., *All Men and Both Sexes: Gender, Politics and the False Universal in England 1640–1832*, Pennsylvania: Penn State University Press, 2002.

Stedman Jones, G., *Languages of Class: Studies in English Working-Class History 1832–1982*, Cambridge: Cambridge University Press, 1993.

Vernon, J., *Politics and the People: Politics and the People: A Study in English Political Culture, 1815–1867*, Cambridge: Cambridge University Press, 1993.

Wahrman, D., *Imagining the Middle Class: The Political Representation of Class in Britain 1780–1840*, Cambridge: Cambridge University Press, 1993.

7 Feminism and citizenship

Feminism concerns the advocacy of women's rights, often in terms of seeking equality with men. The term was first used in this modern sense in the 1890s and it is the period around the turn of the twentieth century that is commonly referred to as the 'first wave' of British feminism. This was the period of the New Woman and the suffragettes, when the campaign for women's rights was more public and visible than ever before. Characterising this activity as the 'first wave', however, begs the question of whether feminism can be said to have existed before it. The suffragette generation themselves acknowledged their debt to their forebears: some sought to write the history of earlier campaigns, or were veterans who had been active for decades. In this chapter, we will focus on the two centuries before the 'first wave'. We will employ the label 'feminist' retrospectively in order to think about the history of campaigners who sought to critique women's subordinate position in British society and politics. These included men as well as women, and conservatives as well as radicals, so may not always look like feminists to twenty-first-century eyes: following the 'second wave' of the movement in the 1960s and 1970s, we tend to associate feminism with the radical left of the political spectrum. In some cases it may not be clear whether the term 'feminist' applies or whether they would have accepted such a characterisation themselves. Nevertheless, the campaigns and campaigners explored in this chapter will differ from the examples of mainstream political activity that we examined in Chapter 5, since they sought to address women's position in society rather than to work within it. In so doing, they broke important ground in terms of making a case for female citizenship.

Early feminism

It is arguably legitimate to apply the term 'feminist' to participants in a debate about the roles and characteristics of women that took place throughout the early modern period. From the fifteenth century, there was a Europe-wide debate known as the '*querelle des femmes*'. On one side, male writers produced bawdy and misogynistic satires, and on the other, defences of women and celebrations of their qualities were published, often by female writers. Historians characterise the period from the mid-seventeenth century as 'proto-feminism', since it was in its early or original form. The impetus for this in Britain came from many sources, including the growth of print culture and the social experimentation and religious radicalism of the Civil War period. The reopening of the theatres after the Restoration in 1660 certainly provided a platform for exploring women's roles, and rebellious daughters, emancipated wives and 'she-philosophers' became stock characters on the London stage.[1] By the eighteenth century, some writers had gone beyond the defensive and were asserting female primacy, with titles such as *Beauty's Triumph, or the Superiority of the Fair Sex Invincibly Proved* (1751). Alice Browne argues that a key achievement of eighteenth-century feminist writers was in rescuing women's issues from satire and making them a topic for serious discussion.[2]

By the beginning of our period some key themes had emerged in feminist writings. First, they discussed the nature of patriarchy. Patriarchy literally means 'the rule of the father', but academic feminists have used this analogy to critique the structural domination of men over women in society. As we saw in Chapter 1, the question of patriarchy was a live issue in the period of the Glorious Revolution, since it concerned the position of the king within the polity as well as the father in the household. Tories argued that the power of both was absolute, whereas critics like Locke argued that it was instead contractual and based upon consent. Second, they discussed institutional arrangements that affected women, notably the institution of marriage and the operation of the law. Third, they thought about female nature and intellectual capacity. To modern readers, it is striking that these writers often addressed all of these issues in a conservative way. They rarely argued that men and women were equal or had the same natures, or even that their traditional statuses were wrong. Rather, they argued that these God-given roles had been abused or undervalued by men, and therefore should be restored to their proper station.

This attitude is certainly perceptible in the writings of Mary Astell (1666–1731), whom Joan Kinnaird has dubbed 'the first major English feminist'.[3] On the one hand, she appears to be a characteristic figure of the Enlightenment, in which women had a prominent role in its early stages. A female writer, who wrote on a range of social, political and religious topics, she was acknowledged as a serious thinker and had many prominent patrons and connections. On the other hand, her conservatism put her out of step with the Enlightenment. She was a high Tory and a committed Anglican, and this had implications for her view of women and the family. Astell was critical of marriage as it was currently practised, and of men who abused their position as husbands. She criticised inappropriate, family-arranged matches, and argued that they should instead be companionate. While this may sound Lockean, her conception of marriage was rather based upon tradition and biblical precept. Marriage was a God-ordained institution and a wife should 'lay it down as an indisputable Maxim, that her Husband must govern absolutely and entirely, and that she has nothing to do but to Please and Obey'.[4] A suffering wife has no recourse but Christian stoicism, taking refuge in her religious devotions. A woman should therefore choose her husband carefully, for marriage is indissoluble. In contrast with Locke, she argues that resisting a husband – as resisting a king – is sinful, since their authority is sacred and inalienable.

Astell's most famous work was *A Serious Proposal to the Ladies* (1694). Here she advocated the establishment of a Protestant monastery, offering a 'Religious Retirement' for women.[5] The disestablishment of the nunneries in England at the time of the Reformation had arguably been a loss for women, as it removed an institution whereby they could live independently of men: indeed, convents were often invoked to discredit arguments in favour of female education.[6] Astell's proposal would provide unmarried gentlewomen with a role in society, and would provide them with opportunities for education and religious devotions. The scheme is consistent with Astell's social and religious conservatism, since it is only for well-to-do and single women, and it projects a traditional view of femininity: women may be spiritually and intellectually equal to men, but they have separate natures that are more suited to domestic duties and religion. Her proposal was well received at the time – receiving backing from the queen herself – and was influential thereafter. The notion of a dedicated institution for single women that provided an alternative 'private' sphere to the patriarchal home was often cited by feminists in the century that followed, and had echoes in the Victorian period with the settlement movement.

The religious focus of Astell's work was typical of early feminism. At the 'low' end of the Protestant spectrum, many of those who argued that men and women were equal moved in Nonconformist circles. Quakers argued that both women and men possessed an 'inner light' and that they therefore had an equal potential to express the word of God. Women were often prominent in revivalist movements, such as the Shakers who had a female prophet in Mother Ann Lee. Millenarian groups like the Shakers, who lived in self-contained communities while they awaited the Second Coming, often proposed novel solutions to women's social role and put them into practice in their living arrangements. Within the Anglican Church itself, the Evangelical revival also emphasised spiritual equality. As we have seen, the Evangelicals promoted a polarised notion of sexual difference, emphasising traditional 'feminine' qualities such as purity, humility, tenderness and charity. This notion of femininity placed women firmly in the private sphere, but also provided opportunities in the public world via the ideal of philanthropy. Women had a special role as missionaries on Earth, spreading the word of God and doing good works on behalf of those less fortunate. There was a fundamental tension in Evangelical femininity, since engaging publicly in moral and religious activities could be seen as a distraction from domestic responsibilities and as exposing women to corrupting influences. Nevertheless, many later feminists came from an Evangelical background and gained from it both practical experience of public campaigning and an ideological justification for supporting women's causes.

The female intellectual was a characteristic figure of the eighteenth century. An educated, opinionated woman was commonly known as a 'bluestocking', after the Blue Stockings Society led by the hostess Lady Elizabeth Montagu (1718–1800). This group derived their name from the unfashionable worsted garment, which emphasised their separateness from the frivolous world of the aristocracy. Both women and men were involved in this circle, and they emphasised that mixed company could be just as serious and moral as male gatherings. In particular, they emphasised the value of conversation, as a means of strengthening the mind and of transcending the division between public and private spheres: as Hester Chapone noted, 'it is a sphere from which not station or circumstances can exclude us'. They sought not only to cultivate themselves but to raise the condition of the female sex.[7] Through intellectual discussion they therefore put Enlightenment into action and had a significant influence on feminist thinkers in the Age of Revolutions.

A further medium for exploring feminist issues in the eighteenth century was the novel. The 'sentimental novel' is most associated with a male author, Samuel Richardson, but his strong, literate heroines provided a model for many female writers that followed. Such novels often took an epistolary form, using the characteristically female genre of the sentimental letter as a space for self-revelation and reflection. In this way, female authors such as Charlotte Lennox, Frances Burney and Mary Hays explored their feelings of oppression and their identities as women. Although the female readers and writers of novels often came in for misogynist criticism for their supposed frivolity and emotionalism, the novel continued to be a powerful vehicle for exploring feminist themes.

Georgian radicalism and feminism

The debate on women in the 1790s was informed by hopes and fears about the French Revolution. Women were on both the conservative and the radical side of the debate. Hannah More and her loyalist colleagues emphasised women's role in the private sphere as being central to the moral regeneration that the nation would require if it were to overcome the revolution. On the radical side, we have seen that many constitutional radicals were committed to a masculine notion of political entitlement, but the Paineite tradition of radicalism had more potential as a way of arguing for gender equality. Thomas Paine argued that political rights should be granted to everybody, based upon their common humanity and rationality: he too was influenced by the Quaker notion of the 'inner light', which suggests that rights are of divine origin and are inherent to the individual to exercise as they please. A conception of equality such as this should have offered much to feminism, but Paine's record in this regard is contested. The title of his great work was, after all, *Rights of Man* (1791). Scholars have debated whether Paine employed the term 'man' to suggest humanity, or whether he conceived of rights in masculine terms. Hilda Smith has argued that writers in this period used supposedly universal terms like 'mankind' in a male sense, providing a barrier to conceptions of citizenship rights that included women.[8] Certainly, Paine had little to say about women in his writings, and those that do are dubious attributions. His earlier career as a manufacturer of corsets did not bode well for his feminist credentials, and is played on in Gillray's 1793 cartoon 'Fashion Before Ease' (Figure 7.1). A scrawny and pockmarked Paine tightens

Feminism and citizenship 123

the strings on Britannia's stays, as she looks on with a concerned expression: the sign on his shop advertises that he offers 'Paris Modes'. Gillray makes an analogy between the body and the political system, since the shapely Britannia's 'good Constitution' is forced into an alien and painful 'Fantastick Form'. Once again, the cartoonist uses the stock figures of a persecuted female and a villainous male to elicit support from the viewer.

Nevertheless, the most significant feminist tract of the age was written in the Paineite radical tradition. Mary Wollstonecraft (1759–97) came from a respectable but poor background, and sought to live an independent life but was frustrated by the lack of opportunities available to women of her class. She moved in London's literary circles and supported herself as a writer and translator. Wollstonecraft also associated with leading radicals of the day and was an enthusiastic supporter of the French Revolution, so she responded to Burke's *Reflections* with her successful *Vindication of the Rights of Men* (1790). She followed this up with what is often regarded as the foundation text of modern British feminism, *Vindication of the Rights of Woman* (1792). This is a

Figure 7.1 James Gillray, 'Fashion Before Ease, or A good Constitution sacrificed for a Fantastick Form' (1793). Courtesy of the Lewis Walpole Library, Yale University.

comprehensive and impassioned attack on society's treatment of women. In so doing, Wollstonecraft goes further than any of her predecessors in rejecting separate spheres and separate natures. Writing in the tradition of Locke, she argued that women were a product of their society and upbringing: 'weak elegancy of mind, exquisite sensibility, and sweet docility of manners' were 'supposed to be the sexual characteristics of the weaker vessel', yet in reality were artificial and only serve to perpetuate women's dependence. In this respect, the *Vindication* is the natural successor to her earlier work on female education, which argued that it should be more practical, rational and virtuous.

To modern readers, the vitriol of her attack on contemporary femininities is striking, since it frequently involves attacking women:

> Pleasure is the business of a woman's life, according to the present modification of society, and while it continues to be so, little can be expected from such weak beings ... Novels, music, poetry, and gallantry, all tend to make women the creatures of sensation, and their character is thus formed in the mould of folly ... The conversation of French women ... is frequently superficial; but, I contend, it is not half so insipid as that of those English women whose time is spent in making caps, bonnets, and the whole mischief of trimmings, not to mention shopping, bargain-hunting, &c. &c.[9]

For this reason, at least one modern commentator has accused Wollstonecraft of misogyny. This is a remarkable accusation to put to the founder of modern feminism, although in a sense it represents a recurring dilemma, since it is often necessary to criticise women themselves in order to reform the society in which they live.[10] Wollstonecraft was certainly frustrated by women of her class and she tends to express admiration for the strong-minded male radicals in whose circles she moved. As Barbara Taylor notes, however, Wollstonecraft was writing in a gendered political idiom that associated vice with femininity and aristocracy, and political virtue with masculine strength and independence.[11]

The *Vindication* should therefore be read as a political work in the radical tradition. She argued that 'women ought to have representatives, instead of being arbitrarily governed without having any direct share allowed them in the deliberations of government', in what was arguably the first serious call for female enfranchisement. She put this demand in the wider context of parliamentary reform, however, since she regarded the whole current system of government is 'a convenient handle for despotism'. In the febrile atmosphere of the 1790s, she boldly used the term 'citizen' to advocate rights for both men and women, proposing

> that society will some time or other be so constituted, that man must necessarily fulfil the duties of a citizen, or be despised, and that while he was employed in any of the departments of civil life, his wife, also an active citizen, should be equally intent to manage her family, educate her children, and assist her neighbours.[12]

Statements such as these demonstrate that there were limits to her rejection of separate spheres. She conceived of women as primarily being wives and mothers and, whereas she advocated giving women wider access to work, these were in stereotypically feminine occupations such as education and medicine. In her later novel *Maria: Or, the Wrongs of Woman* (1798) she developed her critique of the patriarchal institution of marriage, arguing that women should be able to leave their husbands and find a new partner.

Given how provocative and radical the *Vindication* reads today, it is perhaps surprising to note that it was well received at the time. Even conservatives agreed that female education needed reform, that marriage should be affectionate and that excessive sensibility was dangerous. Her reputation among subsequent generations varied. After her death, her husband, the radical William Godwin, published a biography in which he portrayed her unconventional life as that of a romantic heroine, focusing on her affairs, bearing children out of wedlock, renouncing religion and suicide attempts. Partly as a result of this, for much of the nineteenth century she was viewed as an unrespectable amazon and few Victorian feminists would have cited the *Vindication* as an inspiration. Her reputation was rehabilitated by the suffragette generation, and she has been held up as one of feminism's founding figures ever since.

In the period after the Napoleonic Wars, many of the most important and advanced feminist thinkers were Owenites. These were followers of Robert Owen (1771–1858), a factory owner who came to regard society as requiring a complete overhaul. Thinkers like Owen are characterised as 'utopian socialists', since they sought to create the perfect society. Owen believed that all human beings were essentially the same and that everybody could be happy and equal if only the right education and social organisation were in place. His ideas therefore had huge potential as a means of arguing for women's rights, and he tapped into the powerful feminist theme that ideas about gender were artificial and capable of changing. In a sense, his interest in women's rights was incidental to his wider ambition of reforming society: Taylor suggests that he 'was not much of a feminist' personally.[13] Nevertheless, reordering the family and the relationship between men and women were central to his project.

Owen set out his ideas in his 'Declaration of Mental Independence' of 1826. Half a century on from the American Declaration of Independence, he argued that this had only freed people politically, whereas a much more thoroughgoing change had to occur if people's minds were to be freed. To establish the 'New Moral World', he argued that it was necessary to abolish private property, religion and marriage, '*a Trinity of the most monstrous evils*'.[14] This went to the heart of women's condition, since all three patriarchal institutions served to prop one another up. Ambitious as this sounds, Owen did not stop at theoretical speculation and sought to put his ideas into practice. As with religious groups like the Shakers (who were an acknowledged model), he sought to create the perfect society in microcosm by creating living communities. These communities would prove the success of his model, and would multiply until society itself was transformed. Owenite communities in Britain and the United States made great efforts to equalise men's and women's roles, transferring ties from the nuclear family to the community as a whole in order to free women from the obligations of marriage and family. Alas, even in utopia, double standards were still to be found. Although men and women participated equally in work and politics, they were still expected to do the bulk of the 'female' domestic duties. For this and other reasons, most of the communities quickly collapsed.

Robert Owen's ideas, however, continued to be influential. Probably the most far-reaching feminist treatise of the early nineteenth century was written in the Owenite socialist tradition. Anna Wheeler (1780–1840) was born in Ireland and married young to a man who was drunken and abusive. She was only free from him when he died, but this left her penniless so she earned a living by translating socialist writings. She was a close friend of the Irish philosopher William Thompson (1775–1833), and together they wrote *Appeal of One Half of the Human Race, Women, Against the Pretensions of the Other Half, Men, To Retain them in Political, and Thence Civil and Domestic, Slavery* (1825). This was published in Thompson's name, but he always insisted it was a joint production. The *Appeal* is centrally concerned with reforming the institution of marriage, and here Wheeler is clearly drawing upon her own life experience. The use of the word 'slavery' in the title is significant. As we saw in Chapter 5, women had taken a leading role in abolitionism and this gave feminists of the day a vocabulary with which to critique their own situation. For Thompson and Wheeler, this was no mere analogy, since she claimed that British society reduced married women 'to the condition of negroes in the West Indes':

> I say emphatically the slave; for a slave is a person whose actions and earnings, instead of being, under his own control, liable only to equal laws, to public opinion, and to his own calculations, under these, of his own interest, are under the arbitrary control of any other human being, by whatever name called. This is the essence of slavery, and what distinguishes it from freedom. A domestic, a civil, a political slave, in the plain unsophisticated sense of the word – in no metaphorical sense – is every married woman.

As well as critiquing marriage, Thompson and Wheeler argued that women should have the vote. In contrast to the many suffragists in the nineteenth century who focused first on single women, they argued that married women were '*more* in need of political rights', given the oppression that they faced. As radicals, they believed that the vote not only brought practical benefits, but was the 'invigorating charm' that would raise its holder to the status of other citizens.[15] As Owenites, however, they argued that women could only truly be emancipated if society was fundamentally reorganised.

Victorian feminism

Victorian feminism has a very different nature and tone to its predecessors. Certainly it was a far cry from the sexual radicalism and the comprehensive schemes of Wollstonecraft and Wheeler. By contrast, it was striking for its apparent political conservatism, its genteel respectability and the diversity of its causes. Victorian feminists did not tend to attack contemporary femininities, or suggest that women and men should be more like each other. Rather, they often emphasised sexual difference in order to underline women's moral superiority. Great women from history such as Joan of Arc or Elizabeth I, or contemporary women such as Florence Nightingale or Victoria, were held up as exemplars of what virtuous women could achieve (but tellingly, Wollstonecraft was not included in their canon). The longstanding influence of Evangelicalism and the philanthropic ideal are important here, as they suggested that women were more religious, chaste and nurturant. By contrast, Victorian feminists argued that men lacked these qualities, or even accused them of moral and sexual turpitude. This could therefore be seen as a conservative articulation of gender difference, in line with the ideology of 'separate spheres' that was at its height in this period; but it also argued that women should be able to exercise these special qualities in public as well as in the private domain.

Indeed, women were engaging in feminist campaigning on an unprecedented scale. By the 1850s it is possible to talk in terms of a women's movement in Britain. Women were less reliant on male advocates and were acting autonomously. We will see how a range of formal organisations were established in this period, and also publications such as the *English Woman's Journal*, which was founded in 1858. A significant number of women were also living independently. The world of the middle classes created a situation where women lacked a role outside of the patriarchal home, exacerbated by the trend of men marrying late after they had established their financial position. The 'woman question' of the time concerned what to do with all the 'redundant' women that this created. Martha Vicinus has shown how many educated middle-class women instead made a choice to live by themselves, seeking work opportunities and economic independence, and blazing a trail for future generations.[16] In an echo of Astell's ideas from the seventeenth century, some women lived in female communities, developing a practical alternative to the patriarchal home.

In terms of campaigning, the activities of the Victorian feminists can appear diffuse. They tended to focus on single-issue campaigns, often with a prominent figurehead, rather than formulating schemes to reform society as a whole in the way that the Georgian radicals and utopian socialists had done. It was not until the end of the nineteenth century that the various strands of Victorian feminism cohered around the campaign for the vote. Arguably, the situation of women in the mid-nineteenth century was so desperate that practical issues such as divorce reform or access to property were more urgent than abstract issues of political rights. We will also see that many of these practical questions related in fundamental ways to citizenship, and that these campaigns were therefore an important precondition of women's suffrage. Rather than progressing chronologically, it is useful to consider each campaign in turn.

A key focus of Victorian feminists was the law concerning marriage. Successive generations of feminists regarded the legal institution of marriage as being at the root of female subordination. Once a woman married, she ceased to exist in law. The legal entity in this period was the male householder, and when a woman married she was subsumed into his identity, effectively dying a civil and economic death. Under the law of *coverture*, a woman was not responsible in law for her actions and could not sue or be sued. All her property passed to her husband (unless it was kept in a separate trust) and, in a sense, she and their children *became* a form of property: they were 'immovable property' that could not be bought or sold, and in the legal language of the time they were 'in the dominion' of their master. As well as having direct practical consequences for women, this had important implications for citizenship. The citizen was required to be an independent subject with full personhood in legal and economic terms. Electoral law required that they were the head of a household and possessed of a defined amount of property. This gendered model of citizenship therefore excluded women on the grounds of their dependent situation in marriage.

In addition to this, it was virtually impossible to get a divorce before 1857. Although Britain became a Protestant country so that Henry VIII could obtain a divorce, ordinary people could not obtain one. It was possible to obtain a legal separation, known as divorce *a mensa et thoro*, literally divorce from bed and board. This meant that a couple could legally live apart but could not remarry, and the husband retained his rights to his wife's property, so she would have to be desperate or have an alternative means of support to do this. A full divorce, which entailed a full separation and allowed both parties to remarry, was yet more prohibitive. In addition to acquiring a divorce *a mensa*, the man had to sue another man for having a relationship with his wife, known as 'criminal conversation': the woman was not involved in this process as she did not exist in law. After this, the husband would have to obtain a private act of parliament, which was hugely expensive and complex: only a handful of men had ever achieved this and they were necessarily wealthy and well-connected. In most cases, women who were in loveless or abusive marriages had no means of escape.

The campaign to reform the laws on divorce is most associated with Caroline Norton (1808–77). Caroline came from a prominent Whig family and married George Norton, a Tory MP and an aristocratic younger son. When he turned out to have less of a fortune that he had claimed, they became increasingly reliant on Caroline's connections and her earnings as a writer. He was an abusive drunk and denied Caroline access to her children when she refused to subsidise him. Their marital discord became very public when George attempted to sue her friend, the prime minister, Lord Melbourne for criminal conversation: the case was thrown out but Caroline's reputation was dragged through the mud. As the problems continued, she took up her pen to protest about the state of the marriage and divorce laws. Here she drew on her own experience to personalise the plight of married women. A Bill to reform the laws was tabled in 1854 but got no further, so in 1855 Caroline published an open letter to the queen. Here she set out all the contradictions and inequities of the marriage laws, and at times their relevance to her own experience means that her anger is perceptible:

Her being ... of spotless character, and without reproach, gives her no advantage in law. She may have withdrawn from his roof knowing that he lives with 'his faithful housekeeper': having suffered personal violence at his hands; having 'condoned' much, and being able to prove it by unimpeachable testimony: or he may have shut the doors of her house against her: all that is quite immaterial: the law takes no cognisance of which is to blame. As *her husband*, he has a right to all that is hers: as *his wife*, she has no right to anything that is his.[17]

Mary Poovey has suggested that Norton used the language of melodrama, which on the one hand enabled her to present herself as a persecuted female but, on the other, upheld 'the naturalness of female dependence and the sexual double standard'.[18]

Caroline's campaigning contributed to the eventual passing of the Divorce Act in 1857. This was a considerable step forward since, for the first time, women had access to divorce and husbands could lose custody of their children: 'a father's behaviour as a husband began to affect his rights as a father'.[19] Inequalities remained, however. In theory favour would now be shown to the 'innocent' party, but different standards were applied to men and women: men could divorce women for adultery alone, whereas men had to commit additional misdemeanours such as cruelty or desertion. It was prohibitively expensive for working people and the divorce courts were in London, so were inaccessible to most. It was also financially impractical for many women to leave their husbands since the laws around women's property had yet to be addressed, making the Divorce Act ineffective in practice. The success of Norton's publications helped the feminist Barbara Bodichon to persuade the Law Amendment Society to take up the issue of women's property. It was not until the second Married Women's Property Act in 1882 that women were granted 'an indefeasible right to their own property, irrespective of and independent of any husband to whom they are married'. The *Women's Suffrage Journal* hailed this as 'the Magna Carta for women',[20] and indeed it was directly relevant to the question of suffrage since women needed to hold the status of independent economic agents before they could be considered for electoral citizenship.

A further key campaign of the mid-Victorian period concerned the Contagious Diseases Acts. In the 1860s the government was concerned about the high levels of venereal disease in the military, so passed a series of acts in an attempt to control prostitution in the vicinity of garrisons and naval ports. The act legalised interventionist public health measures that were targeted at women: a woman suspected of being a prostitute could be subject to a forced gynaecological examination and, if found to be infected, could be detained in a Lock Hospital until cured. No such measures were directed at the soldiers, since men refused to submit to inspection: indeed, the measure seemed to be concerned with maintaining a supply of healthy women. The government's response therefore appeared to epitomise the sexual double standard. In 1869 a Ladies National Association for the Repeal of the Contagious Diseases Acts was founded, which featured many prominent feminists of the day such as Josephine Butler and Lydia Becker.

The campaign against the Contagious Diseases Acts initially focused on issues of civil rights. Women were being detained against their will and imprisoned without trial, in clear contravention of *habeas corpus*. As the campaign developed, however, it became more focused on the wider double standard and issues of sexual morality. As their paper *The Shield* declared in March 1870, the Contagious Diseases Acts 'subject those submitted to their operation to indecent outrage or cruel imprisonment; they lend the protection of the law to sin, aiming exclusively and professedly at rendering safe indulgence in vicious pleasures'. Campaigners argued that men's sexual vice was at the root of women's sexual subordination. This moral focus was typical of Victorian feminism, which was committed to the notion of female moral superiority inherent in the ideology of separate spheres. For example, many women were involved in temperance campaigning: this was partly motivated by concerns about the effect of alcohol on male violence and family breakdown, but also by middle-class puritanism.[21] More troubling to modern eyes are the connections between targeting male sexual vice and campaigns for social purity. Lucy Bland has highlighted the links between Victorian feminist campaigning and eugenics, whereby issues of male immorality were elevated to wider concerns about the strength of the 'race'.[22]

Finally, Victorian feminists campaigned on the issue of education. The inferiority of educational provision for women had long been a theme of British feminism, since at least Astell. Whereas Wollstonecraft and the Owenites had emphasised that weak femininity was artificially created by education, Victorian feminists were more concerned about the lack of skills and opportunities that girls and women had in comparison with their brothers. There was, however, a fundamental disagreement about whether girls' education should be integrated with that of boys, or whether separate education was more suited to their 'feminine' natures and capacities. This issue went to the heart of the debate on gender difference. It was most perceptible in the campaign for women's higher education, as it was in this period that the first women's colleges were established. The first higher education institution for women in Britain was Bedford College, established in 1849 by Elizabeth Jesser Reid, a liberal Unitarian and veteran of the anti-slavery campaigns. It was followed by a women's college founded by the medical entrepreneur Thomas Holloway, at the urging of his wife, which became Royal Holloway College: the two institutions became constituent members of the University of London and later merged. The period also saw the establishment of female colleges at Oxford and Cambridge, and it is here that the debate on gender and curriculum was most pronounced. Emily Davies and others had campaigned for women to be admitted to Cambridge University and a special Women's Examination was created, but Davies was always adamant that women should be admitted to the full Tripos examinations. This attitude also informed her campaigns for girls' secondary education, since she argued that a separate 'female' curriculum would only perpetuate inequality. Other feminists such as Josephine Butler disagreed, however. Butler campaigned for the establishment of Newnham College at Cambridge, which had its origins in a separate series of Lectures for Ladies and which did not require its students to sit the same examinations as the men. This debate should be viewed in the context of Victorian educational reform more generally, however, since many feminist educational reformers did not see the point in integrating women into school and university systems that they considered to be seriously flawed.[23]

Conclusion

This chapter has surveyed a wide range of campaigns from the Renaissance to the end of the nineteenth century. We can see that a huge amount of activity preceded the generation who are usually regarded as being the 'first wave' of British feminism. In terms of change over time, the development of British feminism was not linear. In a sense, it came full circle: from being politically conservative and committed to the notion of separate natures in the age of Anne; via a period of political and sexual radicalism in the late-Georgian period, when feminists argued that gender difference was constructed and could be overcome; to the age of Victoria, when feminism was again often conservative and informed by the ideology of women's inherent difference. By arguing that women had special qualities that were superior to men, however, Victorian feminists justified their extensive actions in the public sphere, and in this way they achieved a great deal, often by focusing on specific and winnable campaigns. These campaigns broke important ground in terms of female independence, civil rights and access to property, so arguably the subsequent campaign for the vote could not have happened without them. We will resume the story of British feminism in the final chapter of the book, when the diverse threads of Victorian feminism came together in the fight for women's suffrage.

Notes

1 J. Kinnaird, 'Mary Astell and the conservative contribution to English feminism', *Journal of British Studies*, 19:1, 1979, 53–75 (p. 53).
2 A. Browne, *The Eighteenth-Century Feminist Mind*, Brighton: Harvester, 1987, p. 4.
3 Kinnaird, 'Mary Astell', p. 55.
4 M. Astell, *Some Reflections Upon Marriage*, London, 1700, p. 59.
5 M. Astell, *A Serious Proposal to the Ladies*, London, 1694, p. 61.
6 R. Perry, 'Mary Astell and enlightenment', in S. Knott and B. Taylor (eds.), *Women, Gender and Enlightenment*, Basingstoke: Palgrave, 2005, pp. 357–70 (p. 361).
7 E. Eger, '"The noblest commerce of mankind": Conversation and community in the Bluestocking circle', in S. Knott and B. Taylor (eds.), *Women, Gender and Enlightenment*, Basingstoke: Palgrave, 2005, pp. 288–305 (quotation at p. 299).
8 A. Clark, *The Struggle for the Breeches: Gender and the Making of the British Working Class*, Berkeley and Los Angeles: University of California Press, 1995, p. 145; H. Smith, *All Men and Both Sexes: Gender, Politics and the False Universal in England 1640–1832*, Pennsylvania: Penn State University Press, 2002.
9 M. Wollstonecraft, *A Vindication of the Rights of Women*, London, 1792, pp. 7, 166.
10 S. Gubar, 'Feminist misogyny: Mary Wollstonecraft and the paradoxes of "it takes one to know one"', *Feminist Studies* 29:30, 1994, 453–73.
11 B. Taylor, 'Misogyny and feminism: The case of Mary Wollstonecraft', *Constellations*, 6:4, 1999, 499–512.

12 Wollstonecraft, *Vindication*, pp. 335, 333.
13 B. Taylor, *Eve and the New Jerusalem: Socialism and Feminism in the Nineteenth Century*, London: Virago, 1983, p. 40.
14 R. Owen, 'Oration containing the Declaration of Mental Independence', *New Harmony Gazette*, 12 July 1826, 329–31, emphasis in original.
15 W. Thompson [and A. Wheeler], *Appeal of One Half of the Human Race, Women, Against the Pretensions of the Other Half, Men, To Retain them in Political, and Thence Civil and Domestic Slavery*, London, 1825, pp. 6, 66, 107, emphasis in original.
16 M. Vicinus, *Independent Women: Work and Community for Single Women 1850–1920*, London: Virago, 1985, pp. 1–7.
17 C. Norton, *A Letter to the Queen on Lord Chancellor Cranworth's Marriage and Divorce Bill*, London, 1855, p. 12, emphasis in original.
18 M. Poovey, *Uneven Developments: The Ideological Work of Gender in Mid-Victorian England*, Chicago: Chicago University Press, 1989, p. 83.
19 L. Davidoff, M. Doolittle, J. Fink and K. Holden, *The Family Story: Blood, Contract and Intimacy, 1830–1960*, London: Longman, 1998, p. 142.
20 Quoted in Caine, *English Feminism*, p. 119.
21 P. Levine, *Victorian Feminism 1850–1900*, Gainesville: University Press of Florida, 1994, pp. 146, 149.
22 L. Bland, *Banishing the Beast: Feminism, Sex and Morality*, London: Penguin, 1995.
23 B. Caine, *English Feminism: 1780–1980*, Oxford: Oxford University Press, 1997, p. 116.

Recommended reading

Barker-Benfield, G. J., *The Culture of Sensibility: Sex and Society in Eighteenth-Century Britain*, Chicago: Chicago University Press, 1992, chapter 7.
Bland, L., *Banishing the Beast: Feminism, Sex and Morality*, London: Penguin, 1995.
Browne, A., *The Eighteenth-Century Feminist Mind*, Brighton: Harvester, 1987.
Caine, B., *English Feminism: 1780–1980*, Oxford: Oxford University Press, 1997.
Jones, V., *Women in the Eighteenth Century: Constructions of Femininity*, Oxford: Routledge, 1990.
Kinnard, J., 'Mary Astell and the conservative contribution to English feminism', *Journal of British Studies*, 19:1, 1979, 53–75.
Knott, S. and Taylor, B. (eds.), *Women, Gender and Enlightenment*, Basingstoke: Palgrave, 2005.
Levine, P., *Victorian Feminism 1850–1900*, Gainesville: University Press of Florida, 1994.
Poovey, M., *Uneven Developments: The Ideological Work of Gender in Mid-Victorian England*, Chicago: Chicago University Press, 1989).
Taylor, B., *Eve and the New Jerusalem: Socialism and Feminism in the Nineteenth Century*, London: Virago, 1983.
Vicinus, M., *Independent Women: Work and Community for Single Women 1850–1920*, London: Virago, 1985.

8 Popular politics in the age of mass party, 1837–1901

Historians of Britain often characterise the second half of the nineteenth century as a golden age of party politics. This was an era when ordinary people engaged with national political parties and identified with their leaders as never before. It was the period of the Second and Third Reform Acts, which gave the vote to more working men and created a much bigger and less predictable electorate, and political parties quickly realised that they had to appeal to them in new ways if they were going to succeed in the new political landscape. What is remarkable about the Victorian period is how successful the mainstream political parties were at doing this. This was not because they 'represented' the interests of their new constituents in a straightforward way. As Jon Lawrence has argued, we need to be wary of explanations that assume politics reflects its social constituency, since political identities are in fact very fluid and require constant renegotiation. Indeed, as we will see, Victorian political parties 'appealed as much to gender-based as class-based social identities'.[1]

Before we turn to popular politics, this chapter will explore the development of party politics in Britain. A party system is central to modern notions of citizenship. It provides a structure through which individuals can engage with the political system and a range of practical programmes and ideologies to choose from. It also provides leaders with whom to identify, and a sense of identity as a member of a larger political group and as an individual citizen. As in 1832, the question of who should be a citizen was a defining issue in this period. Some historians have argued that the Second Reform Act of 1867 defined the Victorian nation in terms of gender, race and class, by codifying what sorts of people were fit to exercise the franchise. Even after the Third Reform Act of 1884–85, a large proportion of men and all women were still excluded from voting in parliamentary elections. As we will see, however, popular politics was not just the preserve of voters: Britain was a mass democracy in terms of participation in political parties, long before it was in strict electoral terms.

Early Victorian party politics

The two main Victorian political parties emerged from the Reform crisis of 1830–32. The 'Conservative Party' were so-called because of their hostility to reform and their desire to defend the constitution in church and state. The Tories may have been on the losing side, but they adapted to the new political landscape remarkably quickly. Their fundamental rationale was to govern, which is arguably what has made them the oldest and most successful political party in the world. The man who rebuilt the party and re-established its relevance was Sir Robert Peel. Peel was a formidable politician but was not a flashy speaker. Instead he was an efficient administrator, in the managerial tradition of Pitt and Liverpool. His sober political masculinity contrasted with that of the aristocratic Whigs and the flamboyance of his young Tory rival Benjamin Disraeli.

Peel's response to the new political world was the Tamworth Manifesto of 1835. If it had just been an election candidate justifying his conduct to his constituents, it would have been unremarkable, but as a party leader setting out his party's programme it was the first of its type. This broke new ground in terms of the citizen's relationship with the political system, since they were being asked to choose a programme from a government in waiting, rather than just endorsing the king's ministers. In terms of content, it was less remarkable. Peel claimed to embrace the reformed era but sought to avoid 'a perpetual vortex of agitation'. He avoided controversy – not mentioning his role in ending religious disabilities or his preference for free trade – and his policy pronouncements were fairly vague. Instead, he sounded a note of consensus: he would give 'the just and impartial consideration of what is due to all interests – agricultural, manufacturing, and commercial'.[2] Peelite Conservatism would therefore be built on broad support rather than narrow interests.

The formation of the Liberal Party is more difficult to pinpoint. They emerged from the alliance of Whigs, radicals, Catholics, Nonconformists and former Tories who had passed the Reform Act, and long had the character of a coalition. Some historians date the birth of the party to the Litchfield House Compact of 1835, where these various groups agreed to work together against Peel, but they had no unified programme.[3] The Reform Club was established in 1836, but it was not a party headquarters like the Conservatives' Carlton Club. They did not go in for 'whipping' in the 1830s and even the later Liberal Party resembled an umbrella organisation, which sought to win support by rational debate rather than party discipline.

The issue that would draw the Liberals together in the 1840s, and which would ultimately derail the Conservatives, was free trade. The question of import tariffs was hugely controversial in the first half of the nineteenth century, and focused in particular on the duties on grain. During the Napoleonic Wars, the landed interest had enjoyed a domestic monopoly on agricultural produce, so at the end of the conflict the Corn Laws were passed to protect them against cheap foreign imports. Most Tories were 'Protectionist' as they supported the landed interest, but opposition to the Corn Laws became a defining issue for radicals and liberal Whigs. Radicals protested that it kept the price of food high, causing hardship among working people, in order to line the pockets of the landed interest: it was therefore a moral issue and a sign that parliament was unrepresentative. Nonconformists agreed that attacking the entrenched privileges of the elite was a moral question, since they argued that individuals should instead take responsibility for their own welfare and salvation: free trade therefore encouraged self-help and personal regeneration. Utilitarians and liberal political economists had long argued that free trade was an economic policy that would bring about general prosperity, and it was also in the self-interest of the northern middle-class businessmen who were drawn to liberalism. In general, free trade epitomised the ideal of liberty. Liberals were opposed to anything that constrained the freedom of the citizen, so sought to reform the old institutions and vested interests that got in the way of their rights, prosperity and personal development. The Anti-Corn Law League was formed in 1838 by the businessman John Bright and the radical Liberal Richard Cobden. It became a huge nationwide pressure group and provided many Liberal men and women with experience of political campaigning.

Although Peel was a Tory, his own instinct was for free trade and this put him on a collision course with his party. The Conservatives had fought the 1841 election on a platform of protectionism, but Peel then reduced import duties in the 1842 budget. By 1845 it was clear that crisis was looming as the Irish potato crop had failed and England had also experienced a poor harvest. Peel's plan to suspend the Corn Laws lost him the support of his cabinet, so he was forced to resign. His Whig successors also sought reform but were unable to form a stable government so Peel returned and, with their help, succeeded in abolishing the Corn Laws. This disregard for his own party was compounded by religious issues. In 1845, Peel had also proposed increasing the annual grant to the Catholic seminary at Maynooth in Ireland. This was a sensible measure that was easily carried through parliament, but it was insensitive to the Tory backbenchers who had not forgotten his role in Catholic emancipation. The following year, the party divided as the Protectionists split from the Peelites. The former were led by Lord George Bentinck, racehorse owner and defender of the landed interest, while attacks on Peel in the Commons were spearheaded by the brilliant orator Disraeli. The Conservatives fought the 1847 election as a split party, even standing against each other in some constituencies. After the election was lost, the Peelites drifted towards the Liberals, whereas what remained of the party found themselves in the political wilderness for two decades: as the party of religious intolerance and expensive food, they struggled to build a popular base.

Instead, the Liberals dominated the political scene under the leadership of Henry Temple, Viscount Palmerston. Palmerston was an unlikely Liberal, having started out as a Tory who had drifted towards the Whigs despite a lack of enthusiasm for reform. His domestic record was unadventurous, but it did not need to be. Free trade had ushered in a period of prosperity and he achieved widespread popularity because of his foreign policy, which sought to stay out of European entanglements and to promote liberty around the world. The substance of his politics was less interesting for our purposes than were his methods. Palmerston was a great communicator: T. A. Jenkins judges that he was 'a pioneer in the arts of political persuasion'. He used the newspaper press like no previous prime minister, feeding favoured newspapers – and even Conservative ones – with information in order to keep them onside and guarantee favourable coverage.[4] If politics had become print-centred by the mid-century, as James Vernon has argued, then Palmerston knew how to dominate its key medium.[5] He also took politics out of Westminster, embarking on speaking tours of the provinces where he addressed huge audiences. He was engaging and personally genial, as one MP noted in his diary:

> Lord P. outdid himself in gay and sparkling fancy – and skilful banter. He was radiant. In an enormous House, after one o'clock, his stentorian voice rang through the anterooms where many a far younger man was stretched at length and sound asleep. Cheers and laughter followed almost every sentence. I believe he was asleep during most of the debate – at least, he generally is – & I heard he was at Ascot all day.

This aristocratic, uncontroversial and not very 'Liberal' politician succeeded in keeping the disparate elements of the party together and maintaining their popularity. Some historians regard his second ministry of 1859–65 as the first truly Liberal ministry.[6] Arguably his rank was an important factor here, since he revived the old Whig tradition of benevolent aristocratic leadership. His refined masculinity may have been at odds with his times, but demonstrated the enduring power of the disinterested gentleman. The period of consensus and stability over which he presided – sometimes dubbed the Age of Equipoise – came to an end when the question of electoral citizenship returned once again.

The Second Reform Act of 1867

As with the First Reform Act, the Second was the product of a political crisis. Following the death of Palmerston in 1865, the Liberals were led by the veteran reformer Earl Russell. Russell was committed to further reform, as was his chancellor and the leader in the Commons, William Gladstone. Russell therefore proposed a modest reform plan, which would redistribute some seats and reduce the property qualification, increasing the electorate by about 40 per cent. Such a plan would have increased the number of working-class electors but would not have given them a dominant voice: indeed, it may have sought to reinforce the Liberals' dominance of the boroughs. But many prominent Liberals disagreed. Some did not wish to undo the electorate of 1832, which had served the party so well, and others were sceptical about the suitability of the new working-class voters. In particular, Robert Lowe gave a series of speeches in which he attacked the supposed ignorance and corruptibility of the working man. He feared that giving them the vote before they were in a position to use it properly would endanger society: in the wake of the Reform Act he would push for an Education Bill, since it was now necessary 'to prevail on our future masters to learn their letters'.[7] This attitude may seem rather illiberal, but was entirely consistent with their rationale of citizenship. Liberals did not believe that freedom was guaranteed by giving the vote to more people: rather, it should be given to the right people. Only free and responsible people should be allowed to vote, since only the independent could resist corruption and use their power for the general good.

Russell's Bill was therefore defeated and he decided to resign. This let in a minority government of the Conservatives under Lord Derby with Disraeli leading in the Commons. Pressure was growing for reform as the Reform League organised huge meetings in cities across the country. The order of procession for their march in central London on 11 February 1867 reveals the scale of their support, listing dozens of local branches and trade associations. As well as conveying the strength of the popular campaign, this also emphasised their capacity for citizenship. On the page, the march was characterised by strict organisation and an almost-military discipline, with marching bands, banners and various ranks of marshals to keep order. Men were grouped by their trades: printers, cabinet-makers, curriers, tailors, carpenters and so on. This emphasised that these were men who worked, and who were therefore making a claim to manly independence and responsibility.[8] Although the Reform League sought to project respectability, the ruling classes saw only a threat of revolution. The government attempted to ban a monster demonstration in Hyde Park in May, but it was so large that the troops and police kept their distance.

Disraeli responded to the crisis with typical audacity, proposing a more far-reaching reform measure than the Liberals would have considered. With the support of his own party and the radicals, and with the Liberals split, he managed to get the Bill through. The Lords, with their inbuilt Conservative majority, gave no trouble this time. The eventual Act retained the overall shape of the former system, but redistributed some seats and altered the property qualification in the boroughs. Smaller boroughs lost one of their two MPs, which were then given to the counties or to new constituencies such as Burnley and Middlesbrough. There was no attempt to create mathematically equal districts, however, and the two-member system remained in most boroughs. More significant was the revised property qualification, which gave the vote to many urban working men, doubling the electorate and virtually establishing the principle of household suffrage in the boroughs. While this may seem like a sweeping move – which was regarded at the time and since as a 'leap in the dark' – Robert Saunders argues that we have to bear in the mind the specifics of the new qualification. It required that householders had paid the rates (and directly, rather than through their rent): they were regarded as capable of managing their money and therefore responsible and respectable.[9]

Historians have long debated Disraeli's motives in pushing forward this Bill, which was on the face of it so at odds with Conservatism. In part, he was playing party politics. He was clearly trying to score points against the Liberals and his great rival Gladstone in particular. He wanted to undo the Liberal advantage in the post-1832 system: as we have seen, political parties only pass electoral reforms that they think will be advantageous to them. He also sought electoral support for the Conservatives, capitalising on their popularity among northern working men and winning over new supporters by championing reform. This may have been a pragmatic manoeuvre, once he had perceived that reform was inevitable, but his attitude was arguably consistent with what he called One Nation Conservatism. Whereas Peel had been in the managerial tradition of Conservatism, Disraeli belonged in the rival Romantic tradition of Burke and the Young England movement. He had expounded his vision of the political world in his novels *Coningsby* (1844) and *Sybil* (1845). Here Disraeli presented an organic society where the ancient aristocracy fulfilled their paternalistic obligations to the people, who in turn recognised their natural leaders and were loyal to the nation and its institutions. This unified 'One Nation' was at odds with the atomised Liberal social vision of independent individuals who relied only on their own endeavours. It was a backward-looking version of the social order, which sought a return to a quasi-medieval golden age before the Industrial Revolution and utilitarian philosophy. The 1867 Reform Act could therefore be seen as an exercise in Tory democracy, whereby a benevolent elite granted privileges to a grateful people.

Another respect in which the Second Reform Act mirrors the First is its status in the historiography. Whig historians present it as another instalment in the onward march of English liberty: they are unable to give Gladstone the credit so instead emphasise the importance of popular pressure and the role of the Reform League.[10] Tory historians by contrast focus on high-political manoeuvrings and in particular Disraeli's skill in outwitting his opponents.[11] More recently, some historians have emphasised how the Second Reform Act and the debates around it sought to define the citizen. The key work here is *Defining the Victorian Nation: Class, Race, Gender and the Reform Act of 1867* (2000) by Catherine Hall, Keith McClelland and Jane Rendall. Tellingly, none of the authors are primarily political historians, focusing instead on histories of empire, labour and women respectively, and they bring these perspectives to bear on the reform controversy. They argue that the debates sought to fix the definition of who should be admitted to the political nation, and who should be excluded. The citizen of 1867 was the British working man. First, the citizen was British. Hall places the reform debates in an imperial context, particularly against the backdrop of a black rebellion in Jamaica, and shows how the responsibilities of citizenship were entrusted to white Britons rather than other races. Second, the citizen worked. Reformers emphasised how the vote was being given to the working classes, but this was not an inclusive category: as before, the citizen should be 'independent', whereas those who did not support themselves should not be entrusted with the vote. Third, the citizen was a man, since the Second Reform Act did nothing to overturn the exclusion of women in the First.

The debates on reform did, however, focus attention on women's suffrage, to the extent that it became established as a political cause. In particular, the Liberal MP, philosopher and feminist John Stuart Mill became a focal point for the cause. His wife and collaborator Harriet Taylor Mill had long called for women's suffrage, and Mill himself came to the view that sex difference was 'as irrelevant to political rights, as difference in height, or in the colour of the hair'.[12] During the debates in the Commons he therefore proposed that the word 'man' be replaced with 'person' in the legislation. He lost the vote, but women's suffrage

Figure 8.1 John Tenniel, 'Mill's Logic; Or, Franchise for Females', *Punch*, 30 March 1867. World History Archive/Alamy Stock Photo.

had arrived as a parliamentary cause. John Tenniel's *Punch* cartoon 'Mill's Logic; Or Franchise for Females' (Figure 8.1) refers to this episode. The philosopher asks a group of men to 'pray clear the way, there, for these-a-persons', as he ushers forward a group of women. The depiction of gender in the image is telling, as Mill's physically slight build contrasts with the bold women, led by a formidable looking Lydia Becker, implying that women's suffrage upsets the gender order. The image is not solely critical of the suffragists, however, since a John Bullish squire looks on with red-faced hostility, and the new working-class male voters appear dishevelled on the right of the print.

The Third Reform Act of 1884–85

The 1867 Reform Act had some unintended consequences. One was a rise in the cost of electioneering, which placed more pressure on political parties and the candidates themselves: with no secret ballot and more voters, opportunities for bribery and treating increased. Contemporaries also commented on an increase in disorder: there were some notable examples, but this may just have been down to a greater sensitivity to the behaviour of the new electors, as the electoral violence of the Georgian era had never gone away.[13] The new Liberal government therefore reluctantly came to the conclusion that the ballot would reduce opportunities for corruption and disorder. The Ballot Act of 1872 may appear to be a landmark in the modernisation of the British political system, but Matthew

Roberts cautions that we should not overstate this. The secret ballot had long been a radical demand, since working people were particularly vulnerable to intimidation, but most Liberals and Conservatives were of the view that voting was a public trust, and that open voting brought beneficial influences to bear upon the voter. Nor was voting all that 'public' in practice after 1832, since voting took place in dispersed and enclosed booths (although in many constituencies, the votes would be published in a 'poll book' after the event).[14] The year 1872 saw the abolition of the public nomination, shifting instead to a paper administrative process: this further excluded the non-voters, who were of course fewer in number as the electorate increased. These measures were followed by the Corrupt Practices Act of 1883, which criminalised electoral bribery and imposed limits on campaign expenditure.

Around two million men had the vote after 1867, but this still represented only about a third of adult males. Men in rural areas in particular did not benefit from the liberalisation of the borough franchise, and therefore many workers in sectors like agriculture and mining remained excluded. The campaign to extend the franchise to more men therefore continued – and, as we will see in Chapter 10, so did the campaign to enfranchise women. Unlike the previous two Reform Acts, however, the impetus for a Third did not come from popular pressure. There was widespread recognition that the anomalies of 1867 needed to be addressed. Gladstone was also keen to rally his party and head off the demands of radicals within it, such as Joseph Chamberlain. He had been denied the opportunity to reform the system in 1867 and doubtless sought to undo any electoral advantage the Conservatives had accrued from it. Gladstone proposed a simple measure, which would extend the principle of the urban franchise to rural areas. The Liberals had a large majority so the measure sailed through the Commons, as amendments were brushed aside. This included a proposal for women's suffrage, which was defeated by a respectable 271 to 135: suffragists never forgot Gladstone's 'great betrayal' at this juncture.

The problem was the House of Lords, where the Conservatives had a majority and the leader Lord Salisbury was resolved to defeat the measure. He feared that extending suffrage in rural areas would undo the Conservatives' majorities in the counties, and so insisted he would only support a change to the suffrage if it was accompanied by a substantial redistribution. Radicals claimed that this pitted 'the Peers versus the People' and called for the abolition of the Lords.[15] Growing disquiet out of doors and the intervention of the queen brought the parties to the negotiating table. With both Salisbury and the radical Liberal Charles Dilke keen on a sweeping measure, a Bill was agreed based on the principle of single-member constituencies and equal electoral districts.

The Third is the least studied of the nineteenth-century Reform Acts, perhaps because the circumstances of its passing were less contentious than its two predecessors, but its significance should not be underestimated. It gave us the basis of today's electoral geography, based upon constituencies of roughly equal population rather than the old patchwork of boroughs, cities and counties. The spread of MPs better reflected where people actually lived, ending the overrepresentation of the south of England. Significantly, there was a single Act for the whole of the UK rather than separate ones for Scotland and Ireland, although the proportion of men who met the qualifications was higher in England than elsewhere in the Union. Gladstone left Ireland out of the redistribution, to keep Irish MPs on board, so Ireland was overrepresented by population with 103 members.[16] The system was far from mathematically perfect, since most legislators sought to avoid 'arithmocracy' (apart from the Proportional Representation Society, which denounced the measure). Instead, Roberts argues that they sought to preserve a system that represented interests, based on the eighteenth-century principle of 'virtual representation'.[17] The shift to single-member constituencies may have created the 'winner takes all' version of first past the post, instead of the consensus inherent in the multi-member Georgian system and the kind of accommodations that occur when voters have multiple votes. But the new boundaries were carefully drawn so as to differentiate 'natural' communities, ensuring that all interests were represented in the national parliament.

Indeed, when we examine the new franchise it is clear that it would be a mistake to judge the Third Reform Act by modern democratic standards. Women were still excluded from voting, as were around 40 per cent of adult men. Rather than voting being an individual right, it was a public trust that should only be granted to those who were deemed capable of exercising it. The citizen was still defined in terms of his manly independence, so women and certain sorts of men were excluded. This encompassed men who were not heads of household, be they bachelors or men whose occupations prevented this. Male servants were excluded on this basis, and possibly due to enduring concerns about their lack of independence and manliness. Soldiers were too, as they lived in barracks or on service. This was especially ironic, since this era of strident imperialism celebrated martial attributes in men. Sonya Rose argues that 'brute force and military service took the place of property, independence and respectability in the public culture of masculinity and citizenship'.[18] It would take the Great War, however, for common soldiers to be recognised as political citizens in practice.

Popular Liberalism

The arrival of so many working-class voters in 1867 and 1885 ushered in a new style of politics. Electoral politics became more competitive and unpredictable, and political parties had to rethink how they communicated and what they stood for. The Conservative and Liberal Parties, however, were notably successful at adapting to this new era of mass politics. Historians have struggled to explain the British working classes' attachment to mainstream parties. For Marxist historians, the working classes should instead be seeking an autonomous politics, and the Labour Party was late arriving and somewhat disappointing in its constitutionalism. Prioritising social explanations for politics, however, misses the importance of culture in the political world. As we will now see, the Liberal and Conservative Parties had competing political cultures, with which their followers were encouraged to identify. In the era of Gladstone and Disraeli, these party

142 *Popular politics in the age of mass party*

cultures were personified by their leaders: their famous parliamentary double act made Westminster politics more tangible and identifiable. Tenniel captures the difference in their personalities in his *Punch* cartoon 'Rival Stars' (Figure 8.2). Disraeli preens in a theatrical costume, revelling in wit and flamboyance, whereas Gladstone looks on disapprovingly, his seriousness and sense of purpose underlined by his black business suit. The two men represented competing models of masculinity, which they arguably projected onto the parties that they led.

William Ewart Gladstone (1809–98) was the hero of Victorian Liberalism. In order to understand the popular appeal of the Liberal Party, it is essential to explore his image in detail. As Jenkins notes, whereas Palmerston appealed to men's good nature, Gladstone appealed to their higher nature.[19] He was an intensely serious man, who projected an earnest and forceful political style. He enjoyed chopping down trees on his estate and allowed himself to be photographed in his shirtsleeves posing with his axe (Figure 8.3).[20] These images of Gladstone the woodcutter became iconic and were hugely popular among his working-class followers, who saw him as one of their own rather than an elite politician. The image of the woodcutter projects manliness and industry: a wholesome vision of

Figure 8.2 John Tenniel, 'Rival Stars', *Punch*, 14 March 1868. Image owned by the author.

labour for which many industrial workers were nostalgic. The axe was powerfully symbolic for reformers – as it would later be for fascists in the twentieth century – since it chopped away at the dead wood, promising fairness and renewal.

Gladstone was the first Liberal leader to come from a business rather than an aristocratic background. He had originally been a Tory and the process by which he became a Liberal was, typically for Gladstone, a tortuous one. He had received a classical education at Eton and Oxford, where he identified with High Church Anglicanism. Although he championed the rights of religious minorities and won many followers among dissenters – who were drawn to his earnest style – he never lost his devotion to the established church. He was devoutly religious and had a clear moral vision of the world: for Gladstone, politics was a struggle between good and evil, darkness and light. He served as a minister

Figure 8.3 William Currey, 'William Gladstone woodcutting' (1877). Courtesy of Flintshire Record Office.

under Peel and moved with the Peelites from the Conservatives to the Liberals. Free trade was a defining issue for Gladstone, which he continued to pursue as chancellor of the Exchequer under Palmerston. Like many Liberals, he saw free trade as a moral issue, both because it concerned the affordability of foodstuffs but also as competition was the basis of a healthy and vigorous society. The privileges enjoyed by the landed interest were unfair, whereas a level playing field was both a moral good in itself and led to individual self-improvement. This ethos pervaded many of Gladstone's policies. He had an impressive record of reform when in office, including the introduction of elementary education, reform of the army and civil service (so promotion was achieved on merit rather than through purchase), an overhaul of the legal system, the removal of religious disabilities in the universities and the electoral reforms of 1883–85. All of these reforms had a moral edge, since they sought to increase efficiency and fairness, to attack the privileges of traditional interests, and to enable the individual to get on according to their talents and industry.

One issue where Gladstone struggled to define a clear policy and failed to achieve his aims was Ireland. Ireland was a divisive issue for Liberals: they tended to favour national self-determination and religious liberty, but they were also committed to the Union and were wary of Catholics' allegiance to Rome. Ireland had endured great hardship since the famine and the role of Britain within Ireland was increasingly contentious. The Fenians used violent methods to oppose British rule and the political movement for independence benefited from the Ballot Act, since many Irish tenants were now free to vote for MPs who supported Home Rule. Gladstone sought both to combat the violence and to address Irish grievances: he passed the Coercion Act, which allowed suspects to be detained without trial, but also disestablished the church and attempted to reform policies around land ownership. Ultimately he came round to Home Rule but, when he tried to get this through parliament in 1886, many Liberals rejected the measure and the Liberal Unionists split from the party, derailing Gladstone's third ministry and letting in the Conservatives.

Gladstone was at the helm of the Liberal Party for three decades. During this time, his popularity among Liberal supporters was remarkable. Working people hailed him as 'The People's William', who was *of* the people rather than the traditional political class. Gladstone spoke with a regional accent and, unlike Disraeli, never accepted a peerage and remained a commoner. His slightly detached relationship with the Liberal Party and the aristocratic Whigs helped here, since he was seen as being above party politics and not tainted by membership of the establishment. One way that working people could express their identification with their hero was through owning Gladstone paraphernalia: as well as photographs like Figure 8.3, Gladstone's image adorned commemorative plates, Toby jogs and other material articles that could be found in Liberal homes.[21] Gladstone also made himself personally accessible. Like his predecessor Palmerston, he took his message on the road, but he did not just appear at lecture theatres and concert halls. During the celebrated Midlothian campaign of 1879, he travelled between London and Edinburgh by train and whenever it stopped he would spontaneously address the crowds that greeted him. Like the radicals and Chartists had done, he addressed huge numbers of working people in the open air: indeed, historians like Eugenio Biagini view Gladstone as an heir to the English radical tradition.

Gladstone was a formidable speaker and he left a lasting impression on those who heard him. As one of his followers recorded:

> Without an effort – so it seemed to me – the great orator held his audience for nearly two hours. I stood so far off that the features were indistinct, but was spellbound by the music and magnetism of his wonderful voice ... I was only conscious of the presence of a human personality under whose spell I was, and from whom I could in no way escape ... If the things he said were unintelligible to me, the voice brought with it something of an inspiration and of uplifting power ... I felt lifted into a holy region of politics, where Tories cannot corrupt.[22]

Given reactions such as these, historians have debated why Gladstonian Liberalism was able to command mass support. Was his appeal essentially irrational? The quotation above suggests that voters were 'spellbound' by the experience of hearing him, were drawn to his hypnotic personality and were swept along by the experience of the mass rally. For Max Weber, Gladstone was an early example of a charismatic leader:[23] a personality type that is characteristic of modern political systems, and of which the most extreme example is Adolf Hitler. Alternatively, did working people come to a rational conclusion that Gladstone's policies addressed their needs? Under Gladstone, the Liberal Party promoted independence, personal freedom, fairness and self-improvement. For many hardworking and serious-minded working people, this was an attractive package. For those who disagreed, there were always the Conservatives.

Popular Conservatism

If historians have struggled to account for the mass popularity of Liberalism, the popularity of Toryism has been even more puzzling. This was the party of the landed interest and the establishment, which long defined itself by its opposition to the kinds of reforms that might have benefited working people. A working man who votes Conservative is not behaving how a left-wing historian might expect him to. As Lawrence reminds us, however, we should not assume that political loyalties follow social class.[24] Since the electoral success of Margaret Thatcher's Conservative Party in the 1980s, historians have sought to explain the phenomenon of popular Conservatism and this has transformed our understanding of Victorian politics.[25]

This new work has demonstrated that the Conservatives had a large popular following in this period. This was partly due to the popularity of their message and the attractiveness of their political style, which revolved around patriotism, paternalism, Protestantism and the pub. First, the Conservatives were successful at making patriotic appeals. This contrasts with Liberals and socialists, who were often uncomfortable with nationalism and instead promoted an internationalist politics. Conservatives had access to the emotive repertoire of British patriotism in their speeches and their printed and visual materials. This included the Union Jack; beef, beer and plum pudding; the crown and sceptre; and Britannia and John Bull, who by this period was portrayed as a portly Tory squire. Second, the Tories emphasised paternalism. They tended to argue that people should be deferential towards their betters, who in turn would fulfil their traditional social obligations to those below them, particularly through charity. This was a justification for a hierarchical society where everybody knew and respected their place. Tories presented this as an alternative to Liberal *laissez-faire*, which instead lauded personal independence and rejected paternalism as being patronising. Disraeli's 'One Nation Conservatism' should be seen in this light. Social measures such as the Artisans' and Labourers' Dwellings Improvement Act of 1875, which encouraged local councils to rebuild slum housing, could be regarded as a paternalistic measure of the ruling classes seeking to look after working people. This did not mean that the Conservatives believed in a 'big state', however, and in practice they were usually reluctant to intervene at the local level.

Third, the Conservatives made much of their religious appeal. The Tories had always presented themselves as the party of the established church, in contrast with the radical Whig tradition that emphasised religious liberty and the rights of religious minorities. Nonconformists therefore gravitated towards Liberalism, whereas the Tories emphasised the primacy of Anglicanism. In the later nineteenth century, this could have anti-Catholic overtones, which could be a popular stance in areas like the northwest of England where workers faced competition from cheap Irish labour. Orangism, the defence of the Protestant interest in Northern Ireland, has traditionally had close ties with the Conservative Party, and Disraeli was made an honorary member of a Salford Orange Lodge. Finally, the parties' different religious followings related to the politics of sociability. Non-conformists were often teetotal, whereas the Tories traditionally had the backing of the brewing industry. We might expect Blackburn in Lancashire to have been a hotbed of Liberalism and Radicalism, but Blackburn was dominated by Thwaites's brewery. The people of Blackburn worked in the brewery, drank in Thwaites's pubs and voted for Daniel Thwaites himself, who was a Conservative MP from 1875. Blackburn was therefore One Nation Conservatism in microcosm. In general, Liberals had an image of being interfering and censorious, whereas Tories were more comfortable with people enjoying themselves. If the freeborn Englishman chose to go to the pub, the football ground or the racetrack, that was his right. Lawrence argues that this 'cakes and ale' model of masculinity was a big part of the Tories' appeal in the later nineteenth century. After 1900, the emphasis on non-interference shifted to the domestic realm, whereby the Tory voter sought to protect his home against state intervention and socialism. This domestic appeal helped Tories to bring women into their fold, but the emphasis was still very much that the English*man's* home was *his* castle.[26]

The Conservatives' instinct for sociability put them at a distinct advantage in British politics, where elections in particular had always revolved around it. Tory grandees and their womenfolk were often very effective at engaging with ordinary voters through election entertainments. The provision of alcoholic drink, food and other 'treats' was the stock in trade of the electioneer, despite repeated attempts to outlaw it. More generally, the Conservatives were very adept at political organisation. After the First Reform Act, they were quicker off the mark than their opponents at adapting to the new political world. Registration societies were established in the constituencies to ensure that their voters got on the electoral roll, and the Conservative and Constitutional Associations established in this period are still a feature of British towns to this day. During the debates on free trade in the 1840s, they set up County Protection Societies to defend the landed interest, a rival to the Liberal Anti-Corn Law League. As well as this nationwide political machinery, they also established local groups with a social emphasis. Operative Conservative Societies were aimed at working men in industrial districts. These often had Tory notables as patrons and offered social benefits like friendly societies, savings banks and burial insurance clubs. The idea was that these groups would attract people for non-political reasons, but then turn them into Conservative voters.[27]

Given this nationwide network of Conservative groups, there was an effort in the 1860s to coordinate them. John Gorst founded the National Union of Conservative Constitutional Associations (NUCCA), with the intention of bringing these groups together at a national level. Leading Tories hoped to use the NUCCA to their own ends, as a way of controlling the grassroots, but its members had other ideas and proved to be more assertive than they had bargained for. They sought to influence party policy and debated contentious topics such as protectionism and female suffrage. In 1883 a group of Conservatives around Lord Randolph Churchill therefore set up a parallel body known as the Primrose League. It was set up in honour of Disraeli (who had died in 1881) and sought to capitalise on his enduring popularity. In many ways the Primrose League embodied his approach to politics, being named after his favourite flower. As one member put it, the primrose is an appropriate symbol as 'it is a British flower' and accessible to everybody: 'all, from the highest to the lowest, can obtain primroses in their season'.[28]

It is worth focusing on the Primrose League in detail, as this was a huge and important organisation. For a long time political historians overlooked the Primrose League. This may be because it was a political organisation that claimed to be apolitical, and which appealed to women at a time before women could vote. It is also a question of its image: its obsession with the Middle Ages, royal pageantry and the trappings of rank have led some historians to scoff at its 'flummery'.[29] It did indeed revel in history, much like Disraeli had done, and its aesthetic was in the mould of his Young England phase. It looked back to a romanticised vision of the medieval period as a golden age and celebrated the values of chivalry, voluntarism and loyalty. Rather than being backward-looking and escapist, however, Martin Pugh argues that it played a key role in the modernisation of British right-wing politics.[30]

The structure of the Primrose League typified its approach to politics. Whereas the federal structure of the NUCCA resembled Liberal organisations, the League was pointedly hierarchical. Officers held feudal titles like 'Knight', 'Dame' or 'Warden', and the structure of the organisation mirrored social rank with nobles dominating the upper echelons. Although its structure, nomenclature and rituals were reminiscent of the Freemasons or the Orange Order, they deliberately avoided the term 'Lodge' so as not to exclude Catholics, instead naming its branches 'Habitations'. The aim was to be inclusive. Anyone could join who could pay a cheap annual subscription and could swear the following oath:

> I declare on my honour and faith that I will devote my best ability to the maintenance of Religion, of the Estates of the Realm, and of the Imperial ascendancy of the British Empire; and that consistently with my allegiance to the Sovereign of these Realms, I will promote, with discretion and fidelity, the above objects, being those of the Primrose League.[31]

Its ideology was therefore recognisably Tory, although it rarely acknowledged its link to the Conservative Party openly. It sought to attract people who might otherwise have been put off by party politics, and to bring them within the party's ambit. It was highly successful at doing so, gaining around two million members by 1910. They did not primarily recruit voters, or even men, since it welcomed women and children, who could join as 'Buds'. Women dominated the Primrose League at all levels, which is remarkable for a mass political organisation in the period before women had the vote. In general, the Conservative Party often was a more congenial home for women than the Liberal or Labour Parties, which shared a masculinised culture of citizenship based upon the male breadwinner. By contrast, one Primrose League pamphlet criticised Gladstone for not giving 'voting power to properly qualified women' in 1885.[32] It is likely that the Conservatives appreciated that women's suffrage was inevitable and that it should therefore focus on cultivating future voters.

Sociability was key to the League's appeal. It laid on dances, fetes, tea parties, concerts and cycling excursions: the bicycle offered women in particular mobility and independence. Tory grandees would open up their stately homes to working-class members, in a way that Disraeli would doubtless have approved of. For a few pennies, an associate member could access a world of respectable fun, meet new people and be a member of a vigorous public organisation: given the lack of such opportunities for late-Victorian women, all this had an obvious appeal. Pugh judges that its activities were 'political but not boring, educational but not "improving", respectable but not censorious'.[33] It was therefore a characteristically Tory rather than Liberal organisation. In a way, it was merely providing all year round the kinds of political sociability that had traditionally happened at election time, providing a focus for the electioneering energies of Tory ladies in particular. Following the 1883 Corrupt Practices Act, parties had to be much more circumspect about 'treating' and had to limit their campaign expenditure, so the Primrose League got round the restrictions by being an organisation that was not technically part of the Conservative Party.

Conclusion

The Liberal and Conservative Parties were therefore very successful at engaging with ordinary people. Over the course of the Victorian period, the mainstream Westminster parties made a huge effort to organise in the localities, to encourage popular involvement and to present a message that was attractive and identifiable. This was a consequence of the new electoral landscape, as the Reform Acts of 1867 and 1884–85 created a large working-class electorate for the first time, but 70 per cent of the adult population still did not have the vote. As we have seen, Gladstone hero-worship or Primrose League membership went beyond those who already had the vote, to men and women who may get the vote at some point in the future. The parties created social worlds, which allowed ordinary Britons to feel part of something larger and to develop political identities. These identities were highly gendered. The two rival parties offered contrasting models of masculinity and the Conservatives in particular also cultivated a feminised appeal. Popular political culture therefore needs to be central to our understandings of both citizenship and gender.

Notes

1. J. Lawrence, 'Class and gender in the making of urban Toryism, 1880–1914', *English Historical Review*, 108, 1993, 629–52, 629.
2. Quoted in H. J. Hannam, *The Nineteenth Century Constitution: Documents and Commentary, 1815–1914*, Cambridge: Cambridge University Press, 1969, pp. 213, 215.
3. N. Gash, *Aristocracy and People, 1815–1865*, New Haven: Yale University Press, 1979, p. 161.
4. T. A. Jenkins, *The Liberal Ascendancy, 1830–1886*, Basingstoke: Macmillan, 1994, p. 85.
5. J. Vernon, *Politics and the People: A Study in English Political Culture c. 1815–1867*, Cambridge: Cambridge University Press, 1993.
6. Jenkins, *Liberal Ascendancy*, pp. 106, 90.
7. Quoted in A. Ottoway, *Education and Society: An Introduction to the Sociology of Education*, Oxford: Routledge, 1953, p. 62.
8. 'The Only Authorised and Official Programme: National Reform League Demonstration, Monday, February 11, 1867', handbill, 1867.
9. R. Saunders, 'The politics of reform and the making of the Second Reform Act, 1848–1867', *The Historical Journal*, 50:3, 2007, 571–91 (p. 589).
10. G. M. Trevelyan, *The Life of John Bright*, London: Constable, 1913.
11. M. Cowling, *1867: Disraeli, Gladstone and Revolution: the Passing of the Second Reform Bill*, Cambridge: Cambridge University Press, 1967.
12. J. S. Mill, *Considerations on Representative Government* (1861) in *On Liberty and Other Essays*, ed. J. Gray, Oxford: Oxford University Press, 1991, p. 341.
13. J. Lawrence, *Electing Our Masters: The Hustings in British Politics from Hogarth to Blair*, Oxford: Oxford University Press, 2009, pp. 43–4.

14 M. Roberts, 'Resisting "arithmocracy": Parliament, community and the Third Reform Act', *Journal of British Studies*, 50, 2011, 381–409 (p. 386).
15 P. Adelman, 'The peers versus the people', *History Today*, 35:2, 1985, 24–30.
16 M. Pugh, *State and Society: British Political and Social History 1870–1992*, London: Arnold, 1994, p. 79.
17 Roberts, 'Resisting "arithmocracy"', p. 385.
18 S. Rose, 'Fit to fight but not to vote? Masculinity and citizenship in Britain, 1832–1918', in S. Dudink, K. Hagemann and A. Clark (eds.), *Representing Citizenship: Male Citizenship in Modern Western Culture*, Palgrave: Basingstoke, 2007, pp. 131–50 (p. 145).
19 Jenkins, *Liberal Ascendancy*, p. 106.
20 R. Clayton Windscheffel, 'Politics, portraiture and power: Reassessing the public image of William Ewart Gladstone', in M. McCormack (ed.), *Public Men: Masculinity and Politics in Modern Britain*, Basingstoke: Palgrave, 2007, pp. 93–122.
21 A. Briggs, 'Victorian images of Gladstone', in P. Jagger (ed.), *Gladstone*, London: Hambledon, 1998, pp. 33–50; M. Nixon, 'Material Gladstones', in R. Quinault, R. Swift and R. Windscheffel, *William Gladstone: New Studies and Perspectives*, Farnham: Ashgate, 2012, pp. 99–128.
22 Quoted in E. Biagini, *Liberty, Retrenchment and Reform: Popular Liberalism in the Age of Gladstone*, Cambridge: Cambridge University Press, 1992, pp. 390–1.
23 H. H. Gerth and C. Wright Mills (eds.), *From Max Weber*, London: Kegan Paul, 1948, p. 106.
24 Lawrence, 'Class and gender', p. 630.
25 Matthew Roberts surveys this work in 'Popular Conservatism in Britain, 1832–1914', *Parliamentary History*, 26:3, 2007, 387–410.
26 Lawrence, 'Class and gender', pp. 650, 646.
27 M. Pugh, *The Tories and the People, 1880–1935*, Oxford: Blackwell, 1985, p. 8.
28 F. Booth-Barry, *The Primrose League: Its Aims, Object and Work*, Coventry, 1889, p. 3.
29 B. Evans with A. Taylor, *From Salisbury to Major: Continuity and Change in Conservative Politics*, Manchester: Manchester University Press, 1996, p. 278.
30 Pugh, *Tories and the People*, p. 19.
31 *The Westminster Review*, vol. 135, 1891, p. 473.
32 Booth-Barry, *Primrose League*, p. 11.
33 Pugh, *Tories and the People*, p. 28.

Recommended reading

Biagini, E., *Liberty, Retrenchment and Reform: Popular Liberalism in the Age of Gladstone*, Cambridge: Cambridge University Press, 1992.
Clark, A., 'Gender, class and the constitution: Franchise reform in England, 1832–1928', in J. Vernon (ed.), *Re-reading the Constitution: New Narratives in the Political History of England's Long Nineteenth Century*, Cambridge: Cambridge University Press, 1996.
Clayton Windscheffel, R., 'Politics, portraiture and power: Reassessing the public image of William Ewart Gladstone', in M. McCormack (ed.), *Public Men: Masculinity and Politics in Modern Britain*, Basingstoke: Palgrave, 2007, pp. 93–122.
Hall, C., McClelland, K. and Rendall, J., *Defining the Victorian Nation: Class, Race, Gender and the Reform Act of 1867*, Cambridge: Cambridge University Press, 2000.
Jagger, P. (ed.), *Gladstone*, London: Hambledon, 1998.
Jenkins, T. A., *The Liberal Ascendancy, 1830–1886*, Basingstoke: Macmillan, 1994.

Joyce, P., *Democratic Subjects: The Self and the Social in Nineteenth-Century England*, Cambridge: Cambridge University Press, 1994.

Lawrence, J., 'Class and gender in the making of urban Toryism, 1880–1914', *English Historical Review*, 108, 1993, 629–52.

Lawrence, J., *Speaking for the People: Party, Language and Popular Politics in England, 1867–1914*, Cambridge: Cambridge University Press, 1998.

Pugh, M., *The Tories and the People 1880–1935*, Oxford: Blackwell, 1985.

Roberts, M., *Political Movements in Urban England, 1832–1914*, Basingstoke: Palgrave, 2009.

Saunders, R., 'The politics of reform and the making of the Second Reform Act, 1848–1867', *The Historical Journal*, 50:3, 2007, 571–91.

Vernon, J., *Politics and the People: A Study in English Political Culture c. 1815–1867*, Cambridge: Cambridge University Press, 1993.

9 Citizenship, society and the state

To this point, we have largely considered citizenship in political, civil and legal terms. We have focused on rights such as voting, free speech and freedom against arrest, alongside obligations such as obeying the laws and performing military service. This chapter will shift our attention to the social implications of citizenship. Citizens are members of a society as well as a polity, and Britons today are familiar with the wide range of social benefits provided by the welfare state: these include financial benefits for the elderly, the young, the unemployed and the disabled, among many others. The historiography of 'the rise of the welfare state' (and what has arguably been its fall in recent years) is very emotive, given the politically contested nature of social welfare. Geoffrey Finlayson argues that it has traditionally placed too much emphasis on the state, and not enough on the range of voluntary agencies that provided welfare in the nineteenth and twentieth centuries: as well as the citizen's social entitlements, we should study their social obligations.[1] This chapter will do both, but will argue that in order to understand how Victorians and Edwardians understood social welfare, we need to pay attention to the idea of 'society' itself, and how citizenship and personal freedom were conceived of within this new 'social' domain.

In the second half of the chapter we will explore the emergence of the Labour Party, a development that is usually seen to parallel the rise of the welfare state, since its accomplishment is generally attributed to Clement Attlee's 1945 Labour government. We will see, however, that the welfare state had a much older heritage, and the development of a workers' party in Britain was a long process and by no means an inevitable one. As we saw in the previous chapter, working people long remained committed to the existing parliamentary parties, and the ideological roots of Labour were very diverse. Rather than being a socialist party, Labour owed much to radicalism and Liberalism. We have seen how the British radical tradition was characterised by a distinctive model of citizenship, as well as a commitment to a particular model of masculinity. Labour arguably inherited many of these attitudes, alongside connections with a trade union movement that tended to promote the interests of the male breadwinner. We will therefore explore how the concepts of citizenship and gender can shed new light on two key developments in modern British history.

The idea of 'society'

'Society' is a very difficult term to define. It suggests a sphere of human relations that is vast and complex but has a structure and follows certain patterns. This section will suggest that this modern notion of society was a creation of the nineteenth century. Prior to this, the term had many different meanings. As today, a 'society' could be a group or organisation, but it could also connote one's circle of acquaintance. In the eighteenth century, 'social' referred to sociability: you could commend someone for being 'a social fellow', or could enjoy someone's society.[2] When 'society' referred to an aggregate of people, it usually meant the *beau monde*: the society pages of certain newspapers today still describe the world of the elite and its prestigious calendar of events.

Over the course of the nineteenth century, society took on a new meaning. It is therefore useful to study the history of 'the social', in order to understand how this new concept came about, and how people conceived of their lives within this sphere and sought to act upon it. This is distinct from 'social history', which naturalises this domain in the process of studying human life within it.[3] Victorian Britain was a society that endlessly wrote about and classified itself. They came to believe that 'society' was something that could be studied in a scientific way and which had patterns and cycles that could be understood. The nineteenth century witnessed the birth of the 'social sciences', approaches to the human world that employ methods from the natural sciences such as observation, sampling and statistical analysis. In particular, the lives of the poor were placed under scrutiny as Victorian patricians grappled with 'the social question' and how it might be solved. These enquiries were carried out by the characteristic figure of the middle-class male investigator, entering the world of the poor and recording his findings in a supposedly objective way. Figure 9.1, an illustration from the *Illustrated Times*, depicts an enumerator for the 1861 census in an impoverished home: he is at once in the middle of the scene but utterly detached from it, visibly untroubled by the dirt and chaos that surrounds him. Social investigators observed working-class districts in much the same way as an anthropologist might observe a tribe in a distant country, and with a similarly imperial rationale: describing an unfamiliar race with different (and often repellent) practices and beliefs, with a view to governing them. As Mary Poovey argues:

> Empirical observations of specific instances of working-class distress, gathered and interpreted by a middle-class (white male) expert, constitute the basis for understanding that distress not primarily as an individual, physiological problem ... but as a sign of social disorder that required collective (legislative) action.[4]

Social observation therefore constituted problems as 'social' problems that demanded a large-scale, interventionist response.

Figure 9.1 'The Census Enumerator in a Gray's Inn Lane Tenement', *Illustrated Times* 7 (1861), 242. Chronicle/Alamy Stock Photo.

Many of these social investigators were amateurs, gathering social data as members of organisations like the Manchester Statistical Society. Others were agents of the state. Over the course of the nineteenth century, the state gathered huge amounts of information about Great Britain and its population. Government became a science: as James Vernon argues, 'government depended upon the acquisition and analysis of data to determine the most rational and efficient way of organizing the state'.[5] The impetus for this was often military in origin. The Ordnance Survey began mapping the state after the 1745 Jacobite Rebellion, with a view to pacifying the Highlands, and they began to survey the counties of England in order to improve invasion defences during the French Revolutionary and Napoleonic Wars. Over the century that followed, urban areas were mapped in ever-greater detail and surveyors were granted the legal right to enter private dwellings and to fix boundaries and place names. The census too was military in origin, since it was first collected in 1801 with a view to ascertaining military manpower and national resources, and it was collected every decade thereafter. Today the census is a key source for historians and genealogists, since it appears to provide a snapshot of every dwelling and its inhabitants, but as a historical source it presents some complex issues. Far from being objective, the way that census entries were collected owed much to the patriarchal preconceptions of the people who collected it. Families were neatly arranged under the male household head, which may have belied the realities of working-class life. The middle-class men who collected the census believed in the ideal of the male breadwinner, so the occupations of women and children often went unrecorded, creating a skewed impression of the Victorian workforce.[6]

This scientific approach was also applied to charity. We saw in Chapter 5 how the philanthropic ideal gave respectable women a role in the public sphere. The practice of 'district visiting' saw women visiting the poor and the sick in order to distribute material aid, alongside practical advice and Christian moral teachings.[7] By the mid-century, however, there was growing concern that the proliferation of charitable relief was encouraging pauperism and undermining the effect of the New Poor Law, which had been designed to make working people independent. The Charity Organisation Society was established in 1869 with the goal of co-ordinating charitable activity. It sought to ensure that charitable efforts did not overlap, so as to reach more deserving cases and to prevent the undeserving from being over-aided and distracted from self-help. Their guiding principle was 'no relief without enquiry'. Aid would only be given once an individual had been assessed, so district visiting should be accompanied by casework, establishing a practice that is now central to the profession of social work (which is dominated by women to this day). Blending morality and logic, the Charity Organisation Society epitomised the Victorian faith in social science and the reforming power of the investigator.

'Society', then, came to be seen in scientific terms in the nineteenth century. Social life followed patterns that could only be understood by systematic observation, but once they were understood they could be controlled. 'Social problems' such as poverty and disease therefore had to be approached in a rational way. As we will now see, however, approaches to these questions shifted over the course of the Victorian period.

Liberalism and society

This approach to government may be characterised as liberalism. Liberalism in this sense does not refer to the ideology of the Liberal Party, although in many cases they were its clearest advocates: rather, it was 'the common sense of the age'.[8] To a large degree it was defined by its approach to liberty. Classical liberals tended to define liberty in negative terms, as the absence of constraint, so reform tended to consist of the removal of impediments or artificial privileges.[9] For example, we saw in the previous chapter how politicians such as Peel and Gladstone were committed to the policy of free trade. The principle of *laissez-faire* had it that the economic realm had its own delicate rhythms that were upset by intervention. Stripping away impediments such as import tariffs would therefore encourage trade and free competition, leading to general prosperity. At the same time, the policy had a moral edge since it took unfair advantages from the landed interest, encouraged individuals to be industrious and provided cheaper food for the poor.

If the state was to stay out of the economic and social realms, it should be as small as possible. Successive reformers attacked 'Old Corruption' with a view to making the state lean and fair: taxes should be as low as possible and certainly should not end up in the pockets of placemen and pensioners. If the state was to function effectively, its functionaries should achieve their positions on merit rather than privilege: entrance exams were introduced into the civil service and in 1871 the army finally abolished the practice of promotion through the purchase of officer commissions. Political reforms tended to remove constraints on freedom, with the removal of taxes on newspapers, religious disabilities and restrictions on political association. Changes to the electoral system served to remove impediments to the independence of the voter by restricting corruption and inefficiency, and by ensuring that the elective franchise was vested in those deemed capable of exercising it responsibly.

For the liberal state to work, it required a particular type of individual. The most well-known statement of this was Samuel Smiles's *Self-Help* (1859). Smiles argued that the 'spirit of self-help is the root of all genuine growth in the individual'. When individuals do things for themselves it both enables them to be self-supporting, and requires them to exert themselves in a character-building way: it is therefore both an economic and a moral good. But when things are done for them, it removes the stimulus to self-help, leading to moral degeneration. As Smiles puts it: 'Help from without is often enfeebling in its effects, but help from within invariably invigorates.'[10] The best way to help an individual is to remove any obstacles that prevent them from helping themselves: these could include bad laws, unfair advantages enjoyed by others, or (as in the case of the New Poor Law) forms of assistance that supposedly discourage independence. There were therefore positive and a negative sides to self-help: on the one hand, it was meritocratic and potentially egalitarian; on the other, it could be punitive and judgmental. As we saw in Chapter 2, Victorian masculinity privileged the 'inner' man over his external attributes. A man's moral character was fostered through struggle and the daily arena where that could take place was the workplace. Through hard work a Victorian man would not only render himself and his family independent: he would become manly. The concepts of character and self-help were highly gendered and the citizen was ideally a household head, who governed and represented those who depended upon him. The citizen of the liberal state was therefore emphatically masculine.

The freeing of the liberal citizen therefore could only take place if the citizen possessed certain attributes and was capable of governing and supporting themselves. For this reason, Nikolas Rose argues that 'freedom' did not represent the absence of power, but rather an indirect way of exercising it. He argues that the concept of freedom has a history and that it took a distinctive form in the mid-nineteenth century: 'for the first time the arts of government were systematically linked to the practice of freedom'.[11] Civil society, the economy and the polity were increasingly freed, but a free society depended upon individuals conducting themselves in a particular way. Freedom therefore involved a range of strategies to manage individual conduct. The philosopher Michel Foucault coined the term 'governmentality' to characterise this form of power that acts through fostering habits of self-government.[12] Living in a liberal state required 'civil' behaviour. This could be inculcated in direct ways such as education, or by punishing infractions through the apparatus of the law, but it was usually accomplished in more subtle ways.

In particular, the city underwent a transformation in the nineteenth century. The Industrial Revolution had created sprawling cities, many of which had grown in a disordered manner in the absence of adequate local government. Migrants from the countryside crammed into the centres and speculators embarked on a rash of infill building to meet the demand, leading to slums that were overcrowded and unsanitary. Manchester inspired awe and horror in many of those who visited it, who commented on the chaotic mass of humanity that seemed to reflect its commitment to unbridled competition. Many of the streets in central Manchester were filthy, dark and dangerous. Over the course of the Victorian period, however, British cityscapes changed. The passing of the Municipal Corporations Act of 1835 put in place effective local government that was accountable to ratepayers: citizens now had a say in how their city should be run and councils had the power and financial wherewithal to engage in urban improvement. Housing was increasingly planned, underground sewage systems were constructed and public spaces were transformed. Later nineteenth-century Manchester boasted an imposing Town Hall, stately squares, the largest urban park in Europe and streets like Deansgate that were wide, clean and well-lit.

Street lighting was particularly important, since visibility was a key technique of liberal government.[13] Clearly a well-lit street makes people more visible to the police than they would be in a dark alleyway, so uncivil or criminal conduct can be tackled in a direct way. In Manchester, street lighting was run by the Commissioners of the Police until 1851, when it became the responsibility of the council.[14] Visibility also acted on individuals in a more indirect way, however. In the 1780s, Jeremy Bentham had proposed a design for prisons around the concept of a 'panopticon', whereby inmates could always be seen from a central point in the building. Even if they were not being watched, the possibility existed that they were, so they would therefore improve their behaviour: the prison became a place where the individual was not just punished but could be reformed.[15] Over the course of the nineteenth century, this ethos was applied to the living environment more widely, and even to the design of the city itself. The idea was that if people were conscious that they were being watched by the authorities and – more importantly – other people, then they would modify their behaviour accordingly. (There is an analogy today in the widespread use of CCTV and traffic speed cameras: in practice we are not being watched all the time, but we behave appropriately because we *might* be.)

Historians such as Patrick Joyce therefore argue that the process of reshaping the bricks and mortar of the city was bound up with an effort to reshape the conduct of those who lived in it. Dwellers of the opened-up city were constantly exposed to the judgement of others: Rose characterises liberalism as 'government through the calculated administration of shame'.[16] Citizens were encouraged to speak, move and even think in ways that were considered to be 'normal'. The sensory experience of walking down the street was also transformed. Underground sewers carried human waste invisibly away, and indoor abattoirs replaced open livestock markets and the visible slaughter of animals in butchers' shops.[17] In an atmosphere purged of uncivilised sights and smells, citizens were at liberty to practise civility. The liberal citizen was therefore supposed to be governed indirectly: he was free, but that involved developing the techniques to live 'freely' in the liberal society and polity.

New Liberalism and society

Towards the end of the nineteenth century, attitudes towards social problems and political liberty underwent a significant shift. Later Victorian Britain was a time of widespread unemployment, poverty and social tension. Social investigators in British cities were accumulating growing evidence of dire social conditions, the most famous of these being Charles Booth's 1880s study of the East End of London and Benjamin Seebohm Rowntree's study of his hometown York in the 1890s. In the Liberal Party, there was a growing realisation that the mid-Victorian prescription of *laissez-faire* and individual responsibility was no match for the social problems of an industrial society. Thinkers who proposed communal solutions to social problems became influential in the Liberal Party, such as the philosopher T. H. Green and the economists Alfred Marshall and J. A. Hobson, and radicals in the party such as Joseph Chamberlain pushed for a new direction in social policy.

Many Liberals came to reject self-help in favour of a more interventionist approach. As Herbert Henry Asquith noted in 1902:

> with the growth of experience a more matured opinion has come to recognize that Liberty (in a political sense) is not only a negative but a positive conception. Freedom cannot be predicated, in its true meaning, either of a man or of a society, merely because they are no longer under the compulsion of restraints which have the sanction of positive law. To be really free, they must make the best use of faculty, opportunity, energy, life.[18]

This 'positive' conception of liberty proposed that it was not enough merely to leave people alone. A man who lacked education, and who lived in poverty and squalid living conditions, could not be expected to help himself. Rather, individuals had to be emancipated from their social conditions if they were to realise their potential as citizens. Rowntree had proposed that there was a 'poverty line', an objective measure of the minimum income required to support a family. The state should therefore take an active role in providing a basic minimum of social conditions.

This 'New Liberalism' proposed a very different role for the state. Whereas classical liberals had sought to keep the state small and to minimise interference in the social realm, New Liberals argued that the state should intervene in society in a structural way, and that the state therefore had to grow. The Edwardian period witnessed a raft of welfare reforms including free school meals (1906), old age pensions (1908) and the provision of health and unemployment insurance (1911). The concept of social insurance was key to these Liberal reforms. Citizens should contribute to a common fund that would provide them with assistance in the event of emergency. Rather than a 'big state' as such, where wealth was redistributed, social insurance continued to emphasise individual responsibility since citizens were required to be provident and to make contributions, in a similar way to membership of a friendly society. New Liberalism therefore lay somewhere between liberalism and socialism. Taken together, the Liberal welfare reforms of 1906–14 had a huge impact upon the development of British social policy. Britons today tend to date the arrival of their 'welfare state' to the Labour government of 1945, but many of its key features were established 40 years earlier. In order to understand why this happened, we need to focus on these changing ideas about liberty, society and citizenship. Rose judges that, in this second phase of liberalism, the 'normal citizen was to be the social citizen, the citizen adapted *to* society, whose pleasures and aspirations were to be realised *in* society'.[19]

New Liberals hoped that this approach to society would benefit both the individual and the nation as a whole. Asquith argued that such welfare reforms would benefit 'everything, in short, that tends to national, communal, and personal efficiency'.[20] There was widespread interest in the new science of eugenics in Britain at the end of the nineteenth century and grave concerns about the fitness of the race. This came to a head when the British struggled to recruit enough fit soldiers to fight in the South African War of 1899–1902. The poor physical condition of the working class was apparently impacting upon Britain's military and national strength. Part of the impetus for New Liberalism came from a desire to improve the health of the British people with a view to maintaining its imperial pre-eminence. Rather than being a reward for service in the Second World War, the welfare state was arguably intended to enable Britain to fight a war like the First. Either way, we can again see close links between citizenship and military service.

The strong currents of militarism and imperialism in late-Victorian culture were perceptible in contemporary masculinities. John Tosh argues that the later nineteenth century witnessed a 'flight from domesticity', as men turned their back on the stultifying family life of the mid-Victorian period. Marriage no longer held the same attraction for men, and the rise of the New Woman and the advance of women's rights served to undermine domestic patriarchy. Instead, men sought 'comradeship' in male company. There was a proliferation of all-male spaces in this period, including gentleman's clubs and 'male' rooms in houses such as libraries and smoking rooms.[21] A key homosocial institution was the public school. These private boarding schools hugely expanded in the second half of the nineteenth century, where boys would be exposed to muscular sports, Christian morality and a bracing disciplinary regime, as a preparation for manhood and public life. Historians have debated the extent to which there was a 'flight from domesticity' in this period.[22] In part, it depends how far you believe mid-Victorian masculinities were ever that domestic, or whether men's domestic roles and relationships actually served only to underline their dominance of the public world.

While men were seeking emotional intimacy with other men, the notion that this intimacy might be of a sexual kind generally provoked reactions of horror or incomprehension. We saw in Chapter 2 how sodomy was legally, morally and politically problematic in the eighteenth century. As notions of sexual difference diverged, forms of sexual activity that fell outside of the respectable heterosexual norm became ever-more deviant. The notion of citizenship that prevailed by the nineteenth century was highly heteronormative, being based upon a male head of household who exercised authority over the conjugal family. Public figures were therefore vulnerable to any accusation of 'unspeakable' relations with other men, and this was the focus of numerous blackmail attempts and political scandals.[23] The most famous of these scandals was the trial of the writer Oscar Wilde in 1895. Wilde attempted to prosecute the Marquess of Queensbury for libel after he called him a 'sodomite', but when Queensbury's lawyers presented evidence about Wilde's relationships with other men it was he who was arrested. Under the Criminal Law Amendment Act of 1885, any sexual relationship between men was 'gross indecency' that was punishable by imprisonment: Wilde got two years' hard labour, the maximum penalty. Sexual relations between women were not included in the legislation, since the law defined sexual activity in phallocentric terms, and many Victorians regarded respectable women as being sexually passive and thus incapable of having sex between themselves. In the late nineteenth century, the new scientific field of sexology developed our modern vocabulary of 'sexuality'. Sexuality shifted the focus away from bodily acts and towards a more holistic understanding of the self: as Foucault argues, 'the sodomite had been a temporary aberration; the homosexual was now a species'.[24] Homosexuality became a medical deviance, as well as a moral and legal one, but at least it was now defined and publicly discussed. Paradoxically, the very fact that it was demonised and legally oppressed helped gay men to develop an identity and a sense of community.

There was a shift in the tone of British masculinity at the end of the nineteenth century. The empire came to be seen as a space where true masculinity could flourish and many British men craved the promise of adventure and independence that it appeared to present. The public schools instilled a sense of imperial service and in practice a significant proportion of their former pupils went overseas. Even if one did not travel to the empire itself, late-Victorian popular culture offered many opportunities to experience it vicariously. The adventure fiction of authors such as Henry Rider Haggard told stirring tales of British men overcoming foreign 'others', and was notable for its violence, racism and misogyny.[25] The masculine ideal at the turn of the century was the 'stiff upper lip': men should suppress all emotional expression, and should instead exhibit self-control and stoicism. This celebration of masculine composure reached its apogee in 1912 with Captain Scott's ill-fated Antarctic expedition and the conduct of the male passengers and crew during the sinking of the *Titanic*. The self-sacrifice, chivalry and bravery exhibited by these two groups of men was widely celebrated back home, turning these two disasters into moral triumphs.[26] This masculine attitude prevailed as Britain confidently entered the Great War. As we will see in the following chapter, however, Edwardian masculinity was no match for the horrors of the trenches on the Western Front.

The politics of labour

In many historical accounts, the arrival of the welfare state is linked to the rise of the British labour movement and the establishment of the Labour Party. In these narratives, Labour becomes the progressive force in British politics and the working classes abandon the Liberal Party, leading to its decline in the early twentieth century and a more 'social' direction in public policy. As this is the origin story of the British left, it is very emotive and hotly contested. More than any other aspect of British political history, this story has traditionally been told in Marxist terms, as the working class 'matures', achieves political consciousness and seeks autonomous political representation. Labour politics has often been studied as 'labour history', which is closer to social history than political history in its methods, emphasising Labour's origins in long-term social change. Other historians instead focus on political factors and short-term contingencies.[27] More recently, historians of gender have focused on the politics of the British left, and we will see how this offers a different perspective upon the labour movement and left-wing notions of citizenship.

The origins of the British labour movement go back centuries. Workers had long organised among themselves to assert their rights and protect themselves against employers. In the medieval period the guilds sought to protect the interests of skilled trades. Only men who enjoyed the status of 'freemen' were permitted to practise their trade and they also enjoyed political privileges. Before the 1832 Reform Act, many boroughs bestowed the parliamentary franchise on freemen. Today, 'freedom of the city' is a purely ceremonial honour, but the livery companies are still going strong and the City of London Corporation is the longest continuously serving representative body in the world.[28] This somewhat elitist ethos was also present in the trade societies of the Georgian period, which sought to protect skilled artisans against both their employers and cheaper labour, particularly that done by women. Anna Clark argues that artisanal trades had a 'traditional bachelor journeyman culture' characterised by libertinism, violence and misogyny. By contrast, she argues that communities of less skilled workers valued family and marriage more, such as in the northern textile factory districts where women were widely employed. By putting women back into labour history, Clark turns E. P. Thompson's heroic story of the radical artisan on its head.[29]

From the 1830s, trade societies started to refer to themselves as 'unions'. This fraught period of social tension included celebrated cases like that of the Tolpuddle Martyrs, who were transported to Australia for forming a union to protest against their meagre wages. A nationwide protest and petitioning campaign followed, and this pressure eventually led to their pardon. Cases like these helped to establish the legitimacy of unionism and by the mid-century unions were becoming organised and established: nationwide bodies into which members paid subscriptions, which gave unions the financial wherewithal to survive a strike and provide members with friendly society benefits. Historians of gender tend to emphasise the masculinist culture of the early trade union movement. Committed to defending the wage of the male breadwinner, they were often antagonistic towards female labour: they had little interest in the rights of women, whom they only admitted to their organisations in an auxiliary capacity.[30]

The formation of the Trades Union Congress (TUC) in the 1860s was an important step in the development of workers' representation. The TUC initially sought to defend the legal status of unions and the rights of workers to picket, but increasingly functioned as a political pressure group. As we saw in the previous chapter, the working men who got the vote in 1867 largely supported the existing parties. The first two working men got into parliament in 1874, but fighting elections cost money and MPs did not receive a salary until 1911 so it was financially prohibitive as a career. Many working men instead got experience of representative politics by going into local government, which was cheaper and more accessible. By 1886 there were nine 'Lib-Lab' MPs, who were members of the Liberal Party but worked together to promote the rights of labour. It is important to stress the importance of Liberalism to the origins of the Labour Party. Lawrence argues that both parties spoke the same political language, emphasising the rights of the productive classes against those of the idle and the privileged.[31] Some key figures were basically Gladstonian in their beliefs, or had sought to become Liberal MPs but had been kept waiting too long. The origins of an independent Labour Party often lay in a sense of being let down by the Liberal Party in pursuit of similar ends.

Labour politics was also influenced by intellectual developments in the 1880s. These came from various directions including Marxism, utilitarianism and critiques of 'landlordism'. Henry George's criticism of the system of land ownership and rents was highly influential at the time. It was not 'socialist' in a modern sense: rather, it looked to pre-industrial times and celebrated the dignity of labour. This backward-looking, rural vision of labour was typical of a very English version of socialism, such as the Arts and Crafts movement of William Morris and John Ruskin.[32] It was also perceptible in the Fabian Society, which was formed in 1884 and is still active today. The Fabians were a group of middle-class intellectuals who sought to effect change by the force of their ideas: they did not believe in unionism or the need for a separate party of labour. Marxist historians tend to take a dim view of them – Eric Hobsbawm judges that they had 'no place in the British political tradition' – but they were arguably typical of their time.[33] Another group that formed outside of unionism was the Social Democratic Federation (SDF). The wealthy journalist Henry Hyndman was inspired by the writings of Karl Marx, whose works he plagiarised in accessible editions. He decided to form his own socialist party rather than join an existing one, but the SDF was unsuccessful electorally and never developed into a mass movement.

The 1890s were key to the formation of the Labour Party. In this decade of considerable social tension, unions were becoming more powerful and militant, and were fighting long and bitter strikes. The Conservatives were dominant in parliament so the various political groups on the left increasingly worked together. In 1893, the Independent Labour Party (ILP) was formed with the intention of representing labour separately from the existing parties. Lawrence highlights the importance of their 'independence', which as we have seen was a charged political keyword with a long heritage. Some saw the ILP as a rejection of party politics altogether whereas others saw it as a new type of political party where MPs would not be dictated to as they were in the existing ones.[34] In 1899, the TUC set up the Labour Representation Committee, with the aim of sponsoring a labour group in parliament. The unions played a key role in funding the Labour Party and would contribute to electing its executive (a link that continues to this day, although their power over the party was weakened by the reforms of John Smith and Tony Blair in the 1990s). Labour candidates enjoyed electoral success in the fraught 1900s: they had a pact with the Liberals whereby they would not stand against one another, and they thereby benefited from the Liberal landslide of 1906. The 30 MPs adopted the title 'the Labour Party'.

Their electoral manifesto of 1906 gives us revealing insight into Labour ideology:

> To the Electors –
> This election is to decide whether or not Labour is to be fairly represented in Parliament.
> The House of Commons is supposed to be the people's House, and yet the people are not there.
> Landlords, employers, lawyers, brewers, and financiers are there in force. Why not Labour?
> The Trade Unions ask the same liberty as capital enjoys. They are refused.
> The aged poor are neglected.
> The slums remain; overcrowding continues, whilst the land goes to waste.
> Shopkeepers and traders and overburdened with rates and taxation, whilst the increasing land values, which should relieve the taxpayers, go to people who have not earned them.
> Wars are fought to make the rich richer, and underfed school children are still neglected...
> The unemployed ask for work, the Government gave them a worthless Act, and now, when you are beginning to understand the causes of your poverty, the red herring of Protection is drawn across your path.
> Protection, as experience shows, is no remedy for poverty and unemployment. It serves to keep you from dealing with the land, housing, old age, and other social problems![35]

We can see here the range of influences on Labour thinking. Taking the clauses in turn, the first two concern the representativeness of parliament. This was inherited from the radical tradition, which pitted the people against the 'monopoly', and believed that political representation was the key to effecting real change. The third and sixth clauses refer to the power of landlords and the inequity of the rent system, suggesting the enduring influence of Henry George. The fourth clause refers to the rights of the unions, who played such a key role in the formation and maintenance of the party. The fifth and sixth reflect the priorities of the New Liberals, who were concerned with alleviating social conditions for the poorest citizens. These sit uneasily with the last two clauses, which concern free trade and *laissez-faire*, such a defining issue for mid-Victorian Liberalism. Only the seventh and eighth clauses are recognisably socialist, with an emphasis on the inequitable power of the rich and the need for economic redistribution. The Labour Party therefore came from heterogeneous groups and intellectual traditions and has always been a broad church. In the twentieth and twenty-first centuries, various groups would try to claim Labour for Marxist revolutionary socialism, but this does not reflect the reality of its origins. Labour was a constitutionalist parliamentary party, which should be viewed as an heir to the British radical-liberal continuum of the eighteenth and nineteenth centuries.

The party continued to grow and by the 1920s had replaced the Liberals as the alternative to the Conservatives. The growing presence of working people in the political world had an impact upon political culture: Kit Good notes that 'tough working-class masculinity' entered the political mainstream. This was not necessarily gender-exclusive, since early female Labour MPs like Margaret Bondfield were successful at assimilating into this manly political culture and meeting the physical demands of electoral campaigning.[36] Nevertheless, Labour came from a political tradition that was committed to a masculine vision of citizenship. Unionism, radicalism and liberalism all tended to promote the interests of the male breadwinner, and conceived of the citizen as an independent economic agent and the head of a household. We will see in the following chapter how this had implications for the left's relationship with the women's suffrage movement and women in politics more generally.

Conclusion

The nineteenth and early twentieth centuries, then, were a time when citizenship was increasingly viewed in social terms. The question of how politics should act upon the social sphere was controversial and was constantly being renegotiated. In order fully to understand this, we have to historicise the notion of 'society' and how different political traditions conceived of citizenship and personal freedom within it. As we have seen, this led to the emergence of a conception of citizenship that went beyond civil and political rights to social and economic entitlements. Our understanding of citizenship should be yet broader, however. As we have seen, 'citizenship' is not just something that happens when you 'do' politics – by, say, voting in an election, going on a demonstration or reading a newspaper. Nor is it just about being active in one's community, through voluntary action or public service. Citizenship is an everyday lived condition, which affects how we think, what we buy or even how we walk down the street. It concerns our values, identities and behaviours: it is part of our *selves* as members of a society, polity and nation. We have rights within these bodies and duties towards them. From the early twentieth century in Britain, the state had 'social' duties towards its citizens, and it still does, even after they began to be eroded in the 1980s.

Notes

1 G. Finlayson, *Citizen, State and Social Welfare in Britain, 1830–1990*, Oxford: Clarendon Press, 1994, pp. 4, 9.
2 For example: A. Bennett, *Juvenile Indiscretions: A Novel*, Dublin, 1786, p. 310.
3 P. Joyce, *Democratic Subjects: The Self and the Social in Nineteenth-Century England*, Cambridge: Cambridge University Press, 1994, pp. 1–2.
4 M. Poovey, *Making a Social Body: British Cultural Formation, 1830–1864*, Chicago: Chicago University Press, 1996, p. 57.
5 J. Vernon, *Modern Britain: 1750 to the Present*, Cambridge: Cambridge University Press, 2017, pp. 118, 119.
6 E. Higgs, 'Women, occupations and work in the nineteenth-century censuses', *History Workshop Journal*, 23, 1987, 59–80.
7 'On being a "visiting lady"', *Girl's Own Paper*, 1891, pp. 147–9.
8 Vernon, *Modern Britain*, p. 116.
9 I. Berlin, 'Two concepts of liberty' (1969), in *Liberty*, ed. H. Hardy, Oxford: Oxford University Press, 2002, pp. 166–217.
10 S. Smiles, *Self-Help: With Illustrations of Character and Conduct*, London, 1859, p. 1.
11 N. Rose, *Powers of Freedom: Reframing Political Thought*, Cambridge: Cambridge University Press, 1999, p. 68.
12 M. Foucault, *Security, Territory, Population: Lectures at the Collège de France*, trans. Graham Burchell, ed. Michael Senellart, Houndmills: Palgrave, 2007.
13 C. Otter, *The Victorian Eye: A Political History of Light and Vision in Britain, 1800–1910*, Chicago: Chicago University Press, 2008.
14 Joyce, *The Rule of Freedom: Liberalism and the Modern City*, London: Verso, 2003, p. 109.
15 M. Foucault, *Discipline and Punish: The Birth of the Prison*, trans. Alan Sheridan, London: Penguin, 1977, p. 200.
16 Rose, *Powers of Freedom*, p. 73.
17 Joyce, *Rule of Freedom*, chapter 2.
18 H. Asquith, 'Introduction', in H. Samuel, *Liberalism: An Attempt to State the Principles and Proposals of Contemporary Liberalism in England*, London, 1902, pp. ix–x.
19 Rose, *Powers of Freedom*, p. 79, emphasis in original.
20 Asquith, 'Introduction', p. x.
21 J. Tosh, *A Man's Place: Masculinity and the Middle-Class Home in Victorian England*, Yale University Press: New Haven, 1999, p. 171, 182.
22 M. Francis, 'The domestication of the male? Recent research on nineteenth- and twentieth-century British masculinity', *The Historical Journal*, 45:3, 2002, 637–52.
23 H. G. Cocks, *Nameless Offences: Homosexual Desire in the 19th Century*, London: I. B. Tauris, 2003, chapter 4.
24 M. Foucault, *The Will to Knowledge: The History of Sexuality, Volume 1*, trans. R. Hurley, London: Penguin, 1990, p. 43.
25 J. Tosh, 'Masculinities in an industrialising society: Britain, 1800–1914', *Journal of British Studies*, 2005, 330–42 (pp. 339–40).
26 M. Jones, *The Last Great Quest: Captain Scott's Antarctic Sacrifice*, Oxford: Oxford University Press, 2003, p. 229.

27 Matthew Roberts surveys this debate in *Political Movements*, p. 128.
28 'The City's government': www.cityoflondon.gov.uk/about-the-city/history/Pages/city-government.aspx [accessed 1 March 2019].
29 A. Clark, *The Struggle for the Breeches: Gender and the Making of the British Working Class*, Los Angeles and Berkeley: University of California Press, 1995, p. 14.
30 S. Rose, 'Gender antagonism and class conflict: Exclusionary strategies of male trade unionists in nineteenth-century Britain', *Social History*, 13:2, 1988, 191–208.
31 J. Lawrence, *Speaking for the People: Party, Language and Popular Politics in England, 1867–1914*, Cambridge: Cambridge University Press, 1998, p. 148.
32 Roberts, *Political Movements*, p. 131.
33 E. Hobsbawm, *Labouring Men: Studies in the History of Labour*, London: Weidenfeld & Nicolson, 1964, p. 252.
34 Lawrence, *Speaking for the People*, p. 250.
35 Quoted in P. Adelman, *The Rise of the Labour Party, 1880–1945*, London: Longman, 1996, p. 114.
36 K. Good, '"Quit ye like men": Platform manliness and electioneering, 1895–1939', in M. McCormack (ed.), *Public Men: Masculinity and Politics in Modern Britain*, Palgrave: Houndmills, 2007, pp. 143–64 (p. 161).

Recommended reading

Adelman, P., *The Rise of the Labour Party, 1880–1945*, London: Longman, 1996.

Bentley, M., 'Liberalism in nineteenth-century Britain', *History Review*, 12, 1992, 26–30.

Finlayson, G., *Citizen, State and Social Welfare in Britain, 1830–1990*, Oxford: Clarendon Press, 1994.

Harris, J., *Private Lives, Public Spirit: A Social History of Britain, 1870–1914*, Oxford: Oxford University Press, 1993.

Joyce, P., *The Rule of Freedom: Liberalism and the Modern City*, London: Verso, 2003.

Lawrence, J., *Speaking for the People: Party, Language and Popular Politics in England, 1867–1914*, Cambridge: Cambridge University Press, 1998.

Poovey, M., *Making a Social Body: British Cultural Formation, 1830–1864*, Chicago: Chicago University Press, 1996.

Roberts, M., *Political Movements in Urban England, 1832–1914*, Basingstoke: Palgrave, 2009.

Rose, N., *Powers of Freedom: Reframing Political Thought*, Cambridge: Cambridge University Press, 1999.

Tosh, J., *A Man's Place: Masculinity and the Middle-Class Home in Victorian Britain*, New Haven: Yale University Press, 1999.

Vernon, J., *Modern Britain: 1750 to the Present*, Cambridge: Cambridge University Press, 2017.

10 Votes for women, 1865–1928

This final chapter of the book will focus on the campaign for women's suffrage. After a very long and hard-fought campaign, some women were granted the parliamentary franchise for the first time in 1918. This campaign dominates historical accounts of the British women's movement and women's politics in general. In terms of the 'separate spheres' narrative, this is apparently when the pressure cooker explodes: after being trapped in the private sphere throughout the nineteenth century, vivacious educated women burst into the public sphere for the first time in the twentieth, beginning the political history of British women.[1] The suffragette generation is often seen as the 'first wave' of British feminism – which, as we have seen, can serve to obscure the achievements of previous generations of feminists and female political campaigners.

This chapter will tell the story in a different way. Rather than being the beginning of a new story, it is arguably the end of another. The granting of votes for women was the conclusion of a debate about citizenship that had been raging for two centuries, and which had always been conducted in gendered terms. The British state was selective about to whom it granted the franchise and, as we have seen throughout this book, this question was often negotiated in terms of masculinity and femininity. It was only with the granting of equal franchise in 1928 that electoral qualification ceased to be evaluated in this way, so this constituted an end of an era in terms of the history of citizenship. In terms of separate spheres, however, this was not necessarily an ending. Some suffrage campaigners were strikingly conservative in terms of their politics and their views about gender; and in the period after the First World War, many of the freedoms and opportunities that women had acquired during the war were reversed. This chapter will therefore survey some recent work on the history of suffrage and will draw some wider conclusions about the relationship between citizenship and gender over the period covered by this book.

The debate on women's suffrage

The history of the women's suffrage campaign in Britain is a long one. We have seen how Mary Wollstonecraft proposed giving some women the vote in the period of the French Revolution, and how some utopian socialists and early

Chartists supported the idea. In 1851 the Sheffield Female Political Association drafted the first women's suffrage petition to the House of Lords, but in the mid-nineteenth century the vote was just one among many single-issue feminist causes. In Chapter 7 we explored the campaigns to reform the laws around divorce and property, to improve access to education and to abolish the Contagious Diseases Acts. Issues such as these were arguably more urgent and less politically problematic than the vote, which would have seemed a distant prospect at the time. Towards the end of the nineteenth century, however, the vote came to be the overriding priority for the British women's movement, providing the unifying focus that Victorian feminism had lacked. It is worth reflecting on why this should have happened. The vote was, of course, hugely symbolic and represented admission to full citizenship and even dignified humanity. It also held out the hope of real change, since the suffrage campaigners worked within a political culture that had real faith in the efficacy of representative politics. Just as the Chartists had thought that the vote was the means to achieving economic and social change, so suffragists believed that gaining admittance to the process of law-making would bring about a wider improvement in women's condition.

An organised women's suffrage movement began to emerge in the 1860s. The *English Women's Journal* and the group of feminists known as the Langham Place circle advocated women's suffrage, and societies began to form across the country, collecting funds, signing petitions and raising the profile of the issue. The philosopher John Stuart Mill was elected to parliament in 1865 and became a focus for promoting the measure in parliament. He presented a suffrage petition in 1866 and, as we saw in Chapter 8, proposed that women should be enfranchised by the 1867 Reform Act. Other feminists sought to exploit ambiguities in its provisions: an Act of 1850 declared that the term 'man' in legislation should include women unless it specified otherwise, so female campaigners attempted to get on the electoral register. These attempts ultimately failed, but women's suffrage had arrived: political causes needed to be debated in parliament if they were to be legitimate and respectable, and women's suffrage was debated in parliament almost annually thereafter.

It is also worth highlighting the parallel question of women voting in local government. Women lost the municipal franchise in 1835 but this was restored by the 1869 Municipal Franchise Act. Legal contests continued about whether this included married women and whether women should be allowed to stand for local office, until the Local Government Act of 1894 cleared the way for women to participate fully in Poor Law and school boards, and parish and district councils. In general, women voting in local elections was notably less contentious than in parliamentary ones. It was easier to make the case for inclusion in these newly created layers of government than in established ones, and local government was seen as a social rather than a political responsibility, so was easier to square with women's supposed moral and domestic nature.[2] Nevertheless, women gained practical experience of representative politics in this arena, and it contributed in important ways to their sense of citizenship.

The Victorian phase of the suffrage movement has traditionally been neglected by historians. It can appear to be a socially conservative campaign run by respectable ladies and their well-meaning menfolk, and certainly lacks the air of rebellion and drama exuded by militants in the Edwardian period, or munitions workers during the Great War. This image problem partly stems from the very first histories of the movement, some of which were written by former suffragettes themselves and which tended to emphasise their role – and their militant tactics – in the achievement of the vote.[3] More recently, historians such as Jane Rendall have reinstated the importance of the Victorian suffragists.[4] Martin Pugh has focused on the politics of suffrage, exploring its relationship with Westminster parties and voting patterns on the issue, and has suggested that the suffragists had largely won over the parliamentary classes by 1900. All they needed was a willing government with an opportunity to legislate: if anything, militancy made this *less* likely and delayed the process.[5] This interpretation strikes at a foundation narrative of British feminism and has been duly controversial: Pugh's critics claim, among other things, that his narrowly political account misses the social and cultural importance of female militancy.[6]

Nevertheless, it is important to take the Victorian suffragists seriously and the debate with which they had to engage. Suffrage may seem to us like a manifestly just cause but it was not necessarily seen that way at the time. As Brian Harrison and Julia Bush have shown, the 'antis' had widespread support in society and in all political parties.[7] Rather than the anti-suffragists being the anachronism, it was the suffragists who were swimming against the tide of Victorian social and political thought. Indeed, there was widespread female support for anti-suffragism. The Women's National Anti-Suffrage League had thousands of members and mustered over 300,000 signatures for an anti-suffrage petition. Prominent women were involved in the movement, such as the novelist Mary Ward (who, tellingly, wrote under the married form of her name, Mrs Humphrey Ward). Although some anti-suffragists were clearly political reactionaries or misogynists, we should not assume that they all were: antis came from across the political spectrum and were often alarmed at the spread of democracy in general; some were even involved in other feminist causes, such as reform of the marriage laws. As historians, it is important not to approach issues such as this with twenty-first-century assumptions.

In the later nineteenth century, the debate on women's suffrage was usually conducted along constitutional lines, in terms of history and precedent. Suffragists argued that women's exclusion from political life was inconsistent with the true practice of the historic constitution, whereas anti-suffragists disagreed. Laura Mayhall has argued that the suffrage campaigners were drawing on a long tradition of radical protest in Britain, which used constitutional arguments to claim citizenship rights. Like the radicals, they sought the restitution of ancient liberties which they claimed were being withheld, and they protested against the illegitimate 'monopoly' of power and the denial of civil rights.[8] Arguing along constitutional lines emphasised the legitimacy and respectability of the movement. For example, most Victorian suffragists just sought the vote for unmarried women. Widows and spinsters had long been a constitutional oddity, being independent owners of property and yet excluded from voting: widows in particular enjoyed many of the other rights given to men, since in theory they represented a continuation of their dead husband's civil personality. Suffragists therefore maintained the traditional focus on the citizen's independence rather than womanhood as such. Seeking rights for single women was not just a first step. As Millicent Fawcett argued in 1889: 'Wives are bound by law to obey their husbands. No other class in the community is in this position, and it seems inexpedient to allow political independence (which would only be nominal) to precede actual independence.'[9] Effectively, giving the vote to married women would just give more power to their husbands so – in a reworking of the eighteenth-century idea of 'virtual representation' – single women should represent all women. It was easy for the antis to ridicule this argument. Why should a woman vote before and after marriage but not during? Why punish women for fulfilling their religious and biological duty? Decent women might be put off marrying altogether, they argued, whereas freethinkers, mistresses and prostitutes would be enfranchised.

However much the suffrage campaigners tried to keep the focus on political and civil rights, the debate necessarily concerned gender roles. What is striking is that both suffragists and antis often argued *within* the separate spheres paradigm. Suffrage campaigners made arguments based on both equality and difference. For example, Marion Holmes argued in 1909 that women 'need the vote for exactly the same reasons that men need it':

> They are compelled also to discharge their full responsibilities; they have to pay the same taxes, rates, and rent as men. They are expected to fulfil all the burdens and duties of responsible citizenship – yet they are denied the one privilege that makes citizenship a vital and living thing.

In the same pamphlet, however, she drew attention to women's special qualities and roles, suggesting that they needed the vote because they were different to men. Women were 'naturally more law abiding than men', they had 'high intellectual and moral standards', and they understood 'social and moral' issues such as child welfare and housing.[10] This played on the Victorian notion of complementary gender difference, whereby women had superior moral and nurturant qualities. That made them better able to understand the plight of the vulnerable and the unfortunate, which was a powerful argument at a time when the state was increasingly taking an interest in social issues. The antis responded that women should not vote precisely because they were different: women were not temperamentally suited to politics and lacked rational judgement and independence. Moreover, the experience of politics would corrupt women, so they would lose their moral distinctiveness. Critical coverage of the suffragettes in the press focused on the inappropriateness of their behaviour. The *Daily Sketch* commented on the 'shameful' behaviour of the suffragettes outside parliament in November 1910: 'Never before have otherwise sensible women gone so far in forgetting their womanhood.'[11] Whereas the antis argued that politics would change women, suffragists argued that women would change politics. Women would purify politics and 'raise the standard of English national life'.[12] Far from the suffrage campaign being a 'sex war', it was instead the antis who argued that the vote would transform gender relations.

Strategies

Historical discussions of suffrage tactics tend to emphasise the different approaches taken by the two main wings of the movement in the Edwardian period. On the one hand were the 'militants', who dominate traditional accounts of women's suffrage. Militancy was the approach of the Women's Social and Political Union (WSPU), founded and led by the Pankhursts. These 'suffragettes' sought publicity outside of the usual political channels, by focusing on public demonstrations and civil disobedience. On the other were the 'constitutionalists', the majority of suffragists who sought to work peacefully within the political system. They focused on persuading politicians to support the cause, since they had faith in the capacity of the British political system to reform itself. As Sandra Stanley Holton has argued, however, this picture of two separate 'wings' is distorting. She argues that there was in fact much overlap of membership and approaches: both sides engaged in public protest and intellectual debate, and there was a broad alliance of 'democratic suffragists' who sought the same things in similar ways.[13] Rather than two wings, it is useful to talk about constitutionalism and militancy as two strategies, which in practice complemented one another.

The constitutionalists sought to persuade the political parties to enact women's suffrage. They sought to demonstrate the strength of pro-suffrage opinion and the feasibility of winning a vote in parliament. Many long-established societies across the country joined together in 1897 to form the National Union of Women's Suffrage Societies (NUWSS). They were headed by the veteran campaigner Millicent Fawcett, who was a skilful and determined political leader. Fawcett had heard John Stuart Mill speak at an election meeting as a young woman and it 'kindled tenfold my enthusiasm for women's suffrage'.[14] Although nominally neutral in party terms, the NUWSS was dominated by Liberals and worked within the party's reforming tradition. They sought to return as many pro-suffrage MPs as possible by offering support to pro-suffrage candidates in elections. They also engaged in parliamentary lobbying and petitioning, and sought regular private members' bills in order to demonstrate the extent of support across the house. Not all constitutionalists were Liberals, however. Many northern suffrage societies preferred the respectability of the NUWSS to the sensational tactics of the Pankhursts, but supported wider calls for enfranchising working people, and had closer links with the Independent Labour Party and the trade unions.

Whereas the NUWSS was gradualist in its approach, the militant WSPU sought to demonstrate the urgency of the suffrage. It was formed in Manchester in 1903 by Emmeline Pankhurst and her daughter Christabel. Emmeline had been active in the suffrage cause since the 1880s and was motivated to form a new organisation out of frustration with the Labour Party on the issue. The WSPU was a very different organisation to the NUWSS. Whereas the latter was federal in structure and democratic in its operation, the WSPU had no constitution and was run by its leadership. Holton notes that its autocratic structure suited its style of campaigning, which relied on military discipline and charismatic leadership.[15] Militancy was first put into practice in 1905, and was used to put pressure on the incoming Liberal government in the 1906 election campaign. Liberal candidates were heckled and protesters were arrested for disorder, achieving press coverage for the cause. Jon Lawrence has suggested that the suffragettes were here appropriating the masculine culture of election disorder, of which Britain had a long tradition.[16] The violence of elections was highly ritualistic and there was a performative aspect to militancy. It was supposed to be spectacular and was all the more so as women were not supposed to behave that way in public.

Violence became increasingly central to WSPU methods, as they focused on disrupting public events and destroying property. By 1913 this had escalated into a campaign of bombing and arson. Some suffragettes also refused to pay tax and participate in the 1911 census, in order to highlight that, for women, the duties of citizenship did not come with its rewards. Through resistance, women were demonstrating that they were active citizens in the same way that generations of radicals had done.[17] Militancy was also an attitude and a way of life. As Margaret Haig Thomas, Viscountess Rhondda later recalled:

> for me, and for many other young women like me, militant suffrage was the very salt of life. The knowledge of it had come like a draught of fresh air into our padded, stilted lives. It gave us a release of energy, it gave us that sense of being of some use in the scheme of things ... It gave us hope of freedom and power and opportunity. It gave us scope at last, and it gave us what normal healthy youth craves – adventure and excitement.[18]

Amid the thrill of rebellion and self-determination, it is also worth noting the personal cost of militancy. Suffragettes often faced ridicule, ostracism and personal injury, and Emily Wilding Davison died in the cause: she was killed by the king's racehorse at the 1913 Epsom Derby, after she walked onto the course carrying a suffragette flag.

Suffragette violence often focused on the destruction of property, such as the smashing of windows. Breaking the law in this way had several benefits. An immediate one was that it ensured quick arrest, so the women could escape the violence of hostile crowds. It also gave suffragettes their day in court, which they could use as a platform to promote the cause and which would be reported widely in the press. Mayhall highlights the legalistic aspect to the suffragette critique. Suffragettes argued that it was successive judicial decisions that had denied women the vote and they therefore contested the masculine judiciary's authority.

It also served to highlight the many legal incapacities and double standards faced by women more generally.[19] Once convicted, the treatment accorded to suffragette prisoners became a political issue. Suffragettes were not granted the status of political prisoners and from 1909 many went on hunger strike in protest. This presented an acute problem for the government who had no wish to create martyrs for the cause. They attempted to force-feed the prisoners, a violent process that Mary Richardson recalled in her autobiography:

> To my horror ... four of the wardresses, who were all hefty women, lay across my legs and body to keep me pinned to the floor. And now that the victim was trussed up and ready the doctors came in dragging the hated trolley at their heels. One knelt to grip my shoulders, another lifted aloft the funnel that was to receive the liquid, the third knelt by my head and took the long tube in his hand and, little by little, forced the stiff nozzle at the end of the tube up my left nostril. As the nozzle turned up at the top of my nose to enter my gullet it seemed as if my left eye was being wrenched out of its socket. Then the food, a mixture of cocoa, Bovril, medicines and a drug to keep one from vomiting when the tube was drawn out, was poured into the funnel and down into my aching, bruised, quivering body.[20]

The brutal violation of women's bodies in this way caused a public outcry. In 1913 the government instead adopted the policy of releasing the hunger strikers temporarily to allow them to recover, then re-arresting them. The so-called 'Cat and Mouse Act' was depicted in a WSPU poster of 1914 (Figure 10.1). Whereas the huge cat with bloodied fangs represents masculine villainy, the feminine suffragette is portrayed in the mould of the helpless, innocent heroine. The suffragettes were especially effective at visual propaganda and set up an artists' collective called the Suffrage Atelier in 1909, which produced many memorable images. In their imagery of the Cat and Mouse Act and also prisoner force feeding, however, suffragette artists were not above appealing to voyeurism and the chivalric expectations in contemporary culture. Just as Georgian political cartoonists had done, images like these used melodrama to elicit the viewer's support for the female protagonist and what she represented.

Party politics and suffrage

Militancy was successful at generating publicity for the movement, but the key people that the suffragists needed to persuade were the MPs who would vote on the issue in the House of Commons. This was the focus of the constitutionalists, who worked hard to persuade political parties and individual MPs to back the measure. Ben Griffin has therefore argued that it is not sufficient to view the suffrage 'debate' in terms of two opposing ideologies: instead, we need to take into account the political context, party politics and the individual parliamentarians themselves. MPs were, of course, men, and suffragism struck at the patriarchy in which they of all people had a stake, so their willingness to support women's

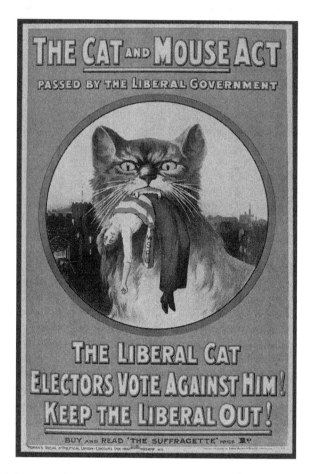

Figure 10.1 'The Cat and Mouse Act Passed by the Liberal Government' (WSPU poster, 1914). Granger Historical Picture Archive/Alamy Stock Photo.

rights depended on the extent to which they thought reform would threaten their privileges. Political historians such as Griffin and Pugh have examined voting patterns on the issue of suffrage, in order to shed light on the extent of support for the issue over time.[21]

The issue of what party suffragists should work with was more complex than it might first have appeared. The Liberal Party would seem to have been the natural ally, since they were the party of reform and home to many intellectuals and progressive thinkers, and many members of the NUWSS were Liberals. The Liberal Party also contained elements that were hostile to suffrage, however. As we have seen, nineteenth-century Liberalism tended to promote the interests of the independent citizen, who was implicitly male. Importantly, the Liberal leadership was a source of frustration. Gladstone did not support the issue and suffragists regarded his failure to give women the vote in 1884–85 as a betrayal. Asquith was famously opposed to women's suffrage and his house was targeted by suffragettes. He feared, probably correctly, that giving the vote to propertied women would just create more Tory voters. This concern served to scupper the Conciliation Bills of 1910–12, which would have given the vote to around a million wealthy women. By 1914 the party was willing to support women's suffrage but the war intervened.

Suffragists had long hoped that the new Labour Party would help to deliver suffrage, with its interest in political reform and progressive causes. Emmeline Pankhurst had been active in the Independent Labour Party but had come to doubt its commitment to the cause. She originally established the WSPU in order to put pressure on the ILP, but eventually split with them and her own politics became more conservative. Instead, from 1910 the NUWSS drew closer to Labour. Its membership became more working-class and Labour made a firmer commitment to the cause, insisting that it would only support franchise reform if it included women. In 1912 the NUWSS established the Election Fighting Fund, which offered electioneering resources to pro-suffrage Labour candidates, but this proved to be divisive. It alienated Liberals in the ranks and some suffragists became frustrated with the new party's underdeveloped electoral machinery.[22]

Instead, it was the Tories who proved to be what Pugh calls the 'unexpected ally'.[23] This may seem surprising, since today we tend to associate feminism and political reform with the left of the political spectrum, but it is important to view women's suffrage in its political context. There were indeed many antis among Conservative ranks but these were declining in number. Most Conservatives came to appreciate that many female voters – and propertied women in particular, who would likely get the vote first – would vote Tory. Whereas in the Liberal Party the grassroots were supportive but the leadership was opposed, in the Conservatives it was the other way around. Disraeli (no fan of conventional gender roles himself) consistently voiced support for the measure throughout his career and the Primrose League, set up in his honour, brought hundreds of thousands of women into the Tory fold. Many suffragists themselves came from a Tory background, such as Frances Power Cobbe and Emily Davies. Others gradually turned to the right, such as Emmeline Pankhurst and many other WSPU members. The party politics of suffrage was therefore complex and it is telling that the franchise was finally delivered by a coalition government, which came into being during the First World War.

War, citizenship and suffrage

Historians have traditionally emphasised the role of the First World War in the awarding of the vote to women for the first time in 1918. Certainly, it had a big impact on the suffrage movement. The outbreak of war divided the NUWSS. Many suffragists were appalled at the outbreak of war, which confirmed their fears that a male political system would inevitably lead to violence, and were drawn to the peace movement. Some joined the Union for Democratic Control, which supported peaceful diplomacy and arms reduction, or the Women's

International League for Peace and Freedom.[24] Others, including Fawcett, were anxious not to appear disloyal and saw the war as means to prove their patriotism. Through service to the nation, they sought to earn their citizenship: by performing a key duty of citizenship they hoped to obtain its rights. The WSPU took this latter course. Emmeline Pankhurst declared that campaigning was suspended and it effectively ceased to exist as a pro-suffrage organisation.[25] Christabel Pankhurst denounced Germany as a 'male nation' and argued that it would be 'a disastrous blow to the women's movement' if it won.[26] This was a common theme in pro-war propaganda: imagery abounded in the press of villainous Huns violating women and murdering children, so Britain should chivalrously rush to the defence of 'feminine' Belgium. Holton notes that some suffragette activity took on a jingoistic tone and some handed out white feathers to men who were not serving in the armed forces.[27] More positively, suffragettes threw themselves into relief work, raising money for hospitals and refugees, and serving as nurses.

Some suffrage campaigning did continue during the war. The Women's Freedom League had split from the WSPU in 1907, as its left-wing members opposed the Pankhursts' autocratic leadership and the WSPU's drift away from Labour, and it did not stop campaigning during the war. Nor did the East London Federation of Sylvia Pankhurst, whose politics had diverged with that of her mother. In 1916 the issue of women's suffrage revived and the government commissioned a Speaker's Report, which declared in favour of the issue. Eventually, a women's suffrage clause was included in the 1918 Representation of the People Bill, which would give the vote to women over the age of 30 who passed a property qualification. The Bill passed with a huge majority and British women could legally vote in parliamentary elections for the first time.

Historians have long debated why this should have happened. Given its timing, it is tempting to link women's suffrage to the work that women performed during the war. The huge demand for men in the armed services, particularly after the introduction of conscription in 1916, created large gaps in the labour market. Women were increasingly used to fill these gaps, particularly in sectors that were essential to the prosecution of the war such as munitions and food production. Women had always worked in factories, but the requirements of the wartime economy meant that they were employed in sectors that had formerly been barred to them due to their being unionised, skilled, heavy or dangerous. The manufacture of munitions was brought under the control of the government in 1915 and nearly a million 'munitionettes' came to be employed in this hazardous work. The employment of women in formerly male industries met much resistance, not least because they tended not to be unionised and commanded lower wages. The practice of 'dilution' broke down a job into several constituent parts, so lower-skilled workers could carry them out: this kept women's wages low, even in areas where they did manage to unionise.

Around a quarter of a million women worked for the Land Army, producing food so as to reduce wartime Britain's reliance on imports. Even women who did not work were urged to contribute to the national war effort at home. Posters urged women to practice domestic economy: 'Don't Waste Bread! Save Two Slices Every Day and Defeat the "U" Boat'.[28] In a total war, the distinctions between the front and the home front broke down, and civilians were both part of the war effort and potential targets of bombing raids by Zeppelins and Gothas. Propaganda such as this did include women in the category of wartime citizenship, but emphasised that the place where they would do this was in the home. Even posters advertising munitions work emphasised the workers' essential femininity, or included departing soldiers to underline that it was the men who were doing the fighting.[29] Women did serve in the armed forces, joining the Women's Royal Naval Service (WRENS) and the Women's Auxiliary Army Corps (WAAC) in large numbers. They performed administrative and auxiliary functions, as British women were scrupulously kept away from combat roles. As the infamous pro-war letter entitled *A Little Mother* put it: 'Women are created for the purpose of giving life, and men to take it.'[30] In practice, however, many women served in harrowing conditions close to the front and well within the range of enemy artillery, and many were decorated for bravery. This was particularly true of nurses in forward field hospitals, many of whom were inexperienced volunteers serving in the Voluntary Aid Detachment (VAD) or the First Aid Nursing Yeomanry (FANY).

There would therefore appear to be a link between women's wartime service and the 'reward' of the suffrage at the war's close, but in reality this is questionable. The women who were awarded the vote were propertied women over the age of 30, rather than the young and working-class women who had performed most of the war work. The war context was important, but in other ways. In 1914, suffrage had been blocked by Asquith's opposition and the complexities of party politics. But in 1918, after such a cataclysmic conflict, the cross-party government was in a position to pass sweeping legislation. The question of women's suffrage was arguably secondary to the award of universal suffrage to the men who had fought for their country in such large numbers. Although in practice there were men who did not serve – by reason of age, physical incapacity, religious conscience or by working in a reserved occupation – in theory conscription made military service a universal duty of citizenship, so its rights needed to be as well. Since the Third Reform Act, around 40 per cent of men had still been unable to vote, including many men in the armed services who did not meet the householder requirements. The exclusion of soldiers from the vote became utterly indefensible in the light of the First World War. The home secretary, Herbert Samuel, had argued in 1916 that such men must be given the vote, but that women's suffrage remained controversial: 'If you make special provision for the soldiers, the sailors and the munition workers, the committee will no doubt consider whether it is possible or desirable to avoid embarking parliament on the great controversy of women's suffrage.'[31] The number of women given the vote in 1918 was comparable to the number of men who were given the vote for the first time. Although the 1918 Representation of the People Act is today primarily remembered for women's suffrage, that was arguably not its main object at the time.

Towards equal citizenship

The First World War had a profound impact upon British gender relations, but historians have debated the extent to which its effects were lasting. Women were presented with a wide range of new opportunities during the war and the experience was in many cases a liberating one. Many women left domestic service to take up war work and never returned to that occupation: after the egalitarian experience of the war, the deference of service was less attractive. During the war, however, the authorities, the employers and the unions emphasised that this was a temporary, unusual situation, and they were careful that the wage and skill levels assigned to women's roles in the workplace were not directly comparable to men's. After the war, the munitions factories closed and the Restoration of Pre-War Practices Act gave returning soldiers their old jobs back. Although women were expected to return to their pre-war roles, in practice post-war femininities were very different. Many women rejected the rigidity of Edwardian social codes, swapping long dresses and corsets for shorter skirts and clothes that permitted freedom of movement. This change is perceptible in the dances of the period, where the militaristic and formal pre-war dances – where the man took the lead and the woman was in closed hold – were replaced by the more expressive and individualistic moves of the jazz age. The 'flapper', with her bobbed haircut, flimsy dress, makeup and cigarette holder, was a world away from the Edwardian lady.

Masculinities too were affected by the war. We saw in the previous chapter how Edwardian masculinities were characterised by chauvinism, aggression and stoicism. In 1914 the outbreak of war had been greeted with enthusiasm and even relief. Britain in 1914 was a divided place, characterised by political strife, strikes, militant suffragism and the Home Rule crisis in Ireland. War was therefore welcomed in many quarters as an opportunity to re-establish the correct order to gender relations and the empire. This was apparently a liberating experience for men, who could experience adventure and escape the pressures of Edwardian society. In reality, however, roles became disturbingly blurred, as women took men's jobs and donned khaki, and men at the front resented those back home. Moreover, Edwardian manliness was no match for the horrors of Ypres and the Somme. Many men were physically and mentally broken by the experience of the trenches. Around a third of army discharges were for 'nervous disorders', a category of illness that had formerly been associated with women.[32] 'Shell shock' entered the medical lexicon, as a way of understanding the effect of modern heavy artillery upon the nerves. Followers of Sigmund Freud identified the root of the problem in Edwardian masculinity itself: men who had been taught to be stoical broke down after suppressing their legitimate feelings of fear. Freudian psychoanalysis emphasised the role of the unconscious, and treated patients by encouraging them to externalise their repressed feelings. Whereas manliness had been a confident and perfectible ideal for men, masculinity in the world of psychoanalysis was fragile and provisional.

Historians have debated the extent to which the First World War represented a watershed for masculinity. Historians such as Alison Light suggest that, having fled from domesticity in the early twentieth century, men were re-domesticated in the post-war years.[33] Such men preferred 'dominoes and home improvement' to imperial and military adventure, and in the anti-war atmosphere between the wars this model of domestic masculinity came to be seen as 'English' in itself.[34] We have seen how the Conservative Party attempted to create a more domesticated and feminised appeal from the later nineteenth century. In the 1920s, however, David Jarvis has suggested that this increasingly caused disquiet among some Conservatives, who feared that men had been put off by this turn away from robust masculinity. He argues that their anti-socialist campaigning and vigorous local electioneering in these years 'reflected a desire to resurrect the essential masculinity of the political arena'.[35] Others agree that there was no turn away from martial masculinity in these years. The persistence of ideas of chivalry and sacrifice in popular culture, particularly in the ways in which the war was memorialised, suggest that Britons were seeking to legitimise masculine violence rather to than reject it.[36]

In terms of the franchise, men now enjoyed universal suffrage but women still did not. The campaign for equal citizenship in the 1920s has received much less attention from historians than the campaigns of 1903–14. The 1928 Equal Franchise Act may appear with hindsight to be a legislative tidying-up exercise and Sylvia Pankhurst claimed that it came 'virtually without effort', but it was by no means inevitable.[37] While former suffragettes memorialised the role of militancy and war service in the achievement of 1918, the NUWSS continued the campaign and re-formed as the National Union of Societies for Equal Citizenship (NUSEC). They continued to use their constitutional tactics and lobbied the government for a decade. The NUSEC did not just focus upon the vote: under the influence of New Feminism, it conceived of citizenship more broadly, pushing for women's rights in areas such as housing, the professions and reproductive health, and achieving successes in the reform of divorce rights, child custody and pensions.[38]

On 2 July 1928, the Equal Franchise Act passed into law, giving the vote to women in the UK on the same basis as men. As Millicent Fawcett wrote in her diary:

> It is almost exactly 61 years ago since I heard John Stuart Mill introduce his suffrage amendment to the Reform Bill on 20 May 1867. So I have had extraordinary good luck in having seen the struggle from the beginning.[39]

A parallel Act granted the same rights to women in Northern Ireland. Women in Ireland already enjoyed the same voting rights as men, having been granted this by their government since partition in 1922. In the UK, female voters now outnumbered male voters: although there are generally more male births than female in a given population, women live longer and many men had perished in the war. Women therefore had a dominant influence on British electoral politics, but this did not lead to the transformation of political life that the suffragists had hoped for. Women's use of the vote in the 1920s and 1930s was notable for its conservatism and, indeed, its Conservatism. Women could stand for election after 1918, but few did. The first woman to be elected, Constance Markievicz, did not take up her seat in 1918 as she stood for the Irish nationalist party Sinn Féin; the Conservative Nancy Astor was the first to do so the following year. As Asquith and others had feared, the new female voters often voted Conservative, the party that had often proved to be the most congenial to them since at least the formation of the Primrose League half a century before. Throughout the twentieth century, women tended to vote to the right of men, and it was the Conservative Party that would give Britain its first two female prime ministers.

Conclusion

How far, then, did the suffrage campaigns challenge the ideal of separate spheres for men and women? It is worth concluding our discussion by focusing on a famous poster, 'The Vote' (Figure 10.2), produced by the Suffrage Atelier around 1911. John Bull claims that his umbrella protects the whole family, but his wife argues firmly that it does not: 'I must have one of my own'. This image therefore contests the longstanding constitutional principle of virtual representation, which suggests that the head of the household 'virtually' represents those who are not directly represented themselves. While the message may appear to be an egalitarian one, the woman holds the hand of their child, who is clearly identified with her by the artist, given how the print has been organised and coloured. The poster therefore argues that the woman needs the vote if children's interests are to be protected, putting forward an argument for women's suffrage based upon the notion of complementary sexual difference. As we have seen throughout this chapter, the question of how the suffrage campaign approached the issue of gender roles, and the extent to which they were affected by the war years, is a complex one. What we can say for certain is that the suffrage campaigners worked within very well-established traditions of citizenship and political protest.

The electoral reforms of 1918 and 1928, taken together, represent the end of an era regarding the history of citizenship. With universal suffrage, the awarding of electoral rights ceased to be the qualitative business that it had been since at least the seventeenth century, when the fitness of voters was assessed in terms of their independence, their household station and their property. And with the granting of votes to women, these criteria were no longer assessed in gendered terms. This is therefore the chronological end to the story told by this book, which has traced the debate about who was fit to be a citizen from the Bill of Rights to the Equal Franchise Act. Of course, there is much more to citizenship than voting: Mayhall argues that the suffragettes did not see citizenship in abstract terms, but as 'an active practice'.[40] The suffragettes can, however, help us to understand *why* the vote was seen to be so important by previous generations.

Figure 10.2 'The Vote' (Suffrage Atelier poster, c. 1911). Granger Historical Picture Archive/Alamy Stock Photo.

The vote was invested with an almost magical power and was symbolic of an individual's standing within the community, as well as being the key to achieve real change. Studying the history of the suffragettes and their forebears shows us why we should not take the vote for granted, in the way that people so often do today.

Notes

1 A. Vickery, 'Golden age to separate spheres? A review of the categories and chronology of English women's history', *The Historical Journal*, 36:2, 1993, 383–414 (p. 388).
2 L. Mayhall, *The Militant Suffrage Movement: Citizenship and Resistance in Britain, 1860–1930*, Oxford: Oxford University Press, 2003, p. 19.
3 For example: E. Pankhurst, *My Own Story*, London, 1914; A. Kenney, *Memoirs of a Militant*, London, 1924; S. Pankhurst, *The Suffragette Movement*, London, 1931.
4 J. Rendall, *The Origins of Modern Feminism: Women in Britain, France and the United States, 1780–1860*, Basingstoke: Macmillan, 1985, chapter 8.

5 M. Pugh, *The March of the Women: A Revisionist Analysis of the Campaign for Women's Suffrage, 1866–1914*, Oxford: Oxford University Press, 2000.
6 See reviews of *March of the Women* by, for example, Hilda Kean in *Women's History Review*, 11, 2002, 315–18; and Jacqueline deVries in *Victorian Studies*, 44:2, 2002, 347–9.
7 J. Bush, *Women Against the Vote: Female Anti-Suffragism in Britain*, Oxford: Oxford University Press, 2007; B. Harrison, *Separate Spheres: The Opposition to Women's Suffrage in Britain*, London: Croom Helm, 1978.
8 Mayhall, *Militant Suffrage Movement*, p. 42.
9 M. Fawcett, 'Female suffrage: A reply', *The Nineteenth Century*, July 1889.
10 M. Holmes, *The ABC of Votes for Women* (1909), in M. Mulvey Roberts and T. Mizuta (eds.), *The Suffragists: Towards the Vote*, London: Routledge, 1999, pp. 23–37 (pp. 27, 35).
11 '120 arrested', *The Daily Sketch*, 19 November 1910, p. 7.
12 Holmes, *ABC of Votes for Women*, p. 35.
13 S. Stanley Holton, *Feminism and Democracy: Women's Suffrage and Reform Politics in Britain, 1900–1918*, Cambridge: Cambridge University Press, 2003, p. 5.
14 Quoted in Holton, *Feminism and Democracy*, p. 32.
15 Holton, *Feminism and Democracy*, p. 41.
16 J. Lawrence, 'Contesting the male polity: The suffragettes and the politics of disruption in Edwardian Britain', in A. Vickery (ed.), *Women, Privilege and Power: British Politics, 1750 to the Present*, Stanford: Stanford University Press, 2001, pp. 201–26.
17 Mayhall, *Militant Suffrage Movement*, p. 40.
18 M. Haig, *This Was My World*, London, 1933, p. 120.
19 Mayhall, *Militant Suffrage Movement*, chapter 4.
20 M. Richardson, *Laugh a Defiance*, London: Weidenfeld and Nicolson, 1953, p. 84.
21 B. Griffin, *The Politics of Gender in Victorian Britain: Masculinity, Political Culture and the Struggle for Women's Rights*, Cambridge: Cambridge University Press, 2014; Pugh, *March of the Women*.
22 Holton, *Feminism and Democracy*, pp. 115, 110.
23 Pugh, *March of the Women*, p. 102.
24 Holton, *Feminism and Democracy*, pp. 136, 138.
25 H. Smith, *The British Women's Suffrage Campaign 1866–1928*, London: Longman, 1998, p. 60.
26 Quoted in Samuel Hynes, *War Imagined: The First World War and English Culture*, Oxford: Bodley Head, 1990, p. 88.
27 Holton, *Feminism and Democracy*, p. 132.
28 'Don't Waste Bread!', poster, 1917.
29 'These Women Are Doing Their Bit', poster, undated.
30 Originally published in *The Morning Post*, 14 August 1916, but widely reprinted as a pamphlet thereafter.
31 H. Samuel (House of Commons, 19 July 1916): *Hansard's Parliamentary Debates* vol. 84, col.1041.
32 J. Bourke, *Dismembering the Male: Men's Bodies, Britain and the Great War*, London: Reaktion, 1996.
33 A. Light, *Forever England: Femininity, Literature and Conservatism Between the Wars*, London: Routledge, 1991.
34 M. Francis, 'The domestication of the male: Recent research on nineteenth- and twentieth-century British masculinity', *The Historical Journal*, 45:3, 2002, 637–52 (p. 641).
35 D. Jarvis, 'The Conservative Party and the politics of gender, 1900–39', in M. Francis and I. Zweininger-Bargielowska, *The Conservatives and British Society, 1880–1990*, Cardiff: University of Wales Press, 1996, pp. 172–93 (p. 188).

36 A. Frantzen, *Bloody Good: Chivalry, Sacrifice and the Great War*, Chicago: University of Chicago Press, 2003.
37 Pankhurst, *Suffragette Movement*, p. 608.
38 Holton, *Feminism and Democracy*, p. 152.
39 R. Strachey, *Millicent Garrett Fawcett*, London: John Murray, 1931, p. 349.
40 Mayhall, *Militant Suffrage Movement*, p. 6.

Recommended reading

Bush, J., *Women Against the Vote: Female Anti-Suffragism in Britain*, Oxford: Oxford University Press, 2007.

Griffin, B., *The Politics of Gender in Victorian Britain: Masculinity, Political Culture and the Struggle for Women's Rights*, Cambridge: Cambridge University Press, 2014.

Francis, M., 'The domestication of the male: Recent research on nineteenth- and twentieth-century British masculinity', *The Historical Journal*, 45:3, 2002, 637–52.

Harrison, B., *Separate Spheres: The Opposition to Women's Suffrage in Britain*, London: Croom Helm, 1978.

Kingsley Kent, S., *Sex and Suffrage in Britain 1860–1914*, London: Routledge, 1990.

Lawrence, J., 'Contesting the male polity: The suffragettes and the politics of disruption in Edwardian Britain', in A. Vickery (ed.), *Women, Privilege and Power: British Politics, 1750 to the Present*, Stanford: Stanford University Press, 2001, pp. 201–26.

Mayhall, L., *The Militant Suffrage Movement: Citizenship and Resistance in Britain, 1860–1930*, Oxford: Oxford University Press, 2003.

Pugh, M., *The March of the Women: A Revisionist Analysis of the Campaign for Women's Suffrage, 1866–1914*, Oxford: Oxford University Press, 2000.

Purvis, J. and Stanley Holton, S. (eds.), *Votes for Women*, London: Routledge, 2000.

Smith, H., *The British Women's Suffrage Campaign 1866–1928*, London: Longman, 1998.

Stanley Holton, S., *Feminism and Democracy: Women's Suffrage and Reform Politics in Britain, 1900–1918*, Cambridge: Cambridge University Press, 2003.

Stanley Holton, S., *Suffrage Days: Stories from the Women's Suffrage Movement*, London: Routledge, 1996.

Conclusion

By way of conclusion, it is worth focusing on an image of an election: electoral rights have been a key focus of this book and elections are a tangible example of citizenship in action. This depiction of the election for the county of Northamptonshire in December 1830 was painted in watercolour by J. M. W. Turner (Figure 11.1). Turner is, of course, more famous for landscapes and seascapes than for urban subjects, but he imbues this scene with the sense of energy and scale for which his work is renowned. The election was a by-election, prompted by the promotion of John Spencer, Viscount Althorp to the position of home secretary in Earl Grey's government. The Whigs had come into power that year with a pledge to pass a Reform Bill and Althorp was a keen reformer. Although the county was dominated by Tories, the two seats were shared between the parties and Althorp was personally popular.[1] The scenes of celebration depicted here reflect this and the banners express the crowd's enthusiasm for reform: 'The Purity of Election is the Triumph of Law', 'No Bribery', 'A Charter of Rights', 'Independence For Ever'. A large Union Flag adds to the sense of patriotic festivity, as the people of the town ritually mark their participation in the national political system.

Although it depicted a real event, Turner did take some liberties with his painting, which should be viewed as an imaginative portrayal. He was not there in person and probably reconstructed the event from reports in the press. These reports attest to the huge and enthusiastic crowd, but record that Althorp entered the town in a 'magnificently decorated' carriage rather than the open chair shown here, which was likely inspired by paintings of chairing ceremonies such as Hogarth's (Figure 3.2).[2] Turner had sketched the town on a previous visit but the buildings around All Saints Church are not rendered accurately, instead providing a frame for his symbolic tableaux. People familiar with Northampton will note that he omitted the large statue of Charles II from the portico of the church, which might have added an ambiguous note to this scene of vigorous democracy. Although it is difficult to make out individual figures in Turner's impressionistic vision, the painting suggests that all classes were present and that the election was a communal event. Only substantial property owners would have been able to vote in county elections, but Turner suggests that civic rituals such as the chairing were socially inclusive. Many women and children are depicted

Figure 11.1 J. M. W. Turner, 'The Northampton Election, 6 December 1830' (watercolour, c. 1830–31). © Tate, London 2019.

in the crowd, or look on from windows and raised platforms. The woman in the bottom left-hand corner is in French national dress: an incongruous figure who is probably symbolic, alluding to the July Revolution of that year.[3] Does she represent the dangers of reform or the greater danger of not doing so?

Turner's own politics were unclear, but his choice of subject during the Reform Bill crisis must have been deliberate. He was depicting the elective process in action, leading to the triumphant re-election of a leading supporter of the movement to reform the franchise. Although Althorp sought to extend electoral citizenship to more people, he was firmly of the belief that it should be allocated selectively: he came from the liberal wing of the Whig party, which believed that the franchise should only be vested in free and economically independent individuals.[4] Turner's lively crowd scene, however, suggests that citizenship involved more than just voting, and that many people who were outside the official category of citizenship had a sense of belonging to their community and their nation. His typically fervent, hazy portrayal suggests that the election is somehow sublime and has a higher purpose and meaning. He seems to be implying that citizens are both individuals and are members of something larger and more significant.

It is apposite to focus on this event, since the Reform Acts dominate accounts of citizenship in Britain in this period. Indeed, they have concerned at least three chapters of this book. As we have seen, however, there is much at stake in the question of how you tell the story of political reform. Whig histories used to tell a triumphant story of gradual progress. It is inarguable that the Reform Acts did incrementally increase the electorate and for this reason there are still traces of this interpretation in accounts of British 'democratisation'. As Laura Mayhall argues, however, it is not possible to claim that the Reform Acts were a victory of liberal democratic citizenship, when the exclusion of women was central to their rationale.[5] Other historians argue that they should not be seen as a continuum: Frank O'Gorman regards the Reform Acts as 'a series of almost entirely unrelated responses', which should be seen in terms of political expediency rather than linear progress.[6] We have seen how the immediate causes of the major electoral reforms of 1832, 1867, 1884–85 and 1918 have to be explained in terms of their political context, but it is nevertheless possible to take a long view and consider them together. Historical events may not follow patterns, but ideologies can. The electoral reforms of the nineteenth and twentieth centuries should arguably be viewed as attempts to fix in legislative terms the category of the citizen, by defining what sorts of people were fit to exercise the franchise, and which were not.

Since this necessarily involved social description, this requires us to connect political history to cultural histories of gender, class and nation. It is therefore worth reflecting here on the ways in which each of these categories in turn have been used throughout the book and what we have learned from exploring politics in this way. Gender has been our primary focus. We have seen how the debate about citizenship that spanned over two centuries was conducted along these lines. The fitness of successive groups of men to exercise the franchise was negotiated in these terms, while unmanliness and femininity served to define the boundaries of who should be excluded. The key terms that commonly defined political inclusion – such as 'independence', 'respectability', property and householding – were commonly articulated in explicitly gendered ways. When campaigners tried to make a case for female suffrage, they had to overturn centuries of political practice that defined political life in masculine terms. Even when they used constitutional arguments, these were gendered to the core. The militant suffragettes may appear to have broken out of this impasse by establishing a new type of politics, but even their use of election violence and crowd protest could be viewed as an attempt to appropriate the masculine culture of popular politics.

A political perspective can shed light on chronologies in the history of gender. The dominant narrative of British women's history was the emergence of 'separate spheres'. Since the 1990s, a key way that gender historians have challenged this narrative has been by exploring the place of women in the political life of the eighteenth and nineteenth centuries. It is clear from this work that politics and women's lives did not take place in different spheres: rather, it has highlighted the more subtle, everyday ways in which women did politics, some of which were not necessarily recorded in conventional source material. The questions of gender difference and separate roles, however, were very enduring. Victorian feminists tended to emphasise that women had different qualities and capabilities to men, and this perspective continued to inform the arguments of the Edwardian suffragettes as they attempted to make a case for giving women the vote.

In the history of masculinity, a key narrative concerns the rise of domestic notions of masculinity in the nineteenth century, apparently replacing forms of masculinity – such as the 'polite' man – that were more publicly validated. John Tosh has charted the fortunes of domestic masculinity, arguing that men's roles within the home as husbands and fathers reached their peak of social importance in the Victorian period.[7] This paralleled developments in the history of politics, whereby citizenship came to be increasingly defined in terms of the man's role as a householder and the head of the family. English constitutional practice had long emphasised that electors were proprietors but, from the late eighteenth century, radicals and reformers emphasised the fundamental 'independence' of the masculine householder-citizen in making the case for extending the franchise. In 1832, this ideology of the excluded became the official rationale of the British state, when a single standard of male, middle-class householding became the qualification for the franchise; this was then reworked for working-class men in 1867 and 1884–85.[8] Tosh additionally argues that there was a 'flight from domesticity' at the end of the century and other scholars have suggested that men were re-domesticated after the First World War. Rather than a to-ing and fro-ing between the home and the public world, however, it is important to stress some fundamental continuities. Men's status in the political world was always underwritten by his domestic stations and familial relationships, even if the precise ways in which it was articulated were subject to change and debate. This is a key reason by it is impossible to disentangle citizenship from gender in the period before equal suffrage.

Social class has also been an important perspective for historians of modern British politics. If this book had been written a generation ago, it would probably have been its primary explanatory concept. The histories of working-class radicalism, trade unionism and the Labour Party were long informed by a Marxist understanding of the relationship between social class and its political expression. Women's history too had its origins in Marxist feminism, and sought to explain the oppression of women in terms of economics and social structure. 'Separate spheres' particularly concerned the middle class and shares its chronology with that of the modern industrial class society, as did Jürgen Habermas's parallel notion of the 'public sphere'. At the end of the twentieth century, however, a fierce debate took place within social history about the nature of class and its role in historical explanation. Under the influence of the linguistic turn, some historians argued that class consciousness could not be regarded as a direct reflection of social circumstances, and that class should instead be conceived of in cultural terms. Class instead became an identity, both individual and collective, which was constructed through language and culture.[9] Language and social description came to be seen as arenas of political contestation. For example, Dror Wahrman argued that the very notion of a 'middle class' emerged from the battles over defining citizenship in the run-up to 1832: so instead of the middle classes making the Reform Act, they were made by it.[10] We saw in Chapter 9 how the very idea of 'society' has a history, and that we need to understand this if we are to explain how citizenship came to have a 'social' dimension by the early twentieth century.

Finally, we have considered citizenship in terms of race and nation. This is fundamental, since citizenship above all concerns membership of a national community. Historical discussions of citizenship in the eighteenth century are inseparable from the ongoing debate about the nature of national identity and the extent to which 'Britishness' came to supersede other national or regional identities. In mid-eighteenth-century concerns about degeneration and foreign cultural contamination, we can see proto-racial conceptions of nationhood. In the nineteenth century, race intrudes more regularly into political discussion, and it is possible to discern eugenic arguments about national strength in movements for social purity and the New Liberal impetus for a welfare state, for example. The empire was an important context for British politics throughout this period, from eighteenth-century mercantilism to the debates around the franchise in the nineteenth. It also played a crucial role in national identities and provided a focus for many extra-parliamentary political campaigns. If this book had been written in north America, empire would doubtless have loomed larger, since 'British studies' has had to reinvent itself as an international, imperial field in US universities in order to maintain its relevance.[11] While it is vital to emphasise the diversity and complexity of 'Britain', it is still possible to tell its story in internal terms: a book about citizenship has to concern itself above all with the nation of which its inhabitants were citizens. Where Britons did consider a wider international context for their politics, their military situation and their national identities, they primarily looked to Europe rather than across the Atlantic, as Stephen Conway has recently argued.[12] Their monarchs were Dutch and then Hanoverian; their political discourse was littered with references from classical Greece and Rome; their ruling classes were criticised for their attachment to Italian opera and French food; their oldest ally was Portugal; and their primary international rivals were France and then Germany.

The European context was particularly pressing at the time of writing, since this book was largely written in the two years that followed the 2016 referendum on membership of the European Union. This focused Britons' attention on issues of citizenship as never before: one side emphasised the importance of political sovereignty and criticised the presence of foreign nationals within Britain; the other side sought to maintain Britons' other citizenship status, as members of the EU, and expressed concern about the rights of EU citizens in Britain in the event of Brexit. As it turned out, the debate proved to be highly charged and polarising. The xenophobia of much of the commentary suggested that British national identity was as much a negative identity – predicated on hostility to the foreign 'other' – as it had ever been in the eighteenth century. On the positive side, the referendum certainly engaged many people in politics who may not previously have shown much interest in it, and focused attention on the rights that we hold as citizens.

It also focused attention on the historic nature of the British constitution. In November 2016, pro-EU campaigners challenged the government in the High Court. They argued that the government alone could not trigger Article 50 of the Lisbon Treaty to start the process of leaving the EU, and that parliament had to vote on the issue. This hinged on some fundamental constitutional questions. Was parliament sovereign? What was the extent of the government's executive powers? Could decisions that affected the rights of Britons be taken without parliamentary approval? Could the courts overrule the government? Because Britain does not have a single written constitution, these questions were up for debate and had to be settled by a court, which had to do so with reference to statute and precedent. Historical precedents were repeatedly invoked during the trail and the court's judgement quoted section one of the Bill of Rights: 'That the pretended power of suspending of laws or the execution of laws by regall authority without consent of Parlyament is illegall.'[13] The Bill of Rights, written in 1689 to protect Englishmen against the kinds of prerogative power that James II had exercised, means that British governments today cannot alter laws without the consent of parliament. If British citizens want to understand the rights that they hold, they therefore need to know their history.

Notes

1 H. Spencer, 'Northamptonshire', in D. R. Fisher (ed.), *The History of Parliament: The House of Commons 1820–1832*, vol. 2, Cambridge: Cambridge University Press, 2009, pp. 744–50.
2 *Northampton Mercury*, 11 December 1830.
3 E. Shanes, *Turner's Picturesque Views in England and Wales, 1825–1838*, London: Chatto and Windus, 1979, p. 39.
4 M. McCormack, *The Independent Man: Citizenship and Gender Politics in Georgian England*, Manchester: Manchester University Press, 2005, pp. 191–2.
5 L. Mayhall, *The Militant Suffrage Movement: Citizenship and Resistance in Britain, 1860–1930*, Oxford: Oxford University Press, 2003, p. 6.
6 F. O'Gorman, 'The secret ballot in nineteenth-century Britain', in R. Betrand, J.-L. Briquet and P. Pels (eds.), *Cultures of Voting: The Hidden History of the Secret Ballot*, London: Hurst, 2007, pp. 16–42 (p. 16).
7 J. Tosh, *A Man's Place: Masculinity and the Middle-Class Home in Victorian England*, New Haven: Yale University Press, 1999.
8 McCormack, *Independent Man*; C. Hall, K. McClelland and J. Rendall, *Defining the Victorian Nation: Class, Race, Gender and the Reform Act of 1867*, Cambridge: Cambridge University Press, 2000.
9 For an overview of this debate, see P. Joyce, *Class: Oxford Readers*, Oxford: Oxford University Press, 1995.
10 D. Wahrman, *Imagining the Middle Class: The Political Representation of Class in Britain 1780–1840*, Cambridge: Cambridge University Press, 1993, chapter 9.
11 See, for example, K. Wilson, *The Island Race: Englishness, Empire and Gender in the Eighteenth Century*, Oxford: Routledge, 2003; P. Monod, *Imperial Island: A History of Britain and its Empire, 1660–1837*, Oxford: Wiley-Blackwell, 2009.
12 S. Conway, *Britain, Ireland and Continental Europe in the Eighteenth Century: Similarities, Connections, Identities*, Oxford: Oxford University Press, 2011.
13 Gina Miller and Deir Tozetti Dos Santos v. the Secretary of State for Exiting the European Union, High Court, 3 November 2016: www.bailii.org/ew/cases/EWHC/Admin/2016/2768.html [accessed 1 March 2019].

Index

abolitionism *see* slavery
Act of Union 1707 15, 53, 68; 1801 80
Althorp, J. Spencer Viscount 184–5
America 8, 15–16, 45, 54, 67, 71–2, 77, 125, 188
Anne 17, 131
Anti-Corn Law League 93, 147
anti-suffragism 169–70
army 14, 38, 42, 69, 81, 144, 156
Asquith, H. H. 158, 175, 177, 180
Astell, M. 120–1, 127, 130

ballot 110, 112, 139
Ballot Act (1872) 59, 61, 139–40, 144
Becker, L. 129, 139
Bell, D. 76–7
Bentham, J. 157
Bill of Rights (1689) 6, 13, 16, 180, 189
Birkett, M. 94–5
Blackadder the Third 51
Blackstone, W. 54–5
Blair, T. 1, 163
Bonaparte, N. 75, 79
Boswell, J. 25, 46
Burdett, F. 70, 82
Burke, E. 75–6, 123, 138
Butler, J. 129, 130
Byng, J. 38

Cameron, D. 1, 2
canvassing 57–8, 92
Cartwright, J. 71, 73, 78
Catholicism 12, 13, 15, 30, 68, 80, 98, 105–8, 134, 146, 148
census 53, 109, 153, 172
chairing ceremony 59–61, 184
Chamberlain, J. 140
charity 93–4, 121, 146, 155
Charles II 12, 184
Chartism 8, 21, 25, 104, 111–16, 168

Chester 56, 59
children 3, 14, 38, 45, 48, 77, 82, 93, 99, 128–9, 148, 155, 170, 176, 180, 185
Church of England 12, 13, 81, 107, 120, 143, 146
citizenship test 1, 3
Clark, A. 31, 114–15, 161
class 6, 22, 32, 36, 46, 72, 81, 101, 104, 107–8, 112–15, 138, 187
clubs 26, 134, 159
coffeehouses 25–6
Colley, L. 15, 68–9, 74, 80
Connell, R. W. 37, 116
conscription 2, 25, 77, 176–7
Conservative party 1, 9, 110, 133–4, 145–9, 164, 175, 179, 180
constitution 7, 15–16, 70–4, 78, 169–70, 189
consumerism 94–6, 101, 124
Corn Laws 27, 114, 134–5
Corrupt Practices Act (1883) 61, 62, 140, 148
Country patriotism 41, 44, 70–1, 113
Cruikshank, G. 82
Cruikshank, I. 94
cultural history 5–6, 9, 36

demonstrations 25–6, 82–4, 115, 137
Devonshire, Georgiana Cavendish Duchess of 51, 62–5, 91
Disraeli, B. 9, 18, 134–8, 141–2, 146–8
divorce 125, 127–9, 168, 179
Duke of York Affair (1809) 81, 85
Dyndor, Z. 95

education 1, 4, 130–1, 136, 157–9, 168
effeminacy 31, 38–9, 64, 70
elections 1–3, 7, 13, 20, 23–4, 31, 51–65, 91, 95–6, 147, 156, 164, 172, 184–5
emotion 3, 4, 7, 15, 26, 48

empire 69, 108, 138, 148, 159–61, 179
England 12, 24, 38, 43, 53, 68, 80, 104, 109
Enlightenment 23, 44, 120, 122
Equal Franchise Act (1928) 3, 10, 167, 179
eugenics 130, 159
European Union 3, 7, 188–9
Evangelicalism 8, 48, 76, 92–5, 121, 127

Fabian Society 162
Fawcett, M. 171, 176, 179
femininity 6, 36, 167, 178, 186
feminism 23, 36, 119–32, 167, 179
Filmer, J. 14
first past the post 7, 52, 58, 141
First World War (1914–18) 3, 42, 77, 141, 159, 161, 167, 175–8, 187
Foucault, M. 156, 160
Fox, C. J. 63, 105
France 2, 8, 9, 13, 15, 26, 38, 42–3, 46, 67–8, 71–80, 97, 108, 167, 188
franchise 6, 45, 48, 85, 109
free trade 112, 134–5, 144, 164; *see also laissez-faire*
freedom of speech 13, 15, 43, 85
French Revolutionary and Napoleonic Wars (1793–1815) 73, 76–81, 134
Freud, S. 178
Fry, E. 93

gender 1, 4, 6, 12, 41, 46, 104, 138, 186
gender history 23, 37, 100, 149
George I 15, 38
George II 38, 42
George III 18, 42–3, 63, 69, 98, 105
George IV 17, 81, 91, 97–100, 107
George, H. 162, 164
Germany 38, 69
Gillray, J. 98, 122
Gladstone, W. E. 18, 137, 140–5, 149, 174
Gleadle, K. 3, 89, 108
Glorious Revolution (1688–89) 6, 12–14, 17, 71–3, 75
Godwin, W. 125
Grey, C. 63, 105–8
Griffin, B. 173–4

Habermas, J. 7, 22–4, 31–2, 88, 187
Hall, C. 108, 138
Harvey, K. 26
homosexuality 39–40, 160

House of Commons 7, 13, 16, 17, 19–21, 45, 52, 92, 109, 140, 173
House of Lords 7, 13, 16, 19–20, 106–9, 137, 140
Hunt, H. 82

immigration 1, 188
independence 3, 20–1, 24, 29, 40, 48, 54–5, 78, 81, 88, 96, 106, 108, 124, 141, 170, 186–7
Independent Labour Party (ILP) 163, 171, 175
Industrial Revolution 22, 53, 138, 157
Ireland 12–13, 30, 39, 68–9, 80, 104, 107, 109, 141, 144, 178
Italy 38

Jacobitism 14–15, 38, 43, 154
James II 12–14, 105, 189
John Bull 41–2, 69, 82, 139, 146, 180
Johnson, S. 70
Jones, G. Stedman 113–14

Kennedy, C. 69, 80

Labour party 1, 141, 152, 161–4, 172, 175
laissez-faire 9, 146, 155, 164
law 3, 16, 43–4
Lawrence, J. 133, 145, 146, 172
Leech, J. 115
Lewis, S. 89–90, 92
Liberal party 9, 18, 93, 110, 112, 134–7, 141–6, 155, 158, 162–4, 171, 174–5
literacy 29
literature 23, 26, 28, 122
Liverpool, R. Jenkinson Lord 106
local government 92, 162, 168
Locke, J. 14, 120, 124
London 28, 44, 46, 161
Lowe, R. 136
loyalism 8, 68, 74–6
Luddism 82, 96

Magna Carta 16
Major, J. 1
Manchester 61, 83–5, 109, 111, 157, 171
manliness 38, 41, 49, 55, 60, 70, 142
marriage 3, 4, 14, 26, 63, 91, 99, 120, 125–9, 169–70
Marxism 22, 88, 141, 161, 162, 164, 187
masculinity 2, 6–8, 25, 32, 35–49, 61, 65, 99–100, 115–16, 134, 136, 142, 146, 149, 152, 156, 159–61, 178–9; history of 35–7, 186–7

material culture 26, 44, 84, 144
Mayhall, L. 169, 172, 180, 186
Melbourne, W. Lamb 2nd Viscount 18, 128
melodrama 100, 114
militia 42, 44, 57, 73, 77, 80, 108
Mill, J. 30
Mill, J. S. 138–9, 168, 171, 179
monarchy 7, 12, 14, 16–18, 37
Montagu, E. 121–2
More, H. 75–6, 122
Municipal Corporations Act (1835) 92, 157
munitions factories 169, 176–7

national identity 1, 4, 6, 8, 15, 41, 188–9
National Insurance 1, 159
National Union of Societies for Equal Citizenship (NUSEC) 179
National Union of Women's Suffrage Societies (NUWSS) 171–5, 179
navy 69, 77
New Woman 119
newspapers *see* press
nomination ceremony 58, 59, 140
Nonconformity 72, 80, 92–3, 106–7, 121, 134
Northampton 58, 184–5
Norton, C. 128–9

O'Connell, D. 107
O'Connor, F. 112
O'Gorman, F. 24, 56, 60, 74, 109, 186
Owen, R. 125–6

Paine, T. 8, 71–4, 96, 122–3
Palmerston, W. Temple Viscount 135–6, 142, 144
Pankhurst, Christabel 172, 176
Pankhurst, Emmeline 171–2, 175–6
Pankhurst, Sylvia 176, 179
party politics 12, 20, 110, 133, 163
passport 1
patriarchy 120, 125, 127, 173
patriotism 8, 38, 40, 67–70, 74, 76, 145–6
Peel, R. 18, 107, 134, 138, 144
pensions 40, 81; old age 2, 159
Peterloo 82–4, 97, 100
petitioning 2, 13
Pitt the Elder, W. 42, 43
Pitt the Younger, W. 63, 72
policing 83, 137, 157
politeness 25–6, 46–7

political history 5, 10, 36–7, 65, 74, 87–8, 100, 104, 161
poor law 92, 111, 112, 156, 168
Poovey, M. 129, 153
poverty 81, 84, 111, 153
press 23, 25, 27–30, 72, 82, 92, 135–6
Price, R. 8, 72–3, 75
Primrose League 147–9
prison 3, 27, 74, 93, 114, 157
property 2, 4, 8, 54–5, 125, 128–9, 172
proportional representation 52
prostitution 63, 99, 129–30, 170
protest 2, 96; *see also* demonstrations
Protestantism 13, 14, 68
public sphere 12, 21–32
Pugh, M. 147, 169, 174

Queen Caroline affair (1820) 97–100

race 46, 115, 138, 159, 188
radicalism 25, 26, 44, 70–4, 81–5, 96, 98, 108, 124, 140
referenda 1, 7, 188–9
Reform Acts 4, 48, 56, 112, 149, 185–7; First ('Great') Reform Act (1832) 8, 15, 21, 24, 53–4, 58, 61, 96, 104–112, 161; Second Reform Act (1867) 9, 133–40, 168; Third Reform Act (1884–5) 113, 133, 139–41, 177
Rendall, J. 138, 169
Representation of the People Act (1918) 176
republicanism 18
right to bear arms 13, 15
riot 15, 51, 59, 96, 98, 108; *see also* protest
Romanticism 41
Rome 2, 39–40, 45, 188
Rose, N. 156–9
Rose, S. 101, 141
Rowntree, J. 158
Ruskin, J. 90, 162
Russell, J. 136–7

Sati 95
satirical prints 28, 63–4
Scotland 3, 12, 15, 42, 43, 53, 68–9, 80, 104, 108, 109, 141
separate spheres 23, 36, 47, 87–9, 100–1, 167, 170, 180, 186
Seven Years' War 38, 42, 43
sexuality 39–40, 130, 160
slavery 39, 93–5, 126
Smiles, S. 47, 156

sociability 7, 58, 148
social history 6, 9, 74, 88, 153, 161
soldiers 69, 77, 79, 83, 129, 141
space 23–6
Spain 43, 46, 70, 71
Stamp Tax 28–30, 72
suffragettes 19, 119

taxation 2, 14, 42, 52, 54, 75, 77, 81, 96, 98, 108, 156, 172
Taylor, B. 124, 125
Thatcher, M. 2, 145
Thomas, M. Haig 19, 172
Thompson, E. P. 161
Tolpuddle Martyrs 161
Tone, W. 80
Tory party 12, 30, 41, 42, 98, 105–11; *see also* Conservative party
Tosh, J. 4, 36, 47, 48, 159, 187
Townshend, G. 28
trade unions 152, 162–4, 171, 176, 178
treating 58, 147–8
Turner, J. M. W. 184–5

Vernon, J. 30, 60, 110, 136, 154
Victoria 18, 90, 127, 131
virtual representation 53, 56, 106
volunteer movement 78–9

Wahrman, D. 46, 107, 187
Wales 12, 24, 53, 68–9, 80, 104
Walpole, R. 37, 40
welfare state 9, 152, 158–9, 161, 188
Wellington, A. Wellesley Duke of 106–7
Wheeler, A. 126–7
Whig history 10, 13, 15, 16, 51, 63, 91, 104, 185
Whig party 8, 41, 42, 72, 75, 98, 105–11, 185
widows 55, 82, 170
Wilde, O. 160
Wilkes, J. 29, 35, 42–6, 67, 71, 78, 84, 105
William III 13
William IV 107
Wilson, K. 13, 69, 71
Wollstonecraft, M. 9, 123–5, 127, 130, 167
women's history 35–6, 46, 88
Women's Social and Political Union (WSPU) 171–7
women's suffrage 6, 10, 101, 131, 138–40, 148, 167–81, 186
Wordsworth, W. 71
work 47, 156
Wyvill, C. 27, 82

yeomanry 83–4